Thinking About Things
and Other Frivolities

Thinking About Things and Other Frivolities

A Life

EDWARD FARLEY

With a foreword by Mary McClintock Fulkerson

CASCADE *Books* • Eugene, Oregon

THINKING ABOUT THINGS AND OTHER FRIVOLITIES
A Life

Cascade Books
An Imprint of Wipf and Stock Publishers
199 W. 8th Ave., Suite 3
Eugene, OR 97401

www.wipfandstock.com

ISBN 13: 978-1-62032-992-4

Cataloging-in-Publication data:

Farley, Edward.

    Thinking about things and other frivolities : a life / Edward Farley ; with a foreword by Mary McClintock Fulkerson.

    xvi + 270 p. ; 23 cm. Includes bibliographical references.

    ISBN 13: 978-1-62032-992-4

    1. Farley, Edward, 1926–. 2. Presbyterianism—Biography. 3. Christianity—Philosophy. 4. Theology—Study and teaching. I. Title.

BX 5995 .F34 2014

Manufactured in the U.S.A.

For Conrad Aiken, *Selected Poems.* Oxford University Press (PB), 1969.
Lines from "Pschyomachia I," Preludes to Memnon, VIII, and XIV
Copyright Holder, Joseph Killorin

For several lines from Edwin H. Zeydel's translation of Sebastian Brandt's *The Ship of Fools* (1944), Dover Publications, NY.

For lines from J. R. R. Tolkien's *The Hobbit.* Houghton Mifflin Harcourt. (reprint)

For Charles Austin Farley,
brother, scientist, lover of nature

Contents

Foreword

I cannot even begin to say how much I have been influenced by the work of Edward Farley. As an entering theology PhD student at Vanderbilt in the fall of 1977, I was in awe of him, intimidated by him, and blown away by his deep, profound, and complex thinking. So it is fascinating for me to read in Ed's memoir about his self-critical reflection on his own life and thinking over the years. Indeed, while certainly not a self-promotional project—he even offers a critical evaluation of his own teaching style—this memoir is a rich and fascinating account of Ed's contributions to theology in its widest and most profound sense and of the life experiences that have contributed to, yet far exceeded the academic world.

It is always helpful and often somewhat surprising to discover more about the world and context in which a constructive theologian emerges, both as a child with the typical complex family background, and as a developing human being with a broad variety of interests. Ed experienced real struggles and joys growing up in a middle class family living through the Depression. He remembers many forms of labor, from yard work, grocery store delivery boy, to theatre usher for thirty cents an hour. His gifts as a musician—a trumpeter, a singer, jazz musician and a pianist—were evident early on. That Ed was and would always be an endlessly curious thinker was also clear early on. His pursuit of intellectual education, ending in a PhD at Union in New York, seemed to always involve ministerial practices, from occasional preaching and interim pastoring, to actual congregational assignments as a Presbyterian minister. Ed's stories of family are rich, including a loving relationship with his wife Doris that began in high school.

Ed's work has always probed possible alternatives to both "conservative" Christianity and "liberal" theologies. Appropriating the positive original connotations of both terms, Ed recalls his early insights engendering criticisms of both Protestant orthodoxy and neo-orthodoxy. His work also constitutes a crucial alternative to what is sometimes termed "radical orthodoxy," and it provides a much-needed and complex theological anthropology to what we think of as liberation theologies (including black, feminist, and queer), which he takes with utmost seriousness. One of the important topics throughout this memoir is the emergence of his consciousness of the familiar marginalizing markers of race, gender, ethnicity and class, along with his willingness to "confess" his myopia in the past to his own related privileges as a white, male academic.

I would hope that the next generation of theologians would further develop Ed's profound theological anthropology, especially with regard to its recognition of the three-dimensional character of agency as individual, intersubjective, and social/institutional. While it is precisely the social/institutional dimension of agency that is recognized by liberation theologies, the combination of the three is crucial to a more adequate account of what sinful deformation looks like in its complexity and, thus, what redemptive alteration would require. Farley's work is crucial to that much needed theological expansion. One of his many groundbreaking insights is displaying the essential role of the intersubjective in anthropology. I appreciate his reflection here on the work of such thinkers as Martin Buber and Emmanuel Levinas in foregrounding the significance of face-to-face relationality, which Ed develops in crucial ways for our theological thinking. Developing this dimension of theological anthropology is an exciting and important way to identify the culturally marked nature of all "communities" and avoid the romanticization of "church" that characterizes quite a bit of contemporary theology.

Another groundbreaking element behind Farley's alternative to orthodox and neo-orthodox theologies is his archeology of theological reflection. His critique of theologies based upon the "house of authority" is really a mind-blower. Longstanding ways that doctrines, confessions, beliefs and theologies in general have been grounded in textual and institutional authorities are charted and analyzed in *Ecclesial Reflection: An Anatomy of Theological Method* (1982). This is not simply a correction of outdated pre-modern (or anti-modern) refusals to historicize and contextualize the so-called revealed texts of Christian tradition. The "anatomy" explores the subtle, ongoing ways residuals of this "reification" continue even in approaches that recognize historical critical method. This analysis plus his later writings expose many complex ways that what should be considered as *mediating* the Divine in fact becomes *reified* and treated as a *substitute* for the Divine, including the ways that symbols of Divine agency become literalized.

Ecclesial Reflection completely rearranged my religious universe, as I came to see the way my own thinking, however liberal, was so dependent upon elements of the "house of authority." Ed's discussion of the development of this critique and his constructive alternative, the medium of ecclesial redemptive existence, is a significant contribution of this memoir. I continue to appeal to "ecclesial redemptive existence" as central for thinking about modes of divine presence, insisting to my Barthian students that with such a claim I am not "reducing" theology to experience. As Ed would say, that experience is a "matrix," not a norm. Without it, Christian faith would have no compelling reason to continue to exist. The subtle and complex articulation of ecclesia provided by Farley in the memoir is a gift.

This memoir is so rich with background reflections on his insights that I cannot cover it all: topics such as Ed's groundbreaking analysis of theological education, which exposes the problematic structure of the "fourfold" organization of studies; his exploration of aesthetics from a theological perspective; the tragic; and his thoughts on the current state of the union. However, the richness of this book is not simply its intellectual wisdom. The sense of humor, humility, and honesty of this man all emerge throughout.

So to fully honor *that* man I must conclude with a personal recollection. In the memoir Ed speaks of his vocational experience as a teacher and faculty member and that includes numerous parties and galas at Vanderbilt. A favorite memory I have of graduate school was one of the theology faculty/student Christmas parties. As Ed notes in the book, the parties were terrific, and faculty and students took turns every year giving skits. The year that stands out for me was the year my entering class performed the skit. Several of us played members of the graduate faculty, and I got to play Ed Farley. As I remember, my borrowed male coat and tie (over a tee shirt) were not exactly Farley-ish. But my fake rubber glasses and mustache were perfect! And I did a fairly good job of imitating his reflective "hmmmmm" as I stroked my mustache. This may be the skit he remembers in the book, or it may be that I am only one of numerous graduate students who had the opportunity not only to be shaped by an incredible theologian, but to enjoy and try to mimic the creative, collegial, and sometimes jazzed up Vanderbilt academic community that Ed Farley exemplified. So I am honored to commend this wonderful memoir.

Mary McClintock Fulkerson
Professor of Theology
Divinity School, Duke University

Preface

"(His) speeches greatly deteriorated in old age.
It weakened his powers, but not his inability to remain silent."

—TACITUS

I must state at the outset that I am not sure what genre of literature fills these pages. I began the project thinking I was writing a memoir. That is in fact what we have in the first three chapters. But chapters 5, 6, and 7 plus the "Problematics" of the Appendix are mostly philosophical essays. The work then is an assortment of personal recollections, "confessions" (cf. Augustine), and essays (cf. Montaigne). I know of no comprehensive term for such an assortment of genres. A work of multiple genres will surely pose a challenge to a reviewer of the work. Among the genres, what deserves comment or criticism, my narratives about a Henry County farm or my essays on poetics or tragedy? My counsel to the reviewer would be to skip the narrative and look for fruits (opinions and analyses) ripe for critical plucking. Note that the Appendix contains a Curriculum Visa which provides information about my schooling, teaching, and publications, and also offers a short bibliography that lists books having to do both with the settings (e.g., Louisville, Nashville) and schools of the narrative and books related to the subjects of my essays in chapters 4 through 7. Offered here then are several books and at least five quite different styles of writing: narrative, philosophical reflections, confessions, op-ed-type analyses, and turgid passages of academic prose. As I saw it, all five were more or less inevitable. I wanted to introduce my children and grandchildren to the history and settings of their family, to times and places of the mid-twentieth century, and to my own story. But whatever else it is, that story is a story of schools, classrooms, research projects, and publications. Thus, I thought it necessary to give some account of the various themes, projects, and "problematics" that constituted my life as a teacher. In merciful mood, I did my best to isolate these accounts in special locations, thus the essays on teaching, writing, and problematics. Accordingly, the reader can know in advance what to seek out or, for that matter, what to avoid. I could not, however, completely ban occasional references to my intellectual and pedagogical activities from the narrative. Thus, readers of the memoir may suddenly find themselves struggling with a passage that makes little sense. (I realize that such passages may not make sense to the academically inclined.) My advice to the reader (the grandchild, the friend, the former student) is to use the book as a kind of dictionary. Select what looks interesting and avoid what will put you to sleep.

If this work combines multiple genres of writing, what then is its unity? I must confess that what unifies the chapters and the genres is the author. If some deconstructionists are right and "authors" and "authorship" best be ignored by interpreters, it has no unity at all. The rather scary notion that I myself am the unity of the various genres makes me conscious of the risks that come with writing a memoir. A memoir proceeds under the dominance of "I" language. I do think this sort of writing can be a useful genre of literature. At the same time, I recall my disdain of "I" style, narcissistic speeches and sermons. But I must live with this discomfort, and hope that the contents, the people, events, and issues, will in some way distract the reader from the hubris of the "I" style.

A memoir need not be simply a self-objectification of the author, a pretension that the "I" is simply something observed, recorded, or explained. Something more complicated than that is going on when a person recollects and records the past. Such authors are working of course from their experiences, their perspectives, the multiple ways they are social and historical beings, but the content of their writing is not simply their perspectives and experiences. To write a memoir is to enter into a constant struggle between the "I" that is specific, even distinctive, in its place, angle of perception, and assumptions, and the contents of experience, the parade of people marching through one's life. On the one hand the "I" struggles not to make itself so central, so dominant, that the contents or objectivities are erased. On the other hand, the author resists turning the events and persons of the memoir into neutralized objects, things depicted as by a camera. Paradoxically, it is only in their presentation to a perspective and to experience that other things come forth as themselves. Perhaps Marjorie Rawlings's *Cross Creek* is one of my favorite books because her intense "I" style, her own way of experiencing, mediates the beauty, danger, and frustrations of life in rural Florida. A time and place, not just Marjorie Rawlings, are disclosed in her writing. The issue is how one can so experience, perceive, remember other things as to open language to their "unconcealing" (Heidegger) being. The instance an "other" enters the picture as something perceived or remembered, it makes its own demands. This may hold even for fictional characters. Novelists often describe how their characters take charge, pursue a life of their own. If the other person (or thing) is not given autonomy or integrity, it begins to fade as an other, its reality blurred by the agendas and ego needs of the perceiver or writer. The other, in other words, undermines, tames, or pushes aside, the narcissistic element so it can get a word in, display and be itself. The memoirist's "I" can overwhelm the "itself" element of actual life. But in the tug of war between the dominant "I" and the integrity of the other, the "I" never disappears. Memoirists cannot cease being themselves. They cannot erase their time and place, their perspectival existence. But they must work hard to keep perspective (biases, negative emotions, stereotypes) from destroying the other. If the others of a narrative are destroyed, the memoir ceases to be a true memoir. The "what" of "what happened" has disappeared. So I accept the terms, the hubris, and self-reference of the memoir, and the space left open for the others.

Closely related to the hubris-alterity tension is another way a memoir can lose its subject. Without close attention and constant self-monitoring, the writer can rather easily assume that memories, narrative, words, even names actually reproduce the others in their very actuality. Thus arises another way in which a memoir can blur or erase the other, not by self-oriented hubris that would dominate the other, but by a kind of naive trust in the appearances. Here the others of the memoir so clearly disclose themselves and are so successfully rendered into language that the chasm between their actuality and their presentation in words is closed. This cognitive over-confidence is an erasure of the others because it empties them of their mystery, possibility, and infinite and ever changing complexity: in short, their concreteness. I try to remember these things but it is a losing battle, a persistent forgetfulness of the others both in their manifest integrity and their elusive mystery.

ONE

Early Memories

"I do not portray being...I portray passing.
My history needs to be adapted to to the moment."

—MICHAEL MONTAIGNE, *ESSAYS*

*"How sweet the silent backward tracings! The wanderings as in dreams—
the meditation of old times resumed—their loves, joys, persons, voyages."*

—WALT WHITMAN, *LEAVES OF GRASS*

"Excitement" is not a word that comes to mind when I think of my life, career, or personality. Of course I enjoy my musical, academic, literary, and familial enthusiasms, and I can be excited by certain events, friends, ideas, and outdoor adventures. But such things are part of the quiet flow of my inner life. I doubt if there are many people whose hearts quicken with anticipation on hearing these recollections are in print. I think of friends and family members whose lives have been fascinating and dramatic, who can tell stories of athletic prowess, going to war, institutional conflicts, crises of injury, the agony of grief and mourning, the challenges of administration or the workplace. Some of my friends were "big shooters" at the top of a business hierarchy or an educational institution: seminary presidents, chief engineers, airline pilots, social activists who spent their days battling societal wrongs and consoling the afflicted. I would be drawn to their stories should they ever write them. My life has some of these features, but lacks the color, drama, and energy of many people I know. My life experience has been a long flow of enjoyments, even excitements, but many of its most meaningful moments are unfortunately the least recordable: for instance, aesthetic enjoyments, insights, and discoveries. In addition to the deep satisfactions that come with marriage, family life, and relations to friends, much of my life story had to do with ideas, writing projects, classrooms, colleagues, books, libraries. I try to convey such things in the essays of chapters 5 and 6 and in the "Problematics" of the Appendix. The "quiet" or uninteresting—some would say geeky—character of my life experience has a few sparks, having to do with my life companion, Doris, children, music, the out of doors, friends. Two major phases organize these memories. The first treats of childhood, adolescence, and the long period of schooling (chapter 1).The second takes up my working life or career from my first teaching position through retirement (chapters 2 and 3).

The one thing all of the periods of my life have in common (except for early childhood) is schools. From kindergarten to my retirement, I have been either going to school or teaching for a school. Furthermore, changing from one school to another, from one elementary school to another, from middle school to high school, from college to graduate school, involved not only a change of setting but a major shift of maturation, challenges, and interests. The breaks with the past and challenges of new situations continued in my teaching years as I moved from one school to another. In my years of study and preparation and in the years of my career, a change of school meant a different neighborhood or city, a new social setting, and new friends. Because going from one school to the other is what created the settings and situations of my personal and also family life, schools will provide the organizing theme of this narrative.

Childhood

The place of my birth was a hospital, the Norton Infirmary in Louisville, Kentucky, a city in which I resided from childhood through my Seminary years. I begin with a word about the time (the 1930s and after) and the place. Louisville was the setting of my early life because it was the city of my father's family and where my mother and father began their marriage. He worked as an office worker in the creosote plant in Louisville before moving to the Ford Motor Assembly plant as an accountant. I spent my childhood and adolescence in an area of the West End of Louisville called Parkland. I have no memory of my first homes: a house on 26th Street, and an upstairs apartment a block from Parkland's small shopping area. I do remember the third home, an apartment above my paternal grandparents. In those years we moved rather often, thus from my grandparents' home on Catalpa to apartments on Olive Street, Virginia Avenue, and Osage. All of these homes were rentals, but when I was a rising sixth grader, my parents bought their first house (Cypress street), located next to the manse (parsonage) of my church. Further, the fist three residences of my memory were within walking or bicycling distance from downtown Parkland with its movie theater, drugstore, fire department, and library, and also my church and the elementary and middle schools I attended. The city center of Louisville and also my high school were both two bus rides away. The 1930s was the decade following the stock market crash of 1929. As an era it was not only a decade of economic depression but cultural transition. Thus, although my father always had a job in this period and we were never in poverty, money was tight, and I grew up without expectations of having any money for extras. In the early 1930s the transition from horse-drawn vehicles to automobiles was almost completed. The Donaldson Wagon delivered bread, milk, and pastries by equine power, and the iron basins providing water for the few horses were still on the streets. As to transportation, street cars had not yet been replaced by motorized buses.

The First Five Years

I am told about but do not remember a few incidents of my infancy. Apparently, whooping cough gave me a "near death" experience as a baby as my mother and her sister maintained an all night vigil of care. Our second house, a block from Parkland's center was high ceilinged, with a long staircase connecting our second floor apartment to the ground floor. This was the scene of a frightening accident (to my mother) when I fell with my stroller down those steps, breaking my nose. Nor do I remember my aunt teaching me to sing the rather haunting song, "Bye, Bye, Blackbird," when I was one year old. My earliest memories have to do with water: being bathed by my mother in a bathtub and sitting in water on the banks of the Ohio River. Most of my early childhood memories are about life on

3

Catalpa Street, the second-floor apartment above my grandparents. My grandfather often took me with him to the fire station a half a block away where he routinely defeated all comers at checkers. This was the time when, because of the kidnapping of the Lindbergh baby—Charles Lindbergh had piloted the first plane across the Atlantic —parents throughout the country were nervous about the safety of their small children. When I was three or four, I had figured out from a kind of map in my head that by walking a half block toward Parkland, and turning right a couple of times, I could return to my backyard by way of the alley. Furthermore, I decided to verify my calculation by walking the route, a journey of eight or ten minutes. That was time enough for my mother, grandmother, and neighbors to think I had been kidnapped, so I arrived in the backyard to face severe punishment. I, simply a curious geographer, never really understood what I had done wrong. When I was about five, my mother began dressing me up in cowboy suits and other regalia to sing at church groups and PTA's in the neighborhood. I recall singing "Farewell to Thee (Aloha Oa?)," a Hawaiian popular song, and since that day I have never liked Hawaiian music. I was told but do not recall that in these years I had an imaginary playmate whose name was Brownie. Apparently, Brownie and I were a duo (cf Calvin and Hobbes).

Parkland Elementary School

Parkland Elementary was located only a few houses from where our family lived. I had attended kindergarten for half a year but was not old enough to follow my friends into first grade, a catastrophe! At this point my mother went into action (as she often did in such situations), taking me downtown to the school board where I was subjected to a few simple tests to qualify me for first grade. My mother and I had been making weekly trips to the Parkland library for a couple of years prior to kindergarten, and I remember requesting books on this or that subject (crocodiles, ships), and by the time I entered first grade, I was a self-taught reader. I do not recall much about the four years I spent in the school in Parkland. The work was not difficult, and I mostly enjoyed playing with friends. In the fourth grade, my teacher discovered that I had some talent for art, so I became an unofficially appointed school artist, assigned to a special desk where I worked on posters advertising school functions, and placed in store windows. I recall doing a silhouette, black on blue, of three wise men on their camels under a crescent moon. Most of my friends were local boys of the Parkland area, but I had one special friend who was an overweight girl whom I felt sorry for because she was snubbed by others in the class. (In her adult years she reminded me of that friendship.)

Old enough to go to school also meant being old enough to attend the Saturday morning cowboy movies in the local cinema, a very loud and messy affair of enthusiastic kids eating popcorn and rooting for the hero. This of course was the high point of the week. Typically, what the cinema offered on Saturday afternoon were the movie itself, a cartoon, sometimes a news program (boring!), and a ten-minute serial adventure that always ended with the hero or heroine caught in some horrible (certain death) peril, the miraculous rescue to take place on the next Saturday. When I was five or six, my parents took me to my first movies in that cinema. I still remember the feeling of sadness both movies left me with. One movie was about an aged navy captain who could not abide the fate of having his rusty ship (a cruiser?) deliberately sunk, so he secretly returned to the ship and was killed by the salvos. A second movie was about a beautiful Native American, Ramona, and I only remember its deep sadness. *The* great movie of my young years was *Robin Hood*, a memorable experience. The books I read from six years on were the standard children's classics: *King Arthur, Heidi, Pinocchio, Twenty Thousand Leagues Under the Sea, A Child's Garden of Verses*. But a new and exciting genre appeared about this time, the comic book. A comic book (*Superman, Batman*) cost a lot of money (five or ten cents) and I could only collect a few of the books. A bout with scarlet fever served to increase my collection. I was confined to bed, did not feel sick, and a few new comic books rescued me from boredom. The only other illness I remember in this period was anemia. I was a picky eater, especially with respect to meat, and large and painful boils appeared sporadically on my arms and legs. The cure was worse than the boils, a big tablespoon of liver extract at meals, the taste of which I remember to this day.

From the third grade on, my parents moved to a different rental house every year, three in all before they bought a house. Because of the moves, I spent the these years living in different neighborhoods and attending different elementary schools. In the first house after leaving my grandparents' house, a group of older boys (eleven or twelve in age) looked after me and occasionally let me hang out with them. I spent much of my good weather time in the backyard building elaborate World War I-type battle grounds (trenches) for my small iron soldiers. The Osage neighborhood was largely Roman Catholic, and our house was across from the parochial school and convent. I did not like the elementary school that year because I was an outsider often threatened (but never assaulted) by the boys in my class. I did like my own neighborhood whose boys had organized themselves into the Corner Gang. Stepping outside of my house on my first day, I was challenged to wrestle a selected boy whom I subdued almost instantly, thus being accepted in the gang. It was not of course a gang in the modern sense. We mostly played softball in the streets, rode our bikes through various neighborhoods of the city, and pretended to defend our turf. A few older boys looked after and offered protection for the younger boys like myself. Fighting and practicing fighting was a prominent activity, but actual fighting rarely took place. In this year on Osage, I was given my first bicycle, a full size bike too large for my ten-year-old frame. I crashed so many times learning to ride it (in the alley) that the neighbors were sure I would not survive the project. Finally, as the sixth grade approached, my parents purchased a house on Cypress Street next to our church's manse, and I attended yet another elementary school, McFerrin. This was a good move for me because I liked the new school, the boys and girls in the neighborhood, new friends, and the chance to play football in the schoolyard in the fall. The sixth grade was the year something new happened at school. The sixth grade boys and girls became interested in each other, boyfriend-girlfriend relations developed, and seasonal parties (Halloween, birthdays) were held.

In these pre-junior high school years, a few things happened that I will only briefly mention. My first memorable *trip* took place when I was eight, a visit to my mother's sister, Lillian, and her family on Long Island, New York. It was memorable not only because of reunions with my younger cousins (Wally and Marilyn) but because of the overwhelming impact, the icy waters, the salty smell, the endless breakers, of the Atlantic Ocean. Aunt Dode babysat my one-year-old brother, Austin, in Louisville, and Aunt Ninny traveled with us.

Visits to the *farm* near New Castle and the house in the small river town of Gratz left vivid memories. At Gratz I could explore small creeks, row a boat on the Kentucky River, fish with my father when he could join us on vacation. My fishing began in those years, and after catching a catfish on a Sunday afternoon family outing at Marshall's slough, I became a lifetime devotee of that activity. We had been visiting Henry and Owen Counties since I was an infant, but in 1937 Ohio floods waters inundated Louisville in late winter. We barely escaped, taking the car through a vast flooded plain on the way to New Castle. I had visited the farm many times during the summers. This was my one winter visit to the farm, which meant no indoor plumbing, no electricity, or central heat, and no playmates. I was put to bed at night with a wrapped-up heated iron for warmth. The kitchen with its huge iron stove was the center of the house in the daytime. Having little to do, I spent many days reading through Hurlbut's *Stories of the Bible*, one of the two books in the house.

Church was an important part of our family life. In those years Sunday school was an hour of rollicking singing of up-tempo hymns. I experienced my first exposure to John Calvin when I memorized the child's catechism and recited it to the minister's wife, thus receiving a copy of the New Testament. Church also meant a huge pageant every Christmas, produced by a gifted junior high school English teacher. One Christmas when I was eight, I played the role of Seth, a crippled boy who was miraculously healed, my first but not quite my last venture in acting.

Christmas was a magic time. Every year a regular sequence of events aroused in me an escalating excitement. The sequence did not begin as early as now (before Thanksgiving). The first sign of Christmas for me was not the cold November days but the first sounds of Christmas carols on the streets of downtown Louisville. A unique thrill and suppressed excitement came with hearing the first carols. The second event in the sequence was the arrival in the mail of Sutcliffe's toy catalogue. I waited for it every year, and when it arrived, I turned into a scholarly rabbi with his Torah, perusing and memorizing every page. The third event followed closely on the second, a visit with my parents to Sutcliffe's store giving me a chance to actually examine what I had found in the catalogue. The fourth event was my church's Christmas pageant and its candlelight service. The fifth event took place a week or so before Christmas. Santa himself would stage some sort of appearance around our house. One Christmas a bearded Santa Claus peered through our upstairs window, my father on a ladder as I learned later. In my innocence and excitement, I never noticed a strange coincidence; the gifts I received on Christmas morning were the very ones I identified in the catalogue and the store. Whatever was going on between Sutcliffes and Santa remained a hidden bit of elvish magic

Music in these years was mostly something I enjoyed listening to in church and at Christmas. I forget when the upright piano first appeared in our house. When it did, I began to experiment with "playing" it, becoming familiar with its challenge. Outdoor *sports* were important in these years, especially backyard or schoolyard football in the fall. In those years, the size difference between the boys made little difference, so I could compete with the best at running and tackling. When I was about eight, my friends and I discovered the downtown YMCA, where we learned to swim and to play a little basketball. I remember only one visit to the doctor at that time. The occasion was an incident at a Sunday picnic. My age group was lined up for a sack race. Each of us was given a waist-high sack that we stepped into and held as we jumped ahead. In my eagerness to win, I jumped before the signal, breaking my big toe. I lined up again, won the race, received a box of candy, and spent the next weeks with a long splint on my toe.

Adolescence

To repeat, schools as well as family and neighborhood marked the major phases of my early life, and with each of them came a new circle of friends plus new interests and activities. Needless to say, the move from elementary school to junior high or middle school was a very big deal, a new epoch in my early adolescence. Many things happened in the three years covering the seventh through the ninth grades: puberty, a serious girlfriend, the beginning of a music "career," my first paying jobs. The school was a fifteen-minute walk from my house. The teachers of math, English, and music were very good. Most subjects were easy for me, but there were exceptions. I was less than enthusiastic about "shop," which presented projects of typesetting for printing or making a small metal handle. I struggled with algebra partly because it was not well taught but mostly because I spent my time in class writing letters to my girlfriend. When I left junior high school for high school, I had a good rudimentary grasp of English grammar, a good beginning on reading musical notes and performing on an instrument (trumpet). Music was more or less at the center of my middle school experience. In my first year, an older boy in our neighborhood died of a ruptured appendix and I was given his cornet. To join the large junior high school band, I had to learn to play that instrument, thus joined a group of beginners taught by the band director. After a few weeks, I had learned enough to become the sixteenth player in the band's large trumpet section. During the course of that school year, I gradually moved up (by challenging the next player above me) to nearly the top. In my second year, I became "famous." These were the early years of the "Big Bands," and Harry James, a trumpet player, was an icon to people like me. I learned to imitate his style, and that year played some of his songs for a school assembly, thus becoming instantly known by most of the students. That performance set the stage for what happened at the end of the year. I ran for president of the student body. A good friend managed my campaign like a professional, with my picture (with cornet) distributed on cardboard badges. I had to write and deliver a speech on stage along with other candidates, but my "fame" gave me a huge advantage and I won the election. Thus, I was president of the study body in my third year. I made the occasional speech to the assembly and was treated like a celeb by some of the younger girls. This fame had a dark side. I began to take my status as celeb seriously, and learned from my friends that I was an insufferable egotist. I forget the language they used. Besides music four things stand out in my three years of junior high school.

I had been working at various jobs for pocket money since I was twelve. Garden work for my grandmother was the first, followed by mowing lawns in the neighborhood. The hardest job of those years was a brief summer job as a grocery store delivery boy. I pedaled a bicycle with a huge load of groceries in a basket over the front tire, each trip covering several miles. I very much enjoyed my job at Winslow's, a drugstore in the heart of Parkland where I had grown up. My friends and I worked there off and on for several years. The job was both challenging and fun. The challenge, especially in the snowy or rainy days or nights of winter, was to deliver medicines by bicycle to homes in distant neighborhoods. The fun was the excitement of getting to know the hundreds of items for sale in the store, using the cash register to sell them, and having free access to the malts and sundaes of the soda fountain. I was fourteen when I worked as an usher in a fashionable, downtown movie theater. I say "fashionable" because ushers, dressed in stiff collars, bow ties, and colorful coats, guided people to their seats with flashlights. The job was difficult because it meant endlessly standing around, and enduring the sights and sounds of the same movie for weeks. It paid thirty cents an hour.

From elementary school on, I had enjoyed the company of girls. My first "girlfriend" was Margie, who lived only a few steps around the corner from our Cyprus house. Ours was a brief, summer-long flirtation, something new to both of us. In the sixth grade, one of my schoolmates was a Jewish girl, Debra. In the fall of that year, we became attracted to each other almost instantly at a Halloween party. Our relation as boyfriend and girlfriend continued throughout our years in junior high school. One of her aunts taught us to dance, and of course the music we danced to was the Harry James band. She was a devoted fan of the female singer (Helen Forest) and I of course thought Harry James occupied a place in the pantheon of pop music deities. In our years at PJH, we wrote letters to each other almost every day, and when possible found private spaces for hand holding and kissing. Her mother was not enthusiastic about our relationship. At the end of the third year at PJH, our relation faded for a variety of reasons, my own celeb self-image being one of them. She went to one of the girls' high schools in Louisville, was president of her senior class, attended the University of Kentucky, married a Jewish classmate, and with him founded a chain of laundries and dry cleaners in Birmingham. I saw her, briefly, only a time or two after our junior high years.

I was fortunate in these years to avoid serious injuries and illnesses. One classmate suffered a debilitating case of polio. Two visits to doctors stand out in my memory of these junior high school years. When I was twelve, five large seed warts (Mosaic warts) appeared on the soles of my feet. One physician proposed to remove the warts with several weeks of acid applications. The next physician simply anesthetized each wart with Novocain and burned it off. The needles poked deeply into the nerve-sensitive sole evoked agonizing pain, and I was admonished by my father (who no doubt had never experienced that procedure) to endure such things more stoically. I had never taken care of my teeth properly, and in those pre-flouride days, they gradually decayed until I suffered painful toothaches and had no choice but to tell my parents. The first dentist I visited seemed to be on drugs and quickly jammed a pick into the pulp of the tooth. After finding a neighborhood dentist (Parkland), I began many weeks of treatment involving drilling out multiple cavities (no Novocain in those days) and teeth extractions, a dreadful experience. I learned later that there were dentists who used a flow of water to reduce the heat of drilling, and other pain-easing devices.

The out-of-doors had always had a special place among my enjoyments. In the sixth and seventh grades, I was (sort of) active in a church-based Boy Scout troop, a project I abandoned after becoming a Second Class Scout. What attracted me most was the occasional hiking, camping, the weekends in lodges and cabins in wintertime. My life out of doors also involved exploring much of Louisville with a friend (Posey Gaslin) on bicycles. A favorite jaunt was to the Ohio River near the Ford Assembly Plant, where we found a rusty oil-carrying barge that we used as a jumping off place for swimming. My friend complained in later years that I insisted on doing this in early March, and I do remember the shock of the icy waters of the Ohio.

Male High School

My three years in High School were the years of my adolescence, a period in which, like most teenage boys, I became more or less loony, beset by exaggerated feelings of sadness, intense anger, and paternal alienation. It was, as I remember it, the worst time in my life. My intense anger was fueled both by hormones and my relation to my father. The physical abuse of earlier times had ceased but personal abuse continued, especially toward my brother. My way of surviving what was a dysfunctional family was typical of teenagers past and present, namely isolation. I worked hard to establish physical distance from the turmoil of family life. I found a way to spend summers away from home as a counselor in a YMCA camp. I moved upstairs to our unfinished and unheated attic, where in wintertime I read late into the night under piles of blankets. Yet in spite of my unhappiness, I was never simply a loser, a marginalized, aimless, wanderer. A number of people, settings, and activities gave these years another dimension: most of all, Doris, who lived next store, a deepening religious piety, a few very close friends, books, Piomingo (summer camp), and music. These things made my teenage years positive, meaningful, even joyful.

These were the years I attended male high school. Going from Parkland Junior High to male high school was more life-changing than any of my previous school moves. Male High was male in the literal sense, all boys and all male teachers. In fact most of Louisville's high schools were gender specific. The building, a fine piece of architecture, is still in existence but Male High School now is a huge suburban complex and is co-educational. The other high school in Louisville was Male's main athletic rival, Manual. Decades before, Manual offered "manual train- ing" in a variety of practical areas and Male specialized in pre-college types of courses. This difference had survived in the mid 1940s but both schools offered solid pre-college foundational studies. Most of Male's teachers were solid educators and some were brilliant. Its athletic teams were among the best in Kentucky. I am embarrassed to confess that, in spite of solid teaching, my academic life at Male was virtually non- existent. For some reason, it never occurred to me that doing homework was necessary or even important or that what I learned and my level of grades might have something to do with my later studies in college. Why such obtuseness? I did sense that my parents expected me to attend col- lege. (I would be the first member of my immediate family to do so.) But notions of doing homework, being accepted into a college, obtaining scholarships, excelling in courses never found their way into my loony teenage brain. The result was poor performance in math and science courses, mediocre performance in such courses as Latin, and sometimes A level performances in history and literature. (In my first year at Male, the teacher read my assigned paper to the class. Of course its subject was, of all things, music!) Homework, then, was not allowed to intrude on my world, a world of religion, Doris, music, and books. Books were very much a part of my world, and I read poetry and novels every night in my attic retreat. But I did graduate, and because admissions standards and costs were never very high in the colleges I knew about, I did eventually go to college.

Music is the topic of one of the essays in chapter 6 of this work and I shall try to avoid repetition. But music occupied a central place in my high school years and any account of my adolescence that omitted it would distort the story. In these years my musical tastes and activities were divided between two very different musical genres: the popular mu- sic of the Big Band era, and, the classical music of church choirs and the symphony orchestra.

The Big Band genre was in the picture prior to my arrival at Male. I had played that music doing trumpet solos in the assembly of my junior high school. And when I was fourteen, my mother saw a notice in the newspaper inviting tryouts for a Big Band. My parents took me, cornet in hand, to the tryout. I played well enough to be invited to join, but not with the cornet. Big Bands had trumpet not cornet sections. And our financially pressed family could not simply go to a store and purchase a trumpet. School had just ended, so I looked for and found a summer job in a movie theater. I worked all summer, saved the money, and at the end of the summer took my approximately one hundred dollars to a music store downtown and bought a rather mediocre trumpet. I joined the band of about eight teenage musicians the next week. The band, expanded in size, became the Kenny Hale Orchestra. I played second trumpet to Herbie Hale, a gifted musician, and replaced him as first trumpet when he was drafted into the army. We played every weekend at a teenage club, Gremlin Corner, and for High School dances, in parks, the USO of the military, and occasionally went on the road to play college proms. Eventually I left the Kenny Hale band to be the sole trumpet player in a band playing Saturday and Sunday nights in a night club outside of Louisville. We played from a huge collection of arrangements, and there were no rehearsals. I either had to learn to sight read the music on the job or give up the project. Sight reading thus became a musical skill that stayed with me ever after. The upside of my weekly band jobs was that I always had money for dating, for buying music-related things such as a record player, and even for savings. The downside was serious sleep deprivation when after late-night music gigs, I rose in the early hours for pre-school marching band practice at Male.

I was acquainted with another genre, classical music, simply because it was the music of the church choir, and in the 1940s, the Big Bands sometimes played arrangements of the lyrical themes of the great Romantic composers such as Tchaikovsky, Rachmaninoff, and Chopin. When my voice changed, I sang bass in the church choir. Sometimes I tried to play simplified versions of classical pieces on our home piano. In my junior high school years, my mother and I attended the concerts of the Louisville Symphony Orchestra, and in high school, a friend of mine and I would attend the rehearsals of the orchestra. I sensed at this time that the "real" music of my future would not be popular but classical music. All this is background to the main musical event of my high school years. One of my ways of surviving my adolescent unhappiness was to create chord patterns and melodies on the piano, and out of these musings came a short composition which combined both classical and popular elements. Once again, my mother, ever alert to opportunities for her children, noticed in the newspaper an announcement of a competition for young composers. Why not submit what I had done? So began a project pursued over the winter months of expanding and orchestrating the initial piece into several movements of a symphonic poem, writing out the parts for each instrument. Of course, I did not know what I was doing. I depended on my ear to tell me if I was breaking the rules of musical theory. I did self-teach myself orchestration and the ranges and appropriate keys for the instruments. Such work needed more privacy than our crowded dining room, and the pastor's study in our church provided the secluded space I needed. It was a tiny room with a desk, a chair, and a heater but no piano. I spent many weekday evenings of that winter in that room orchestrating the piece I had written. As I remember it, the work was embarrassingly bad, but for a sixteen-year-old, it was probably fairly good. I was one of four or so Louisville young people who "won" the composition, and the judge, the head of the music school at Indiana University, recommended that the winners perform their compositions and that the symphony should play my work. Thus, the symphony performed the piece at an all-school concert and again on the radio. When this happened, there was the expected hoopla, pictures and articles in the newspaper. After that I was invited to conduct the Atherton High School (Doris's school) orchestra in a performance of the work. An important consequence followed this whole affair. Robert Allen, our church organist and a cellist in the Symphony, offered to give me piano lessons and teach me music theory. I didn't study piano very long (a few months), and did not get beyond playing Bach's two-part inventions, but this was enough basis for enjoying piano playing for the rest of my life. The theory book we used was not rudimentary enough to serve as an introduction to music theory thus did not provide the foundation I needed.

Piomingo was a YMCA camp located on high cliffs overlooking a huge bend of the Ohio River near Brandenburg, Kentucky. The large, now abandoned log home of a Kentucky politician (Van Buren) was nearby. The camp consisted of a central area (office, mess hall, social hall-gym) and five outlying clusters of log houses, each with a central lodge. I knew about the camp as a member of the downtown YMCA. My first stay at the camp should have been for the summer. I was accepted as a junior counselor, and was beside myself with excitement at the prospect of a summer in the forest away from my family. It was not to be. The polio epidemic of 1943 closed the camp after only two weeks. But I did spend the next three summers at the camp as a counselor, an unforgettable experience. The need to be away from home plus the lure of the forest must have been powerful to draw me away from Doris (except for occasional weekends) and from playing trumpet in Louisville night clubs. Part of the lure and charm of Piomingo was my best friend of those days, Dan Hunt (see "Friendships").

I did many things at the camp. I was the camp bugler, waking the camp in the morning with reveille and putting it to bed with taps. I taught lanyard making (a stretch), worked in the nature lodge with snakes and other creatures (a delight), and in the social hall (weights and boxing). During the afternoon rest for the campers, the counselors usually played competitive sports. I often did a three-mile run, played touch football, and two-on-a-side volleyball. Because my companion (Dan) was six feet tall and a gifted athlete, we were rarely beaten. In a one-on-one basketball game with Dan, his shoulder caught my chin, the result being three very loose lower teeth, a trip to the dentist in Louisville, and a painful summer eating soups and soft food. When I was in graduate school in New York City, those teeth abscessed, requiring root canal work at the Columbia dental school. Camp life included a few memorable and sometimes even dangerous adventures. One of them was a Tom Sawyer-Huck Finn trek on the Ohio River. Dan and I had been given a counselor's leave for an afternoon and evening. Our plan was to follow the railroad track along the river eight or so miles to a small river town, grab a huge log at river's edge and float back down to camp. The hike and the floatation took much longer than we anticipated and it was just getting dark when we saw lights ahead *in the middle of the river*. The lights were a dam and we and our log were bearing down on it. We swam to shore, and then our real adventures began. The river shore was all dense forest, and we had no choice but to strike inland searching for our railroad track. That search involved feeling our way through an utterly dark forest and crossing a huge field of thorny blackberries. Those misadventures took up most of the night, and we arrived at camp in the wee hours of the morning. A few years ago Dan and I revisited the camp, and were surprised to see in a picture of former counselors *Tom Cruise*.

Religion was an important part of my high school years (see chapter 6). "Religion" in the sense of personal piety, strong beliefs, and being part of a church congregation found its way into many aspects of my life: friendships, Camp Piomingo, my relation to Doris's father, Dewey Kimbel, books, and even music. I was moved both by religious poetry and also the occasional novel: for instance, *The Chain* or *Dr. Hudson's Secret*

Journal. Music and religion were interweaved in the choral music sung by the church choir. The choir was directed by Robert Allen, a Louisville educator, and was made up of both adults and young people. I remember being very much moved by the cantatas we sang at Easter and Christmas, for instance "The Crucifixion," by John Stainer. Both my piety and fascination with the beliefs and narratives of religion prompted me to weigh the pros and cons of a religious career (ministry). Religious piety was an important part of my relation to my best friend, Dan Hunt. He worked for an inner-city mission and I sometimes helped out in a Sunday school class or weekend youth retreat. He had committed himself to ministry as a life vocation, but in high school I was pulled in the two directions of ministry or music. Twice in my high school years I delivered a sermon to the congregation and was praised for "sincerity" and "having a good voice." I doubt if there was much else to deserve praise.

It will come as no surprise to those who know me that from my sixteenth year on, *Doris* was my life's very center. Two years younger than I, she was my next door neighbor and a PK, a "preacher's kid." It did not take long for us to find ways of being together. I "tutored" her in Latin and taught her to dance. (I had almost nothing to offer on either subject.) Our serious relation began with a New Year's Eve party, a foursome which included her sister and a long-term friend, Bill Hopper. We were a couple through high school and college, and became engaged during my last year at Centre College. The only things that threatened our plans for a life-time together were my recurring and sometimes long absences. These included my frequent weekend band gigs, my summer residences at Piomingo, my first two years away at college, and my weekend absences when we both attended Centre. We agreed that she would date during those times, and we were fortunate that our relation survived such an arrangement. Our relation from the start was a mixture of close, intimate friendship in which we shared our deepest feelings and the passions of adolescent romantic love. She was not enthusiastic about becoming a "minister's wife," a fairly defined role and sexist pattern prevalent in Protestant congregations at that time, and that too was a small obstacle to our plans. Yet neither of us could imagine life without the other one and it has continued that way ever since.

My senior year at Male ended in January. For reasons I hardly remember, Dan Hunt and I decided to celebrate the occasion by spending a week or so in one of the lodges at Camp Piomingo. My father drove us there, the car loaded with food, winter clothing, and chess board. The first day the weather turned bitterly cold and snow covered the ground. The large fire we kept going kept us warm only if we remained close to it. Beyond five or so feet from the fire, the cabin temperature was close to freezing. In mid-week, my father and Doris arrived to rescue us from being snow-bound only to learn that the cold hadn't bothered us and we were having a great time walking the silent forests, playing chess, cooking meals, and talking. College in Danville did not start for me until September and I needed a job to build up money for the first year's tuition. My father made that possible, connecting me with the personnel people at the Ford Assembly Plant where he worked. My job was in the mail department and included doing the mimeographing for the office on a maleficent machine that never worked very long without some repair. I'm afraid I let my father down by resigning to go off to Piomingo in late spring. He (and Ford) had assumed I would stay through the summer. Piomingo's lure was so strong, I unthinkingly was responsible for an awkward situation for my father. Thus, I spent one more summer at camp before heading to Danville, Kentucky and Centre College.

Centre College

Centre College had been the locale of a Presbyterian Seminary in the nineteenth century and still retained a connection with the Presbyterian church. Because of its stunning pre-World War II reputation in football and other sports, it was well known beyond Kentucky. It was academically a "good" college, although most of its faculty would not rank with professors at Chicago, Stanford, Yale and other prestigious schools. Its faculty was solid in the sciences, thus it had a good pre-med program. Offerings in the social sciences (sociology, anthropology, political science, economics) were weak, but that in part simply reflected the state of those fields at the time. Philosophy, taught by the religion professors, was close to non-existence. Art (one professor) was good as was drama (one professor), and music (four or five teachers) was neither very strong nor weak.

That I would continue my education beyond high school was both a familial and personal expectation. That I chose Centre for my college studies was a signal that I would not pursue a musical career. Otherwise, I would have enrolled in the music school of Indiana University. Attending a college other than Centre was never a consideration. The reason was my "second father," Dewey Kimbel. He never pushed Centre on me nor did have to. In the 1920s, he had been one of Centre's famous athletes, lettering in three sports and active in a variety of campus activities, and he had shared with me many stories from his years there. The college scene in the years following World War II (the late 1940s) was very different from today. Only a small percentage of the population attended college, and the rapid expansion of colleges and universities was only just beginning. The cost of going to college was low. Centre's tuition was less than $500 a year, and few students graduated with significant debt. Admission standards were low, and applicants with mediocre High School GPA's (like me) had no trouble being accepted. The year I arrived at Centre was the first year World War II veterans flooded college campuses and they swelled the Freshman class.

When I arrived on campus in the fall of 1947, my high school frame of mind about study, classes, education had changed. This new thing, "college," was to be taken seriously. It actually cost money, and study there had to do with the opening or closing of future doors of opportunity. So for the first time in my life, I settled down to serious academic study. I also did other things, far too many things. But I did study, and to a degree even learned some things. What follows here is a summary of my activities at Centre, my overly busy way of facing up to the challenge of the being a college student. When I think back on my college years, I find the pace and number of my activities almost ridiculously excessive. My life at Centre included acting, a Big Band, the debate team, an interim pastorate, a fraternity, various college committees, outdoor treks, a noon-time prayer group, and a course of study that led to graduation in three years and a summer. Other than my A-type personality, I find it difficult to explain such a pattern. I really thought that was what "going to college" was about. Twenty-five years earlier, Dewey Kimbel, my mentor and pastor, had spent his years at Centre in a similar way. A wiser strategy (for me) would have been to slow down, take four years to complete college, study piano (not voice), learn a modern European language, major in classics rather than philosophy/religion, and resist the temptation of serving a church.

Philosophy/religion and music were my double major. Citing my shaky and minimal exposure to music theory, I persuaded the department to allow me to skip the first year (ten hours) of music theory and enter the second year. I had no trouble with the subject, but I had missed a lot of basics. Trumpet was my instrument, but the small department had no trumpet teachers so voice became my performance instrument and required a series of private lessons ending with a recital. In the freshman year, I joined a newly formed Big Band that played for school dances, but I soon lost interest in it and the band itself did not survive very long.

Acting came as a complete surprise. After I had read an assigned poem in a speech class, the professor who was Centre's drama and also debate coach (West Hill) took me aside and said, "I want you to play Oscar in *The Little Foxes* (Lillian Hellman) this winter. And I said, "Okay." Doing that play was a new and exciting experience: rehearsals, make-up, hanging out with "actors," having to actually slap the face of my "wife" on stage, reading reviews of one's work. The next year, I played Eilert Lovborg in Ibsen's *Hedda Gabler*. This play was well reviewed by the local critic. But although I enjoyed acting, I was never a natural. It never occurred to me to do the things any real actor would do to prepare for the part: read through the play, get a sense of the character one was playing, become that person on stage.

West Hill, a graduate of Male High, was a wounded veteran, shot in the lower spine and kidneys after D-Day. He walked with a limp, was still undergoing treatment, and later on died of complications from his wounds. He and I became good friends, and it was natural that, given my interests, I would join the debate team. Being a Centre debater had many perks, the main one being a deep South trip every winter to such places as coastal Mississippi or Miami. We targeted tournaments in those places, and took on the big universities. Debating was one of the things I could do fairly well and my partner and I won most of our debates, Fraternity brothers and close friends were part of the team of six or eight debaters, so the trips were occasions for various mishaps, adventures, pranks. In one tournament, after debating all morning on pro and anti sides, my partner stopped in the middle of a speech, his eyes glazed over, and he asked, "Which side am I debating on?" Needless to say, we lost that debate.

Through high school, religion had been an important dimension of my personal life, hence it was natural to connect with college men and women of the same mind. We formed a noon-time prayer group, volunteered in a small congregation up in the hills. Sometime in my freshman year, it became clear to me that my future would involve some sort of ministry and thus would require post-college study in a seminary. To my surprise, I discovered that at this Presbyterian college, being a "pre-ministry student" meant a significant scholarship. Centre then added an academic scholarship to that, so my tuition was covered for my second and third years. The executive of the Presbytery of Louisville asked me if I wanted to be the interim preacher at a small Presbyterian church in Carrollton, Kentucky, on the Ohio River. Driven by my own egocentrism (having a congregation at nineteen years old), I foolishly said yes. It was a difficult thing to do. In the first months, I hitchhiked the ninety or so miles across Kentucky, spending the night at the hotel in town. Eventually, I bought a Model B Ford (1933), and that made things easier. The congregation was small, and, aware that it was on its last days, was tolerant of having a college-student leader. The whole venture was foolish, partly because of what it took out of me in time and energy, and partly because that was the one year Doris was on campus, and the church took me away from her on the weekends. The result was that she became the dating favorite of Centre's most prestigious fraternity, the Phi Delts.

When I arrived on campus, it never occurred to me to join a fraternity. I knew they were on campus—Dewey Kimbel had been a Beta —but fraternities were not on my mental horizon as part of the "going to college" scene, and I did not go out for rush. Nor was it surprising that no fraternity went after me. But late in my first year, a defunct Centre fraternity (Phi Kappa Tau) was reorganized. When several of my friends became interested in being part of the reorganized fraternity, I joined them and we were hauled off to Lexington to be initiated. Each frat on campus had its own distinctive aura and reputation: drinkers, jocks, social elites. Ours, I think, had the aura and reputation of nerds. That is, we routinely had the highest GPA average among the fraternities, and only a few of us drank alcohol. I enjoyed the friendships made in the fraternity, and in my third year at Centre served as its president.

My third and last year at Centre was for emotional and personal reasons my most difficult year, partly because of my weekend treks to Carrollton and partly because, as the year went on, I became convinced I was losing Doris. It was natural for her to choose Centre as her college. Her father was a former BMOC (Big *Person* On Campus?) there. And after her "monogamous" high school years with me, her family urged her to date other men. My treks to my church opened up the weekend for her to date and even develop serious relationships with a variety of men, two in particular. She was enormously popular, constantly pursued by, to use a sixteenth century term, various swains. I had agreed to the arrangement, but each week became more despondent over what I perceived would be the outcome. Just before Christmas, we broke off our relationship, with devastating pain on both sides, but at Christmas time, found a way to reunite and even became engaged. That ended her Centre dating, but her second semester would lack the excitement of the first. Both of us attended summer school in Danville, which enabled us to finish college (in her case, the University of Louisville) in three years.

I found a way to ease the strain of study and the pressure of activities by occasional treks to the local countryside. In those days Danville was a tiny college town, and farms abutted the edge of the campus. In the fall, winter, and spring, a biology major and I would search the creeks for snakes, or simply enjoy hiking through snow-covered fields. A number of our captured snakes ended up in Louisville, cared for by my budding scientist brother, Austin. Many of my college friends are described in the appendix, "Friendships." My closest friend was my roommate of the second two years, Jim Brown. Jim had been a neighbor in Parkland. A year or so older than I, he was drafted into the army, thus lived in the veterans' barracks at Centre. I joined him in a tiny room in those barracks. Andy Blane from Hopkinsville was smart, a Baptist pre-ministry student, and a varsity competitor in tennis and golf. He eventually pursued graduate work in Russian studies and became a professor at Hunter College in New York City. Mayo Smith, a fellow debater and fraternity brother, eventually attended the Presbyterian seminary in Louisville, and after several years in the pastorate, worked as an editor in Presbyterian publications, retiring with his wife, Joanne, in Stanford, Kentucky. Bobby Jones, a fraternity brother and fellow debater, worked as a regional sales person and died from injuries in an auto accident not many years after graduation. Four professors at Centre were also good friends: West Hill (drama and debate), Charles Hazelrig (English), Arnold Come (religion), and Jameson Jones (religion).

Louisville Presbyterian Seminary

Louisville Presbyterian Seminary originated from two conservative streams of nineteenth century Presbyterianism: the "Old School" (traditional Calvinism) of the northeast, and the traditionally conservative religion of the southeast. In the nineteenth century, two Kentucky Presbyterian schools, one in Louisville, the other in Danville, merged to create Louisville Presbyterian Seminary. A mutual religious conservatism made the merger possible. However, in the early twentieth century, the Modernists more or less won the fundamentalist-modernist war in the Northern Presbyterian church, and the fundamentalist strands of the church broke off into separate denominations. This event was a moderating influence on the "Old School" Seminary in Louisville. Thus, by the time I arrived at the end of the 1940s, the faculty was staffed by both Modernist and Calvinist faculty members. The school had survived an earlier period of conservative-moderate conflicts and for the most part was a moderate rather than fundamentalist school. Thus, it had an aura of ecumenism and a diverse faculty which included representatives of radical historical criticism (J. P. Love, A. B. Rhodes) and traditional Calvinism (Andrew Rule), and many professors in between. Two general features gave a certain structure to the curriculum and therefore to the faculty. The first was displayed in its slogan, "an ancient Gospel for a modern world." Judged by its curriculum and the fields of its faculty, the "Gospel" meant more or less the two testaments of the Bible and the "modern world" meant the twentieth century and the everyday life of the churches. This was why, in my time, almost nothing was offered in the history and theologies of Christendom between the close of the New Testament canon and the current era. No primary texts from the long history of Christianity were assigned in classes, not even Calvin! (This ahistorical curricular structure was corrected in the 1950s.) The second feature arose from the first, a very strong emphasis on practical (especially pastoral) theology. This emphasis was not only apparent in the areas of preaching, Christian education, pastoral care, and field education but throughout the curriculum.

Almost all of the faculty were strongly committed to teaching and sustained a pastoral relation with the students. The teachers I became close to were Harry Goodykoontz (practical theology), Arnold Black Rhodes (Hebrew Bible), and Julian Price Love (biblical theology.) The professor of theology, Kenneth Foreman, was a gifted linguist, wordsmith, and wit. He taught theology "homiletically," that is, distilling complex theological arguments, doctrines, and texts into applicable and often amusing adages. He never subjected a text or idea to extended analysis, digging for presuppositions, nor did he follow the implications of ideas into larger structures (systematic theology). He was not in his writing or teaching a Paul Tillich or Karl Barth, but he was a much loved, highly respected teacher who worked hard to connect the mystery of faith or tradition with everyday life.

In my final months at Centre, I decided to settle for myself the conflict going on between traditionally conservative Christians, pastors, or
theologians and what came to be called historical criticism on the issue
of the Bible's authority. I knew little about the latter, although it had been
around since the eighteenth century. This had been one the main issues
that triggered the fundamentalist-modernist wars of the early twentieth
century in the mainline denominations of the Northeast. I was briefly
exposed to the modernist (historical-critical) side in religion classes at
Centre, but the textbook versions of the issue were too brief and too
general to settle the matter. I simply wanted to know whether the "inerrancy" of every story, every text, every passage in the Bible could stand
close inspection. I selected certain pericopes of the New Testament, for
instance the resurrection stories, found in all four Gospels. It became
quickly apparent that these narratives offered different accounts of the
same events. Further, the differences reflected viewpoints and even the
historical situations of the authors. This meant of course that the writings
had originated not in a supernatural communication that overrode the
author's perspective, personal convictions, and fallibility. The author (or
the text) may have been "inspired," but the "inspiration" did not produce
or guarantee inerrant or mistake-free historical accounts or theological
views. No flow of miraculous interventions in the authors' brains guided
their hands as they wrote. The passages may carry insightful messages;
they could not, given the irreconcilable details of their content, be the
result of a transfer of "truths" from God's mind to the mind of the author.
Coming to this conclusion was less a trauma than it was the opening of a
door that allowed me to peer into the tangle of social conditions, linguistic usages, and contents of biblical passages. With this simple negation
of an ancient paradigm of authority (the paradigm of an equally distributed set of truths throughout the passages of the Bible, each of which
was necessarily free from error), everything changed: the very nature of
scripture, the meaning and challenge of interpreting its passages, the very
character and task of theology itself. Now there arose before me the possibility of a different paradigm and with it many new tasks of inquiry.

Doris and I planned to marry at the end of my first year in seminary, leaving her with one more year of college to finish. Our choice of
a Seminary was Union in Richmond, Virginia. I knew little about the
school, but living independently from our families was probably what
drew us to Union. It was not to be. Doris needed to finish her college degree at the University of Louisville. Attending Union would have placed

us in serious debt. Our plan was to marry and live in married students' housing at Louisville Seminary. Nor was that to be. The Seminary had no space for us. At that point, my father, still working full time at Ford, spent endless nights and weekends turning the attic of our Cyprus house into a very nice livable space, with plumbing, heat, walls, and ceiling. When we did marry at the end of my first year at school, we had a place to live, and Doris could spend that year finishing college. I don't think I ever properly thanked my father for such a great gift. In the second year of our marriage, we continued to live with my parents. Doris graduated from the University of Louisville and found a tedious office job filing records. We spent every Saturday night as well as two summers in southern Indiana near Madison, where I served two rural churches, Jefferson, and Smyrna-Monroe. Doris and I returned from our honeymoon to a sparsely furnished farm house near one of the churches (Jefferson). The next summer we lived with different parishioners and I sometimes helped out in farm work. During one summer, I rose at dawn every day to read my Greek New Testament. I had great affection for these farming families and regret I lost touch with them after heading for graduate school.

During the summer following my graduation, I worked at several jobs, and as usual I was caught up in an excessive schedule of activities. Once a week I taught an introduction to philosophy course at the University of Louisville. On weekends I preached at a church in Winchester, Kentucky, and in connection with that we visited Doris's sister in Lexington. The killer job was working the seven to eleven or graveyard shift several nights a week in the psychiatric ward of a local hospital. Because of the summer heat (no air conditioning in those days), it was almost impossible for me to sleep beyond a few hours in the morning.

In my seminary years, I had spent significant time reading a number of works by the Swedish theologian, Nels F. S. Ferrè. I was fascinated by his mix of process philosophy with Lundensian (*agape*) theology, and his powerful criticism of Calvinist notions of divine sovereignty. Ferré taught at the Divinity School at Vanderbilt, and we decided a year's study with him would be a good start on graduate work. But this was not to be. Shortly after we had made these plans, I received a call from Bob Johnson (Robert C. Johnson), a Presbyterian pastor in East Tennessee who would eventually serve as Dean of Yale Divinity School. He too wanted to spend a year at Vanderbilt working on a PhD and was looking for someone to fill in for him both at Tusculum College, where he taught several courses a year, and in the pulpit of his church. It was "an offer I couldn't refuse," a chance to get started teaching and also build up capital toward graduate school. After accepting the offer, we finished up our summer responsibilities and headed for Greenville, Tennessee.

The year in Greenville was a happy one. The college was teetering on the edge of non-existence, and its leadership was anything but impressive. Doris, a new college graduate, was hired for several jobs: "campus nurse," dorm counselor, Dean of women, and I enjoyed teaching a course or two each semester. We lived in the women's dormitory at the college, and struggled all year with armies of mice that took up residence in our apartment. The college was located in one of Tennessee's most beautiful areas, the foothills of the Appalachians, and with our new friends on the faculty, we enjoyed many driving treks on Sunday afternoons. A major downside of the year was a messy surgery for a pilonidal cyst on the end of my spine, which took a year to heal. Two important, life-shaping decisions were made that year. The first was to begin enlarging our family, taking on the responsibility of looking after an infant in our graduate school years. The second was to apply to the doctoral program at Union Seminary in New York City, the joint PhD program with Columbia University. That decision was strongly influenced by Bob Johnson, who had recently completed a master's degree there and could tell stories about studying with Paul Tillich and Reinhold Niebuhr. When we left Greenville at the beginning of summer, I had been accepted at Union, and Doris was pregnant with Mark, the due date in early February. After a brief visit to Doris's parents in Bossier City, Louisiana, and a vacation with her sister, Ginny, and her husband, Bob, in New Orleans, we headed for New York city.

Union Theological Seminary/Columbia University

In the summer of 1955, Doris and I loaded all our possessions onto a homemade, two-wheel trailer behind our car began the long drive to the Big Apple. Our emigration, transport, and poverty reminded me of the Okies in Steinbeck's *The Grapes of Wrath*. We were soon stopped by state police for not having lights on the trailer, thus had to spend most of our cash fixing the problem. (It would have been smarter to dump the trailer and our pitiful belongings.) We used up our last pennies getting through the Holland tunnel, and just before dawn on a bridge to Long Island, we ran out of gas. A compassionate stranger rescued us, bringing us gasoline and sending us on our way to Lillian and Wallace Murray on Long Island. So began our wonderful but low-budget three years in New York City. We found an apartment four blocks from Union at the end of Harlem's main artery, 125th Street, and while we were shocked by its cost, we felt lucky to find it at all. Doris, a few months pregnant with Mark, was hired by the Union library, and I joined a small group studying "theological German" with a former judge who had recently emigrated to the United States. After three weeks of the small group seminar, I received a notice that the German exam (a translation of several passages from theological works) for graduate students would be given that week. I took the exam in order to get some sense of what it was like and miraculously passed it, thus dropping out of the course and putting off until later the language study I needed for facility in German.

Union Seminary was at the time one of several prestigious theological schools of the Eastern academic establishment. Its reputation came from its history, its library, its link (for graduate students) with Columbia University, and its faculty of superstars in a number of fields. In the early twentieth century, its professors (e.g., Charles Briggs) were at the center of the fundamentalist-modernist controversy taking place among mainline Protestant denominations. In the following decades, its presidents (Henry Sloan Coffin and Henry Pit Van Dusen) were highly visible religious and educational leaders in the country. Union's liberal tradition continued in such figures as Reinhold Niebuhr, who had been a Socialist Party candidate for a political office, John Knox and F. C. Grant in New Testament, Paul Tillich, and many others. In the mid 1950s, the theology area included David Roberts, a specialist in existentialist philosophy who died shortly before I arrived, Tillich, Daniel Day Williams, Robert McAfee Brown, Richard Kroner, specializing in the philosophy of religion, the historical theologian Wilhelm Pauck, and Jack Hutchison, who was chair of the small department of religion at Columbia University. This group was not in any sense a school of thought, but its members did share two things: a Christian orientation, and, political and theological liberalism. Reinhold Niebuhr was for a time tagged with the fuzzy term *neo-orthodox*, because of the remnants of the Reformed tradition in his work, his social realism, and his sharp criticism of the "social Gospel" of Walter Rauschenbusch. But "neo-orthodoxy" was clearly a misnomer applied to Reinhold Niebuhr. Williams was a liberal from the "Chicago School," a proponent of process philosophy and a disciple of Henry

Nelson Wieman. The central figures in Pauck's theological orientation were Martin Luther and Friedrich Schleiermacher. Bob Brown was just beginning his journey toward what would be a social activist career and many well-written works on liberation, feminist, and Black theologies.

My initial response to Union as a place and an ethos was not fear and anxiety—it probably should have been—but surprise, fascination, and awe. When I wandered about the library reading room perusing the almost uncountable series of translations and reference works, I felt like "some watcher of the skies when a new planet swims into his ken" (Keats, account of how he felt on first reading Chapman's translation of the *Iliad*). Ocean-like were the myriads of volumes whose texts, authors, and analyses contained deeps I would never sound. Doris and I were Okies as we approached the new world of New York City, and I was an innocent, an academic rube wandering about in a new world of learning. At this point, Union posed for me a challenge and a decision. Should I use the years at Union to "catch up," fill in the gaps of my previous education, sharpen the historical, linguistic and philosophical tools I needed to become adept in centuries-long traditions, philosophical options, and conceptual mazes, or should I postpone such things and hurry through my graduate program of study as quickly as possible? It was not a hard decision to make. We would soon be a family of three. I was anxious to do what I so much wanted to do, namely to teach. Life in New York City was not an easy one and we needed a normal family life as soon as possible. Thus, I would not lengthen my graduate years studying languages or take years completing a dissertation. I would work hard to finish things up, and after graduate school I would focus on whatever I needed to be a teacher-scholar.

Before Mark was born, Doris and I would take our car on a weekend night (a risky thing to do since we might lose our parking spot) along Broadway and choose a movie to attend. After he was born, we bought a television, black and white of course, for Doris to watch in the evenings. I worked more or less seven days a week and most evenings. I discovered among the maze-like spaces in the library a small room hidden away on the top floor that even had an old typewriter. It was like having my own office, and I spent evenings and much of the days there. Four decades later I returned to that library to consult certain materials pertaining to theological education. The room was still there, still unused, and still available to me for space and privacy. The most important thing that happened in our first year was Mark's birth in Columbia-Presbyterian hospital. Just before Doris went into labor, I took and passed my French exam. The labor Doris went through with her first baby was difficult and very long, and I joked that I could have learned the French language while pacing in the waiting room. Mark's first months were not easy for him as he struggled with severe colic. After his birth we settled into a daily routine. While I worked at school, Doris would take Mark in his stroller twice a day, rain or shine, for long walks in the parks around Union. Courses in that first year opened up new vistas of subject matter, especially the required ten hours of history of religions at Columbia. At the end of the year, I passed with honors the general exams required of all Union-Columbia PhD students. The money we had accumulated prior to coming to New York City, a Union scholarship, a theology prize from Louisville Seminary, and work in a church in Queens enabled us to finish the year without debt. My Queens job as a "youth minister" and occasional preacher I owed to my friend, Bob Lynn, a graduate student in education who was Union's field education director.

Our second year in New York City began with an unexpected beneficence. Bob Brown invited me to be his tutor assistant, a position involving both teaching and grading papers. It also meant a nice stipend and, more important, Union housing. A gift from John D. Rockefeller to Union, an apartment building next to what is now the Church Center, was just being completed. Our apartment was to us a mansion and included a small room for our new baby, Mark. We had given up our other apartment to spend the summer in Louisville, where I served a small Presbyterian church and studied for my general exams. Returning to New York, we found the new apartment not quite ready, thus Doris and Mark stayed for six weeks or so with Lillian and Wally Murray on Long Island, and I stayed in the city, joining them on weekends. Almost all of the occupants of the apartments were young instructors or tutor assistants and their spouses, and close friendships formed over the year. One of those couples became lifelong friends, Jack and Shirley Forstman. Union and Columbia was an exciting environment for me, but Doris and I together had little money to enjoy one of the world's great cities. A few museums, the Bronx Zoo, and rare evenings at Birdland (jazz) were about all we could manage. Throughout our three years in New York, we enjoyed regular visits from both our families (our parents, cousins, Ginny and Bob) and friends. Through the generosity of our visitors, we sometimes were able to enjoy a Broadway musical. The Murray home on Long Island was our home away from home, a place for fairly frequent visits. From the first year on, a circle of friends formed, which included both graduate students in the area of theology and the tutor assistants and young faculty members at Union. My special friends were Jack Forstman, Bob Lynn, Ted Roche, Joe Elmore, Larry DeBoer, Charles Nielsen, and of course, on the faculty, Bob Brown. I owe my initial encounter—yes, "encounter" is the right word—with John Fry to Bob Lynn. John, the editor of an adult education magazine in the Presbyterian curriculum called *Crossroads*, was looking for someone to write a series of articles, "Ideas We Live By." Bob told John he should talk with me. A meeting was set up and our talk was mostly a constant stream of loud laughter. I did write the series and gained a lifelong friend.

I finished my course work in the first semester of the second year and took my specialty exams (philosophy of religion and ethics), again passing with honors. That left me with the task of finding a dissertation topic. The graduate program (in theology) was broad enough to include ethics, and the topic that attracted my interest was a specific but at the same time very broad problem, the ground or basis of (theological) ethical claims. I gave that up when I discovered someone else (probably dozens of people) was working on the same subject. My second topic was the rather vague problem of "supernaturalism," at least as a framework for understanding God and the activity of God. Traditional liturgical and even theological language tended to be supernaturalistic, speaking of God as "acting," "in heaven," as a being. After much consultation and many changes, I finally reduced this problem to something also vague, the question of God's "transcendence." On the advice of my advisers, I worked out a fairly typical research project, an inquiry into how a select- ed group of contemporary theologians interpreted transcendence: thus, Paul Tillich, Charles Hartshorne, H. N. Wieman, Reinhold Niebuhr, and Karl Heim. It was, I think, a good selection because of the wide range of frameworks represented. Thus, the problem of how to understand how God differed from what was not God could be studied using very different conceptual frameworks: philosophy (Hartshorne), science (Heim), philosophical naturalism (Wieman), continental philosophy (Tillich), and a powerful ethical vision (Niebuhr). The project of mostly descriptive chapters of these figures was something I could finish, so I thought, in my time at Union. The problem (vagueness) of the topic was conceptual. "Transcendence" is of course a metaphor and a contrast term to "immanence." It was an often used concept in the theological movements of the twentieth century, but it was infrequent throughout the history of Christian theology. If I had been familiar with the so-called "church fathers," the medieval scholastics, the Christian Neoplatonic tradition, and other movements, I would have seen that the metaphor, "transcendence," was an umbrella term for a variety of different notions and problems: God as that through which everything else existed (God as creator), the negative theology of Pseudo-Dionysius, and the Hebraic tradition of God's radical goodness, justice, and love. My faculty advisors did not assist me in sorting this out, probably assuming that the concept had a self-evident clarity, and thus were satisfied with the investigative device I had proposed, the selection of representative theologians as the main research and textual project. Decades later, taking up this problem again, I did not find "transcendence" a useful category.

The third year at Union was spent partly in several income-producing jobs and working on the dissertation. As to the jobs, I continued as a tutor assistant in the theology area, and was hired to do the same thing at Columbia, assisting Jack Hutchison. In mid-year I became an interim minister of a small but thriving Presbyterian church up the Hudson River at Blauvelt. The income from the three jobs was greater than my salary at my first teaching position, and we were enabled to finish our stay in New York without debt. The church in Blauvelt became more and more central to our family, and in our final summer, we lived in the manse next door. I worked on my dissertation in my "cell" on the fourth floor of the library until we moved to Blauvelt, where at the end of the summer I completed a rough draft. In Blauvelt we enjoyed visits from both sets of our parents, and took occasional trips to local lakes and even to West Point. At Union Jack Forstman and I were both nominated by Union to be Kent Fellows, and both of us were accepted into that society. In most cases this would carry with it monetary assistance, but I was just finishing my course of study and being a Fellow meant access to its annual meeting but without a scholarship.

The third year at Union was not only a dissertation year but a year of job seeking. Finding a teaching position in the middle 1950s did not pose the challenge it did in later decades. In the 1950s there *were* jobs to be had. Because of a growing population, returning veterans, and the new importance of college in the country's ethos, new colleges were being formed and existing colleges and universities were expanding. In some schools, departments of religion were being newly created and existing departments were growing in size. In the spring I made trips to Hood College and to Smith College and both schools offered me a tenure-track position as an instructor. I was probably foolish to turn down the job at Smith. (The department chair thought so.) I did so because 50 percent of my teaching would have been a required course, "Protestant, Catholic, Jew," and there was little opportunity to teach philosophical or even theological subjects in the electives. I had rushed through my doctoral program, and thus hoped my first years of teaching would be given to my own subject and to deepening my grasp of the textual history of philosophy and theology. Bob Newton, a fellow student at Union who had taken a job at DePauw University in Indiana, called and asked if I might be interested in coming to DePauw. The department combined philosophy and religion (perfect!), and offered a huge range of subjects to be taught. After a visit to DePauw and meeting with the department chair, Russell Compton, and the young faculty that had recently gathered there, I was offered and accepted a position as instructor. Although I had insisted all along that I would be leaving the church for a teaching job, the Blauvelt church refused to search for a new minister, hoping I would change my mind. In the final weeks of the summer, I remained in Blauvelt finishing a rough draft of the dissertation, while Doris and Mark left to spend time with her sister in Indiana.

The three years in New York and at Union were sea-change years for Doris and me. We arrived at Union as teetotalers, mostly innocent of *haute couture*, more or less politically indifferent, with little sense of issues between major political conflicts. We left enjoying an occasional wine, and while not really politically savvy we had a growing alertness to the issues at stake in various national-level controversies. We were still cultural innocents, but the worlds of art, music, food were gradually getting our attention. We had spent six years of our marriage in relative poverty, living the marginalized life of graduate students. From now on, we could devote ourselves to house, family, and a stable job.

TWO

First Jobs

"He grinds divinity of other days
Down into modern use; transforms old print
To zig-zag manuscript, and cheats the eyes
Of gall'ry critics by a thousand arts."

—WILLIAM COWPER, *THE TASK*, BOOK II

From graduate school to retirement, I taught in three post-high school institutions of education: DePauw University, Pittsburgh Theological Seminary, and Vanderbilt Divinity School. To live and work in those settings was the fulfillment of a long-held dream (see "Vocation" in chapter 5). Hard to believe as it is, that life and setting was interesting, even exciting, and carried with it its own reward. Its everyday activities included cognitive and personal interchanges, and when successful, the facilitation of understanding in others (teaching). Salaried or not, these are the sorts of things I would have done anyway, given the opportunity and wherewithal. As with all human enterprises, disappointments, conflicts, frustrations, and drudgeries were part of the deal. The bureaucratic machinery inevitable to any large institution could be intrusive, time-consuming, and distracting. Colleagues and administrators could be inept, power hungry, even mean. Through the decades of the twentieth century, higher education in the U.S. mirrored the larger society's racism, sexism, and homophobia, and could embrace policies that were counter to its own broad aims. I am very much aware that I was part of these things and made my own contribution to education's darker sides. My persisting attitude toward this darker side of higher education was that such things are simply inevitable to life in the world and they increase with social complexity. This is not to say that I was uncritical or simply indifferent to change.

But while inevitable, human ineptness and even nastiness are not defining or exhaustive features of universities. I did not experience life in the university (or seminary) as simply a grim, frustrating waste of time but as a constant succession of interesting challenges: teaching most of all, student friendships, highly able and sometimes quirky faculty colleagues, gifted administrators, and campus events. The social values of the university encouraged freedom, creativity, even critical analyses of the university itself, all of which are the very conditions of genuine and fruitful inquiry and teaching. Values and commitments of this sort are rooted in the university's primary aim, to provide both liberal arts and specialized, professional education in a variety of fields, sciences, and specialties. An aim of this sort creates a rather distinctive environment, an ethos of cognitive plurality, an overall structure that gives to each academic field a certain legitimacy. This structure presupposes a commitment by the university to many different ways of knowing, inquiring, and even teaching. Research and critical inquiry give rise to a constantly changing body of knowledge, thus change itself is part of the ethos of the university. The university's "liberalism," the intellectual and cultural commitment to diversity, is born here. As I experienced them, faculty members and colleagues had mutual respect for each other—there were, of course, exceptions—and their relations to each other sometimes produced cooperative pedagogical and scholarly projects and even friendships. This ethos is part of the reason why the universities, again mirroring trends and events in the broader society, could embrace the morally liberating movements of the mid-century, thus adopting the values and agendas of feminism and civil rights. In saying these things, I caution myself against idealizing the university. Like other institutions, universities tend to embody the prevailing traditions, policies, and social structures that prevail in the present. Thus, they not only have become mileux of bureaucratization but their organization and ethos promoted the racism, chauvinism, elitism, and homophobia of the broader society.

In addition, they tend to freeze the customs and policies of traditional pedagogy (teaching methods) in which teachers are content to imitate their own graduate professors and give little critical attention to what they do in the class room. There are then tensions between their commitment to social and intellectual diversity, freedom for research and teaching, and the values which make up a democracy and their myopia to their own problems (see the essay "Schools" in chapter 6). Overall my four decades of undergraduate and graduate teaching have been a positive, sometimes deeply fulfilling experience.

Depauw University

DePauw University is located in central Indiana (Greencastle), about forty miles west of Indianapolis. It was a university possibly because its Methodist founders often created not just colleges but universities. Unlike most universities, it had no degree-granting professional schools, but it did have a small music program that offered a master's degree that qualified it as a university. DePauw still maintained official relations with the Methodist Church but it was fast losing its Methodist features. It had a Methodist president, a Methodist chair of the philosophy-religion department, several Methodist faculty members in the department, and close relations with the local Methodist church. Further, there were faint signs of the Methodist taboo against drinking alcohol, ignored of course by both the fraternities and the faculty. Academically, it did not rank with the very best of the colleges (Connecticut Wesleyan, Oberlin, Smith, Haverford, Reed, Williams, Macalester), but its departments of psychology, literature, and philosophy-religion were large enough to be staffed by a variety of specialist scholars in each field, and a portion of the faculty was research-oriented. I was disappointed with the quality of its administration, often the subject of ridicule by the "young Turk" faculty members. DePauw was also a strong "Greek" (fraternity) system and a portion of the male students lived in the houses.

When I visited DePauw for my interview with the department, I was shown the housing available to young faculty. Buying a house was beyond our means, and rental properties were rare. What remained was "the Barracks," campus quarters used by soldiers on campus during World War II. Three tiny apartments organized each one-story building. About half of the young faculty of the philosophy-religion department lived there. The apartment had no bath, only a small shower, was heated by a stove in the living room, and its windows did little to shut out the cold of an Indiana winter. But because the rental cost of $30 a month drew lightly on our funds, we were able to accumulate a down-payment on a house purchase after our first year. I tried my best to describe the barracks to Doris, but she thought I was exaggerating the downside and didn't realize what was in store for us. Her first inspection of the Barracks—I was still in New York—was of course a shock. We were a family of three when we moved into the Barracks, but with Wendy's birth in April, we would become a family of four.

Whenever our family moved to a new school and city, the first year was especially significant. This we expected since it meant the challenge of a new job, family adaptation, new friends, and new living quarters. Our first year in Greencastle was packed with challenging, exciting, and even harsh events. The philosophy-religion department was in a period of expansion with four new faculty, all males of course. Leon Pacala and Bob Newton had arrived the previous year, and John Eigenbrodt (New Testament) and I joined the department in the same year. Yale and Union were the supplying graduate programs: Pacala and Eigenbrodt from Yale, Newton and I from Union. None of us had finished our dissertations, and we differed significantly from each other in our theological orientations. Eigenbrodt, a fine musician (organist) was an Episcopal priest, New Testament scholar, and gourmet. Pacala had grown up in a Romanian family in Indianapolis, a northern Baptist who combined a commitment to Aristotelian-Thomist philosophy and Barthian theology. Newton and I were typical Union graduates, historically oriented and without alignment to any one major theological movement. The first semester for me was a highly pressured time given to preparing for teaching four different courses. Only one faculty member, a near retirement "Boston Personalist," taught philosophy, and Pacala and I joined him in that venture. My exposure to "world religions" at Columbia was minimal, but it was sufficient for me to be assigned that basic course. I ended up working hard to stay ahead of the class week by week as I taught Hinduism, Buddhism, and Chinese "religions."

In the break between the fall and spring semesters, our lives suddenly became, shall we say, more interesting. Dan Hunt, my best friend in my high school years, lived in Indianapolis and it was natural that he and I would get together to reminisce and renew our athletic adventures.

The semester had ended and Doris and Mark were visiting her sister. Dan and I were playing a vigorous game of one-on-one basketball when I was suddenly thrown to the floor, nearly unconscious with pain. It turned out to be a ruptured Achilles tendon. A general surgeon in Greencastle (who had never done the surgery) re-attached the tendon. Thus began a very long period of recuperation: eight days in the hospital, casts of various sorts for six months, months of loosening up of a frozen knee and ankle and learning to walk again. My second semester and part of the summer were spent on crutches. Doris had to drive me everywhere except for a brief time when someone loaned me a car with an automatic transmission.

The most important event of that year was the birth of Wendy Lee Farley in Greencastle hospital. A fine GP and family doctor taught Doris hypnosis and Wendy was born via natural childbirth plus hypnosis. We had hoped that Fortune, Nature, or whatever would provide a sister for Mark, and so it happened. Wendy was taken home to the Barracks where the kitchen sink served as her bathtub. Sporting a huge cast, I slept on a sofa bed in the living room, and all of us (especially Mark) suffered flu and colds most of the winter.

I had finished a rough draft of my dissertation the previous summer but the work needed extensive revision. Daniel Day Williams, hoping I would give closer attention to Henry Nelson Wieman, had grumpily approved it. Finding ways to get to the office every night, I finished the revisions and in the spring after Wendy's birth, Doris and searched the country side around Greencastle looking for typists. I mailed the finished work to Union/Columbia and the date was set for my orals in time for me to graduate that spring. What I mailed to the committee must have been the ugliest *looking* dissertation ever submitted to Columbia. Typing errors abounded and because typists did not always use a new ribbon, the text of some chapters was faint. When the time came, I boarded a plane to New York at Louisville, negotiated subways, climbed the many steps to Lowe library on my crutches, passed the oral, and qualified for the degree. Did I pass because my crippled condition evoked sympathy from the committee that included Columbia University philosophers? I graduated that spring, and for obvious reasons did not attend the ceremony.

Three events stand out in my memory of our first summer in Greencastle. First, Don Hartsock and I had become good friends. He was the pastor of the Presbyterian Church in town, a superb athlete (he regularly beat me at handball until my injury ended such sports), and a charismatic and caring human being. He prodded me to join the Presbytery of Indianapolis, a move that involved leaving the southern branch of the Presbyterian Church for the Presbyterian Church USA. He and his family planned to vacate Greencastle for the summer due to a study leave, thus he invited me to preach for him in the interim and our family to live in the manse, a virtual mansion compared to the Barracks. Second, we were able to purchase a small house on the outskirts of Greencastle with the help of small loans from Doris's uncle and Ginny and Bob. Third, Westminster Press agreed to publish my dissertation on transcendence. Thus, I spent significant time that summer replacing the final chapter of that work and making editorial revisions. As the next school year began, our lives had become much easier. We had roomy, functional living quarters and I was out of the cast and learning to walk.

Our stay in Greencastle lasted five years. As I review those years, the following events and persons especially come to mind. Academically, the courses I taught plus certain special reading projects marked a beginning of my post-graduate school continuing education, namely serious textual studies of movements and figures in Western philosophy and theology, and developing a little knowledge of the origin, possible importance, and flawed elements of certain key themes of Catholic and Protestant Christianity. In these years, I found ways to teach or study key figures of ancient Greece and continental philosophy (Kierkegaard). I spent most of one summer on Plato, a life-shaping experience.

One of the ongoing delights of these years were the many friendships with people on and off campus. The department of philosophy-religion continued its expansion and at least five of its faculty I counted as close friends. In addition to them, friendships formed with faculty in other departments of the university: music (Art Carkeek), classics, history, and English. Because of my almost life-long love affair with English-American literature, my friendship with E. K. Williams in the English department was almost inevitable. He and I found a way to jointly teach (a rarity at DePauw) courses on themes of tragedy and human evil using as texts works such as *King Lear*, Kafka's "The Burrow," and Dostoevsky's *The Idiot*. Don Hartsock left the Greencastle church and he was replaced by Dennis Shoemaker, a smart, competent, and angry minister. We became good friends, playing the occasional golf game and conducting an ongoing theological dialogue. During these years, I was active in the Indianapolis Presbytery, serving one of its churches as an interim preacher. Both Shoemaker and Williams vacationed regularly in Michigan. Thus, our family made northern Michigan (e.g., Crystal Lake) our primary summer vacation spot. John Fry and I had become friends in the Union Seminary years. He continued at the Witherspoon Building in Philadelphia, taking on the editorship of *Presbyterian Life*. Because of Fry, I became a regular consultant on adult education, making occasional visits to Philadelphia.

My musical activities had almost completely ceased in the period of post-college graduate study. This abatement continued at DePauw with one exception. When a college-sponsored production of Menotti's opera, *Amahl and the Night Visitors*, was announced, I tried out and was given the role of one of the three kings, the bass voice of course. It was an exhilarating musical experience.

Our final year in Greencastle, like so many other years, was marked by extreme highs and extreme lows. The low was the unexpected death of Doris's father at the young age of sixty-four; the high was the birth of Amy Catherine Farley. The two things were in fact connected. In the late period of Doris's pregnancy, there were signs of premature delivery and the doctor put her to bed. While she was bed-ridden, news came that her father was hospitalized with a serious coronary. He was only momentarily lucid, living only three days after the initial attack. Her mother and sister, fearing her trip to Louisville would risk a premature birth event, were hesitant to call her. Her father died shortly after she was informed of what was happening, and all of us attended the funeral in Louisville. It was a devastating loss not only for Doris but for me. And it meant that Doris's mother was on her own in Louisville, depressed, traveling by bus, living alone. But she was able to come to Greencastle for the birth of Amy, and actually hopped up and down with joy when she learned that Doris had given birth to a baby girl.

Some months prior to these events, something had happened to further complicate this period of joy and sorrow. I was urged to apply to the Lilly Endowment for a grant it had announced for study in the philosophy of religion. This was a serendipitous opportunity for me since it could mean a year in a German-speaking locale and the chance to study both Latin and German and work out some basic theological issues. I hesitated to apply, knowing the enormous difficulties of living in Europe with a newborn and coping with a new language. Doris well knew the risks and problems but urged me to apply anyway. When I received the grant, I began to study Latin in a serious way. My friend, Bob Johnson, and his family, were living in Basel that year, and he proposed we take over their apartment when they returned to the states. Basel then would be our German-speaking locale. We were almost overwhelmed in our preparations to go abroad, not only by the death of Dewey Kimbel and the birth of Amy, but an academic project which needed to be finished. At the encouragement of Prentice-Hall, Leon Pacala and I had begun a textbook project, a large book of readings from classical sources on the major doctrinal themes of Christianity, each section and author requiring a short commentary. Neither of us was particularly qualified to do such a project, but we had selected the authors and texts, and in these final months prior to leaving the country, the pressure was on for me to finish my portion of the introductions. I did finish the introductions and mailed them to Pacala. He had become the academic dean of Bucknell University and it was very difficult for him to complete this project. Although Prentice-Hall was willing to publish the work, I am glad that it never happened. The era of "the history of Christian thought" and of "Christian doctrines" studied in undergraduate education was ending. The work would have been out of date by the time it was issued.

In these months both Doris and I were ambivalent about our options for our initial weeks in Basel. I needed a jump-start on speaking German, and the best opportunity was to spend a couple of months at the Goethe Institute in Germany. What we should have done was to find a way for Doris and the children to spend that period with relatives while I did language study in Germany. But there were problems with all of these plans. If Doris had stayed behind, she would face a trans-Atlantic flight with three small children, one of whom was an infant. Doris's mother could not manage the family in her tiny apartment. Doris's sister was showing signs of psychological breakdown and the family situation was highly unstable. Thus we chose to take our apartment in Basel where the family would reside, and except for a few weekend visits, I would live in Germany. It was not a smart decision. We boarded a Swiss Air flight for Zurich where Pete Pedersen, an American student at Basel, met us. So began a year which can only be called both an *annus mirabile* and an *annus horribilis*.

I had a number of items on my agenda for the year in Basel. The most general item was simply to live and breathe the cultural, aesthetic, and academic airs of Europe. Paramount was my wish to do what I could not do in my rush through graduate school, develop a working knowledge of Latin and German. Theologically, I wanted to examine the doctrinal structure of the Reformed (Calvinist) strand of Protestantism, elements of which still lingered in the neo-orthodox theologies of the mid 1950s. I was somewhat frustrated by what appeared to be vague and elusive styles of theological inquiry in those theologies. I had no special attachment to "orthodoxy," but I did want to know what it was all about, its supernaturalist cosmology or time-frame that presupposed a "Fall" in the past, a rectifying event (incarnation), a divinely caused intervention in the future. If such things called for "demythologizing" (Bultmann, Tillich), I wanted to be clear about the myth itself. At the same time, though vague about the whole enterprise of theology, I knew that whatever else it was, theology was not simply textual inquiry, expertise in the historical periods or individual thinkers of the past and present. Theology in its primary sense was an activity of thinking: uncovering presuppositions, making judgments, distinctions, and gathering evidence. This may sound like a "rationalistic" mindset at odds with my ever-present poetic orientation. But very little is claimed or illuminated about theology by these formalistic terms. When we consider what goes on in the rites, emotional experiences, and activities of religious communities, we quickly become aware of a tangled language of metaphor and deep mystery. Compared to the mysteries themselves, my reflective activities in that year were formal, a kind of clearing of weeds. Every day I spent part of the afternoon in reflection. Abandoning my textual and linguistic studies for part of each afternoon, I applied an open-ended, dialectical analysis to authority, knowledge, reality, method, evidence, and norms.

The German language was an initial challenge. That meant language study at the Goethe Institute located, unfortunately, in northern Germany (Kassel). I made the long train ride back to Basel on two week-ends. After a bout with the flu, I opened a letter (a letter!) from Doris informing me that she had broken her leg. Her mindset was so fixed on what I needed (language study) that she was going about her daily tasks on crutches and with a little help from a German cleaning woman. I left Kassell immediately, traveling most of the night, arriving in Basel in the early morning hours. Doris was on crutches over two months. The fracture was only the first in a long series of injuries and illnesses afflicting both Doris and the children: an infected toe requiring surgery for Doris, measles, mumps (Doris got that too), flu. Our Godsend was Babette, a sixty-ish German woman who helped out several hours a day until Doris was off of her crutches, and then she would come once a week—she loved the children—without pay to have a bath and clean the house. Although she herself was desperately impoverished, living in the hayloft of a barn in a small German town, her constant concern and project was *"die Arme,"* the poor of Assisi, for whom she would collect clothing and transport it on her bicycle for delivery to Italy.

Two positive things about our everyday life in Basel were the setting, a high-rise (*Hochhaus*) overlooking the Rhine river in a Basel suburb, and the many friends we made that year: several American families (the Pedersens, Calians, McKelways), a Jewish couple, an Americanized Swiss neighbor who had been the personal assistant to the Swiss actress, Jean Tierney. All of these families helped us out in our crises. Our closest friends were the Pedersens, with whom we did some traveling in Switzerland, France, and Bavaria. In the spring of the year, Doris and I spent two weeks camping through Italy. We drove our Volkswagen visiting the major cities such as Milan, Assisi, Florence, Rome, Naples and Venice. It was a Europe-on-$5-a-Day- trip, but it introduced us to countless artistic, architectural, historical, and even musical wonders.

At the University, I settled down to reading seventeenth-century texts of the "Protestant scholastics" in the Reformed tradition and various German secondary sources. Neither the Lilly Grant nor DePauw University put pressure on me to publish my studies, thus it could be a year of theological maturation, tool-acquiring, and historical broadening. The Theological Seminar at Basel was awash with American students for an obvious reason, Karl Barth. He offered an English-speaking seminar, aided by his assistant, Fraulein Kirschbaum, and an American disciple who seemingly had memorized the *Church Dogmatics*. I lost interest after several weeks and began to attend the more rigorous and lively German-speaking seminar he offered. Our sequence of illnesses excepted, our daily life had its comforts, even high moments. We traveled occasionally to the Alps and lakes of Switzerland, to beautiful Swiss cities such as Zurich, Lucerne, and Bern, celebrated Christmas with fondue and real candles on the Christmas tree, socialized with friends, and enjoyed reading books ordered from Blackwell's in Oxford, England. Mark's school year as a new student and a foreigner to boot was difficult for him, but he began to pick up Swiss as well as German as the year progressed.

The life-changing event of the spring began with a phone call from Pittsburgh. The president of Pittsburgh Theological Seminary, Don Miller, called to inquire whether I might be interested in joining the faculty there. My former mentor and also good friend, Bob Johnson, had been invited to become dean of the Yale Divinity School and a position in theology needed to be filled. In my years at DePauw, I had been approached by several schools, and in those cases, I either terminated the discussions early or the school itself found someone else. But a move to a seminary meant taking up the theological vocation for which I had been preparing. I had been teaching a *potpourri* of subjects (world religions, philosophy, literature) and was ready to focus on the pedagogical and intellectual challenge of "being a theologian." Shortly, I was on a plane bound for Pittsburgh, leaving Doris with a measles-ridden set of children. The offer to join the faculty as an associate professor was made and accepted. Thus, our family plus luggage, crammed like sardines into our VW, traveled across France visiting Paris and the Loire valley castles, and stopped in a small town near Oxford where I worked at the Bodleian library. We then proceeded for a brief vacation on the North Sea in Arbroath, Scotland. Struggling as usual to make ends meet, we flew back to the states on a prop plane of Icelandic Airlines. A friend, Dennis Shoemaker, met us at JFK airport. We traveled by train to Pittsburgh, finding a house to rent for that first year, and then reunited with our parents in Louisville. In early September, we were settled in Pittsburgh facing a new life in a new place.

Pittsburgh Theological Seminary

Presbyterianism in Pittsburgh had been throughout the twentieth century divided between two distinct denominations, the United Presbyterian Church and the Presbyterian Church USA. Pittsburgh was the hub of the United Presbyterians and the location of their primary seminary, Pitt-Xenia. This denomination and its seminary leaned to the conservative side of mainline denominations. The Presbyterian Church USA had emerged from the fundamentalist-modernist debates of the early decades of the century on the modernist side, and in the 1960s its Witherspoon Building leadership was attuned to the liberation (civil rights, anti-Vietnam War) movements of the 1960s. In the era which followed, the more conservative wing of the Presbyterian Church would punish that leadership and the denomination for its radicalism. But in the 1960s the seminary in Pittsburgh (Western) more or less embodied that ethos. Two or so years prior to my arrival on the faculty, the two denominations merged and Pittsburgh Theological Seminary was created by a merger of Western and Pitt-Xenia seminaries. The faculties of each school largely reflected their respective denominations. The faculty from Western Seminary was the larger group, more or less in charge of things, and the majority of the student body came from the Presbyterian Church USA. There was a small but self-conscious and vocal group of orthodox or Calvinist students whose mentor was one of the Pitt-Xenia faculty members. The academic dean (Gordon Jackson) of the newly merged school was from Pitt-Xenia but in his liberal views, he resembled the Western faculty more than his own. The first president of the new seminary was Don Miller, a New Testament professor from Union Seminary in Richmond, Virginia. His background was another fairly conservative Presbyterian denomination, the southern Presbyterian Church USA, and he was less than sympathetic with the activist trends and "transgressive" (Rieff) behaviors of the 1960s. Presumably his appointment was meant to satisfy the laity, clergy, and seminary faculties of the two Presbyterian communities in Pittsburgh with a "moderate conservative" leader, but it was clear that he was from the beginning on a collision course with the formerly Western faculty and also the academic dean. His response to the situation was to partition areas of responsibility between "administration" and "faculty," a policy that left the faculty and the academic dean free to pursue curricular, student body, and extra-curricular matters. This arrangement repeats a fairly standard pattern in denominational seminaries, in which the president is an "outside" (fundraising) development officer and the academic dean an "inside" educator.

Our seven years in Pittsburgh marked a significant break with the past in a number of ways. For the first time since our marriage, Doris and I were not struggling financially. Furthermore, we were able to build a spacious house in a beautiful setting. Doris's life was at that time taken up with the domestic challenges of looking after three children, and graduate study, career, even church and Presbytery activities would all come later. I too experienced a break with the past. I now had a house and yard to landscape and maintain. With my friend and colleague, George Kehm, I renewed by passion for the out of doors, canoeing and fishing. And eventually, my musical life would reawaken with chances both to sing in choruses and play jazz on the trumpet. Moving to a denominational seminary carried with it a new ecclesiastical visibility, the result of which was an increase in my denominational-level activities: conferences, papers, lectures, and consultations in other cities. Teaching at a seminary also involved a changing pedagogical and research agenda, internal school conflicts, and close relations with a number of students. I will not attempt a chronology of these years but select few highlights.

The first year in Pittsburgh was like other first years a special time. Our return to the states from Europe took place in late summer and our September arrival in Pittsburgh meant that, for the time being, we had to rent a house. Thus Mark was placed in yet another school, and I realize now the difficulties our mode of life made for him. Mark went to five different schools prior to high school, and being taken into the inner circles of the entrenched boys was always a challenge. The major event in our family that year was a terrible trauma, and I still wince in pain as I remember it. Amy was two years old. We were visiting the Sunday morning service of a local Presbyterian church. In the supervised care for children, the heavy lid of a toy box fell, severing the tip of her finger. (Doris suffered a similar accident years later.) I will not go into details. The finger was surgically re-attached, and so began many weeks of sleepless nights and post-traumatic memories for all of us. One of our activities that first year was more upbeat, searching for a house to purchase. It was not easy. After weeks of perusing what was available, we finally discovered a beautiful neighborhood in the hills across the river only a fifteen minutes drive from school. There we found a lot (almost the last one) on a cul de sac at the end of the street. We sold our Greencastle house, repaid our loans, and with the help of the seminary worked out a mortgage enabling us to build a house on that lot. The cost was $26,000. With its basement garage and other rooms at that level, it was three stories. It was a tree house. We looked into tree tops from our dining room and living room. In the forest were deer, pheasants, hawks, and a season-changing array of avian species. Over the spring and summer, our house gradually rose on the lot. I visited it almost every day, and almost always found things that were overlooked or ineptly done. We moved into our new house before fall classes and for the first time began to experience the stability, even luxury, of a living space, neighborhood, and beautiful environment. This move introduced me to a new set of challenges and even pleasures: house maintenance, landscaping, gardening, and repair (undertaken on my father's visits).

Our life in these Pittsburgh years was, like our year in Europe, a mix of pleasures and pains. As to the pains, the most severe incident was of course Amy's severed finger. But there were others. One Christmas time, Mark broke his arm skating on a neighborhood pond, and later had an emergency appendectomy. A toothpick pierced Wendy's foot so deeply that it required surgery to remove it. A physician friend in our neighborhood wrote the needed prescription to relieve her post-surgery pain. Doris had some anxious moments preceding surgery to remove a cyst from her ankle bone, a procedure involving a long recovery. Such things were painful and traumatic, but none compared with the death of Doris's sister, Ginny. Ginny and Bob and their two sons were our closest family. In today's parlance, Ginny was bipolar, but the miracle drugs that ease that disorder were not available in the 1960s. Even prior to our year in Switzerland, she had grown more anxious, depressed, and prone to erratic behavior. Her anxiety was intensified when a long overlooked melanoma was discovered and surgically removed. We never knew whether the physician had communicated to her a prognosis of her condition. The outcome of all of these things was her death in her Evanston home from an overdose of sleeping pills. Leaving the children in Pittsburgh, Doris and I headed in different directions: she to Louisville and her mother, I to Evanston and the Nichols family. Doris, I am sure, was more traumatized than her mother, and I regret not being with her in those days following Ginny's death. Ginny was never simply a "sister-in-law" but one who had been a teenage friend, next door neighbor, and especially loved friend. Thus, I experienced her death as a loss of part of my life. It was much more than that for Doris, and the trauma and loss remains with her to this day. For our remaining time in Pittsburgh, the Evanston family continued the tradition of an annual Christmas visit.

Although the new house, family, and school responsibilities added up to a busy schedule of activities, there was now both opportunity and time for music. A major event in our family was the purchase of a console sized piano that I enjoyed playing in spite of my sparse training and limited prowess. I returned to singing by joining the Bach choir of Pittsburgh. Among its concerts I enjoyed most of all the performance of a version of Christopher Smart's (eighteenth century) *Jubilato Agno*. That choir opened the door to singing in a performance of Verdi's *Aida* by the Pittsburgh opera company. And after many years of inactivity, I began to play trumpet again. A small group of jazz-oriented musicians from the seminary and the University of Pittsburgh wanted to get together to play jazz. I had been a *note* player in the Big Band era, but had never done jazz improvisation. I made a beginning at this challenging art in these Pittsburgh years but did not get very far. We gathered on Saturday nights at our house, and occasionally played for parties and coffee houses. The one genuine jazz musician of the group was a quantum physicist from the University of Pittsburgh who played both trombone and piano.

Teaching theology at one of the denomination's seminary plus my former connections with adult Christian education and various editors in the denominational center in Philadelphia gave me a certain denominational visibility. Thus, I wrote a second adult education series for *Crossroads* and an article in *Presbyterian Life*. Westminster Press decided to publish the series, and it appeared under the unfortunate title, *Requiem for a Lost Piety*. I gave the annual lectures to the Presbyterian Association of Christian Educators. Since the lectures included sharp criticisms of certain concepts in vogue at the time, they (and replies to them) were published in the journal, *Religious Education*. Then there was "the Ghost Ranch story." Taking their cue from Jessica Mitford's *The American Way of Death*, the Presbyterian "radicals" of the Witherspoon Building had issued a pamphlet entitled, "The Christian Funeral," which relativized or dismissed most of the burial practices that provided income to funeral homes. This deeply offended the professional organization, National Select Morticians, and the denomination proposed a dialogue between representatives of both sides. This sounds a bit like a Hollywood comedy but it was much more than that. The denomination asked three people: a psychologist, a biblical scholar, and a theologian (me) to meet with the morticians and, as it turned out, their pastors. The appointed place was Ghost Ranch, thirty or so miles north of Santa Fe. Judged by their talk, one would think that the only reason they applied makeup for "viewing," embalmed the dead, did "grief counseling," sold expensive coffins, and conducted burials was their desire to imitate Jesus and continue first-century Jewish burial practices. Marketing and profits were not in the picture. The psychologist (Paul Pruyser) taunted their pretense at being counselors. The biblical scholar tried to sort out Jewish burial practices recorded in the New Testament, and I offered a theological analysis of death and the variety of ways the religious community might mourn. Needless to say, the two groups were never on the same page. But the incident had one positive feature, Ghost Ranch itself. The conference was the first of many visits there by our family, including a month in which I served as "theologian in residence."

At school my time and energies were taken up with teaching future clergy in the Master of Divinity program and a few future teachers in a small PhD program, with growing tensions and conflicts in the faculty, and with the theological puzzles that began in my year in Switzerland. At the center of those puzzles was the question of what grounded the whole enterprise of theology, the very phenomenon of faith itself, and thus the status of the beliefs and practices that constituted the life of religious communities. The traditional Catholic and Protestant answer to that question was to affirm a truth-grounding authority: hierarchical, philosophical (the "proofs" for God in the Thomist strand of Catholicism), confessional, and biblical. I had long ago abandoned this traditional answer. The historical origins, ambiguities, fallibilities, perspectives, and the presence of institutional corruption in every historical period of the religious community undermined biblical verses and passages, Synodical confessions, papal bulls, and the vast complex of tradition as inerrant locales brought about by direct divine communications. What then was the reality articulated in hymns, sermons, liturgies, and biblical texts? Even though I had abandoned "authority" theology and piety, I had not simply dismissed tradition, scripture, or councils as having no role at all theological thinking. All religious communities have traditions, convictions, narratives, and recurring practices. What accounts for their transformative power, their elements of realism and hope? How could an ancient event and its texts and traditions transform a community or its individuals? I began to search for a way of inspecting the "reality convictions" of the religious community that was neither an appeal to an authority nor an introspection on the "religious experiences" of individuals. So I asked how one could take seriously the experiential side of religion (e.g., liberal theology) as something evoked by "objectivities." It was at this point that my studies in continental philosophy (superficial at the time) entered the picture. The phenomenological movement and its founder, Edmund Husserl, had been doing just this sort of thing, developing a method that opened up the way objectivities and experiences were necessarily linked. To use Husserl's language (which at first sounds like psychology), there was a necessary connection between meaning-intending acts and contents that were not simply those acts. For instance, when we aesthetically respond to something beautiful, when we experience anything, even dream, we are not simply experiencing our experiencing. This rather vague insight pushed me to spend a full sabbatical year on Husserl's German texts. The few English translations in existence at the time were not useful, and were in fact responsible for the standard caricatures of phenomenology. Over many months, I labored over Husserl's *Ideen I* and *Logische Untersuchungen*, refining an instrument of inspecting or uncovering experience-contents connections and looking for ways to expose the link between faith and what evoked it.

In my last year at PTS, a growing suspicion—call it an insight—gradually undermined my initial project. My colleagues had taunted me (quite rightly), asking whether I had discovered my philosopher's stone, "a distinctive consciousness and content of the act of faith." The question calls in mind the centuries-long caricatures of Schleiermacher's work as a psychologically driven reduction of faith to "feeling." Rather suddenly I realized what my formulation of the problem, my inspection of the faith, had missed. Whatever "reality" is faith's referent and foundation, it is not directly delivered to an individual's "consciousness." Faith itself, like all human acts and experiences, takes form and originates in something already structured by something distinctively real. That something is the gathering of human individuals in relation to each other, an "intersubjectively" formed network of shared experience. That insight was not, I think, yet another way of bestowing "authority" on the community, but it did try to understand how the distinctive being-together or *koinonia* of communities carried cognitive content. ("Narrative theology" seems to make the same point. However, lacking philosophical analysis, it has the look of a modern form of authority theology.) In other words, communities, religious and otherwise, are not simply preservers of folklore and ancient myths but can be embodiments of specific and distinctive insights. This seems to be the case not only with very large and complex communities such as "Israel," first-century Christianity, Pali Buddhism, or a Native American tribe, but for smaller units such as a slave community on a pre-Civil War plantation, a family, or even two people in a relationship. The interpersonal structure that constitutes such communities opens their participants to specific insights into things that are not simply shared prejudices. With this insight, I realized I needed another tool of analysis, one designed to uncover the deep structures of a community's intersubjectivities. The tool was lying close at hand in the authors and texts I had been studying, the social (intersubjective) analyses of Husserl,

Alfred Schutz, Heidegger and many others. Eventually this tool was refined and expanded with the help of Jewish philosophers such as Buber, Rosenzweig, and Levinas. When I had that tool in hand, I would be ready for the first "academic" writing project since my dissertation. That project came to publication not when I was in Pittsburgh but after I had moved to Nashville and Vanderbilt University.

In the turbulent years of the 1960s, the real conflicts were going on in the jungles of Vietnam, the American ghettoes, the small towns of the South, and the halls of government. Church sponsored coffee shops were awash with government agents, and Senator McCarthy was discovering "Communists" behind every door in Hollywood, the universities, even the military. Both students and faculty at PTS were active in varying degrees in various events of protest. The school had its share of conflicts, but for the most part they were not over civil rights or Vietnam. Nor were they conflicts between the two faculties of the merger. One conflict arose under student pressure to end the old required curriculum. After vigorous faculty debate, PTS like so many other schools backed off from its heavily structured pattern of study. The tension between the president and the dean seemed to be heading toward the removal of the dean from office. Most of the old Western faculty supported the dean, and one group spent significant time on oppositional strategy. The faculty was thus "politicized," an unfortunate, energy-draining, time-consuming development. I was active in these strategic plots but never at ease with them.

I knew something about the Vanderbilt Divinity School from my relation with Bob Johnson and my interest in Nels Ferré's work, and some of my Pittsburgh colleagues and I had attended a Schleiermacher conference there. Furthermore, Jack Forstman, my closest friend from Union-Columbia days, had gone there to teach. Thus, amidst the *Sturm und Drang* of Pittsburgh seminary, I was pleased and flattered to receive a call inviting me to interview for a position on the faculty. Several things about that new environment attracted me: friends on the faculty (especially Jack Forstman), a very impressive chief administrator (Walter Harrelson), an established PhD program, the academic setting of a university, and a philosophy department where several serious scholars worked in Continental philosophy. I was frustrated with what looked like an endless situation of internal politics at PTS and a move to Vanderbilt seemed like a kind of rescue from such. After a visit to Nashville, the offer came and

I accepted it. The President at Pittsburgh made no attempt to keep me on the scene, but even if he had made some dramatic counter-offer, it would not have kept me in Pittsburgh. Thus my family and I transitioned from the period of "early jobs" to three decades of teaching at Vanderbilt and life in Nashville.

THREE

Nashville

Nashville! One city and many cities.
  City of schools and studios, high rises and spires.
  City of the Loveless Café and Meres Bulles,
      Tootsies and the Schermerhorn. The Bluebird and the Black Poodle.
  City of North Nashville and Belle Meade,
      Lower Broad and Radnor Lake, Germantown and the projects
  City of pickers and preachers, scholars and street people,
      actors and executives.
  City of the Scene, the Tennessean, the Contributor.
  City of the Sounds, the 'Dores, the Tigers, and the Titans.
Nashville! Here we come, curious, excited, leery, but on our way.

—EDWARD FARLEY

I n 1969 our family packed up and moved to a new city for the third and
last time. Prior to that move, we had lived in Greencastle (Indiana)
and Pittsburgh. For the coming decades, Nashville would be our home. It
was not completely unknown territory for us. As a child Doris had spent
a few years in nearby Bowling Green. Only a year or so earlier, our family
had enjoyed a week's vacation at Dale Hollow Lake in Tennessee, and
I had recently attended a Schleiermacher conference at Vanderbilt. The

common thread running through the following sections on academic matters, family life, and retirement is simply Nashville itself.

The Divinity School At Vanderbilt

Founded in 1875, Vanderbilt University was to be the major southern university of the United Methodist church, providing also a school for the education of ministers. In 1914–1915 the university and the Methodist Church parted ways, a severance that created a non-denominational Divinity School not unlike schools at Yale, Chicago, and Harvard. The preceding forty years had been marked by controversies between those committed to a "modern" university staffed by a faculty that represented the exploratory rigor of the sciences and the members of the biblical department and ministers on the Board of Trustees. Thus the idea of a dogma-free modern university had already shaped Vanderbilt's ethos when it shed its Methodist connection to become a non-denominational institution. The biblical department evolved into the Divinity School, which early on embraced the scholarly and scientific ideals of open research and teaching. The school continued to educate ministers but its approach to biblical and historical studies reflected continental (German) scholarship, and on such issues as civil rights, it was more a "Northern" than "Southern" institution. This was the background in a number of incidents in the 1960s, one of which was the "Lawson Affair," when most of the faculty resigned their positions to protest of the university's removal of the first black student to study at Vanderbilt, James Lawson. The Divinity School itself came close to expulsion, an event prevented by the intervention of several nationally visible scientists and physicians plus Harold Vanderbilt. Other incidents as well contributed to the school's reputation as a "liberal" institution. Controversy swirled around certain writings of the Swedish theologian, Nels F. S. Ferrè. Some of the school's biblical scholars were contributors to the Revised Standard Version translation of the Bible and were labeled "communists" in a local newspaper. In the 1960s, a Seminary connected with Oberlin College decided to close, and a small merger took place in which six or so Oberlin professors joined the Vanderbilt Divinity School faculty.

The invitation to me to join the faculty grew out of an earlier, painful and largely personal conflict in the faculty. Ray Hart (theology) and Robert Funk (New Testament) had pressed the faculty, perhaps aggressively,

McFague began her career with literary-theological interests, and moved from an early focus on metaphor to feminist and ecological theology. Hodgson taught and wrote over a broad spectrum of historical, theological, and ethical texts and issues, a range of interests which included nineteenth-century theologies from Baur to Hegel, contemporary liberation and black theologies, and works in education and even literature (George Eliot). Forstman began as a Reformation scholar, moved to works on Schleiermacher, and spent his retirement years on Paul and Christian origins. My range of teaching and writing was similarly broad, including a four-volume series in systematic theology and works on theological education, aesthetics, and various subjects in practical theology. These five theologians quickly became united as colleagues and worked hard to create a coherent and helpful program for future teachers of theology. These five theologians quickly became united as colleagues and worked hard to create a coherent and helpful program for future teachers of theology.

When I learned the details of the Hart incident, I feared I would be caught up in yet another conflicted, politicized situation, but this was not the case. This new faculty merged easily with the faculty in place, and for thirty or so years worked together as a group of colleagues and friends. Whatever resentments and political structures had arisen in the mid-1960s gradually faded as the new faculty found its identity. This is not to say there were no conflicts, disputes, or even alienations. But fortunately, these things took place without the creation of semi-permanent faculty factions. Contributing to the faculty's working together was the short era of Sallie McFague's deanship in which, with the help of a Lilly grant, she held various retreats and conferences on the subject of a new curriculum. This "young faculty" of the 1970s did become old and eventually retired almost as a group, thus leaving the school with another "new faculty." Within the faculty, there were special groups of friends. The "theological speculation society" was a small group which pooled their resources to invest in stocks and bonds. One group of close friends included the Harrelsons, Forstmans, Harrods, Knights, and Farleys. Another group formed when several families purchased some Hickman County acreage together (Bev Asbury, Darrell and Nancy Ray, Farleys, Charles and Donna Scott). Throughout my time at Vanderbilt, I enjoyed both collegial relations and friendships with John Compton, Charles Scott, and Don Sherburne in the philosophy department and Paul Dokecki at Peabody, and in my last years of teaching and in my retirement friendships with Alice Hunt, John

Thatamanil, and Victor Anderson. To have colleagues and resources in the Vanderbilt philosophy department was a delightful surprise. The strength of the department was not only the impressive scholarship and pedagogy of its faculty but its sheer size and variability. The department included specialists in process philosophy, analytic philosophy, American pragmatism, and existential and phenomenological philosophy. I sometimes audited their courses, and friendships developed with a number of them. Most of the chapters of *Vanderbilt Divinity School* (Dale Johnson, editor.) focus on the last three decades of the twentieth century, the period of my tenure at the school. Since I discuss my research and writing in other parts of this book, I omit it from the following recollections about the school's leadership (deans), student friendships, and selected events.

Deans

In the typical university, the dean of a professional school is not simply an "outside" person focused on public relations and financial stability but the chief academic officer. The job is comprehensive and calls for a variety of skills. All the Divinity School deans of these decades faced an especially formidable challenge. The university's administration and Board of Trustees were both appreciative and leery of the Divinity School, an ambivalence brought about by the school's high academic reputation, its publicly visible social liberalism, and its inability to pay its bills. The latter violated the ETOB principle of the university, "every tub on its own bottom." Appreciation was expressed in recurring statements by chancellors praising the school as the "moral conscience" of the university. In spite of a fairly strong endowment compared to other schools, no dean prior to the 1990s was able to avoid a serious end of the year deficit. The school's alumni were loyal but their clergy income was far below that of engineers, lawyers, and doctors, hence annual alumni support was minimal. Further, the general orientation of Nashville wealth and power was not overly enthusiastic about a religiously and socially liberal school. Added to these financial worries were the perennial tasks of maintaining a faculty known for its scholarship, keeping the school competitive with denominational schools as a place for ministry study, and attracting and supporting a growing population of students.

Walter Harrelson, Sallie McFague, Jack Forstman, and Joe Hough were the deans of my tenure at the Divinity School. Harrelson, a Hebrew

Bible scholar highly respected in various university circles, assembled "the new faculty" of the late 1960s and 1970s. I served on the search committee for a new dean when Harrelson resigned, and the committee quickly made Sallie McFague its first choice. As far as I know, she was the first woman to serve as the primary administrator of a seminary or Divinity School in the country. She was not enthusiastic about the outside or development aspects of the office but found a development officer who was exceedingly adept at such things. This allowed Sallie to focus on the faculty and the curriculum, aided especially by grants from the Lilly Endowment. Her deanship turned out to be brief. The university decided to host a worldwide tennis competition, the Davis Cup, one of the competing teams being the *apartheid* Union of South Africa. The students, faculty, and Sallie promptly staged a series of public protests against the university, an act which prompted the president of the university to remove her as dean. The next dean, Jack Forstman, also came from the school's faculty. Unlike Sallie he enjoyed making a case for the school to potential supporters in and beyond Nashville. He thus formed ongoing personal friendships with several families and individuals, and was the first dean to evoke serious support from wealthy donors. Jack too was a "scholar dean" who continued his research and writing in nineteenth- and twentieth-century German theology. In Joe Hough's tenure as dean, the school began to balance its budget. A number of factors contributed to this, including Joe's own adeptness, gifts as an administrator, and his energizing presence in every aspect of the school's life.

Friendships

Outside of my family, my closest friends over the years have been the students, faculty, and administrators in the schools where I have taught. At DePauw I was only a few years older than my students, and several student friendships (Bob Williams, Walter Lowe) developed that persist to this day. The same holds for my Pittsburgh years. But there was something special about VDS which evoked close and lasting friendships with students and faculty. Faculty-student friendships formed in the PhD program as students studied in small seminars and pursued faculty-guided research. In those years many MDiv students were not recent college graduates and the age difference between them and "the new faculty" was not great. The ethnic and national plurality of the student body and the growing population of women fostered friendships with women, African-Americans, Asians, Roman Catholic priests, monks, and nuns. These friendships were not simply "academic"—that is, project or class based—but deeply social and personal. In many cases they continue to this day. Student and faculty friends partied together, made trips to the wilds of Hickman County, celebrated birthdays and even births. We teased each other mercilessly in annual parties given by the theology and ethics areas. In one of the annual Galas, a student (Ted Brown) dressed up in a Superman suit with a large E on the front, leaped on the stage and announced that "Ecclesial Man" would rescue the school from its dire situation. In another skit, a trial was held in which my character, played by a student, was charged with complicity in breaking the arm of one of the women students (Betty DeBerg). She really had broken it on one of our sailing adventures. In another skit, a student took on my persona and delivered a lecture filled with my verbal and pedagogical eccentricities. One group of friends lived at the Disciples' House and would occasionally gather on the roof there for a beer before heading out to attend a Sounds game. At one student party, a student (Cindy Jarvis) took on the difficult task of teaching me how to dance to rock music.

One tradition created by student-faculty friendships was the annual Gala, a night of food, drink, music, and dancing, that for several years included an ambitious skit put on by either students or faculty. One year I ended up as producer, writer, and director of the faculty skit. "Peter Pilgrim" (Peter Hodgson) was a new student being introduced to various aspects of Divinity School life by way of a series of mostly musical skits performed by faculty members. The music was taken from a variety of sources (Gilbert and Sullivan, *Porgy and Bess*) but I wrote alternate lyrics for all of the numbers. A few years later we considered doing a revival of that skit but wisely decided the school had changed too much for the humor to work. I continue to enjoy these memories of the relationships, antics, and simply great fun with several generations of students. Such things did abate in my later years when I approached my sixties and the age gap with the students increased. Friendships remain and reunions occur between students and their teachers of decades ago.

One of the major events of the 1970s was the appointment in the area of New Testament of John Donahue, a Roman Catholic priest and Jesuit. It was an event not only because of what he added in scholarship and personal presence but because it drew many priests, nuns, and monks to graduate work at the school. Thus began our "priestly" era, the time of the Jesuits. One group of Jesuits lived together, becoming frequent hosts for great parties. The most famous Jesuit was "Monk" Malloy, who later became president of Notre Dame. Another Jesuit, Paul Lakeland, became chair of the religion department at Fairfield University, and a Franciscan (Bill McConville) later became president of Siena College.

Conflicts and Transformations

In the decades of the last third of the twentieth century, several events or trends gave shape to what the Divinity School would later become. First of all, it continued to exist. It had survived its near demise in the "Lawson Affair" of the 1960s, continuing to be a "liberal" school in a socially and religiously conservative region. Second, although its student and even faculty constituency was primarily Protestant, it gradually became ethnically, racially, religiously, and gender diverse. In the 1970s women constituted 28 percent of the student body but by the year 2000, the number had grown to 58 percent. The school had appointed a woman dean; a men and women's dialogue retreat had taken place (1983); and soon the school had appointed a number of women to tenure-track positions.

In these years, black students constituted about 10 percent of the student body and a few black administrators and faculty were on the scene. At the same time, the presence of black faculty was minimal (one professor), and from the perspective of black students and women, the new diversity had not had much effect on the school's curriculum and pedagogy. The faculty and many students were myopic in grasping how teaching could embody racial and gender experience. Such was the background of the protests and conflicts of 1986–1987. A small group of students more or less managed a series of events which included manifestoes, accusations of racism, demands for change, plenary student-faculty sessions, and visiting figures (C. T. Vivian, Will Campbell). The incident was painful to me and apparently to other faculty. I felt caught between my "liberal" self-image and my myopia about the concrete situation and experiences of blacks and women. Because of my "liberal" self-image, I was aware of my too passive activity in these matters in the 1970s and after. I was not totally inactive in gender and racial issues. I had come into conflict with the personnel and policy committee over our need to offer Sallie McFague a tenure-track appointment. At this time, the school had no women faculty members at all. I had volunteered to explain the school's policy on inclusive language in the fall orientation. And my colleagues and I in theology were determined to bring women into the PhD program. But like other faculty members, I failed to see that changes of this sort (body count, growth of diversity) required a transformed pedagogy. Thus, my Introduction to Theology course (which I never did very well) was traditional, and it never occurred to me that it could show how "thinking theologically" might include racial and gender sensibilities. The protesters wanted both greater numbers of minorities and women on the faculty and a curricular and pedagogical recognition of gender and racial issues. I do see various kinds of myopias (insensibilities) not only as widespread but in a certain way inevitable. Myopia, the failure to know about and appreciate the concrete situations and feelings of others as individuals and groups, is a partner of separation, distance, and lack of contact. For instance, the faculty and students (also the protesters) were myopic to the needs and situation of handicapped people. Peggy Way was the faculty member who voiced this issue to the administration and faculty. I (and my colleagues) had no antipathy to handicapped people but we were myopic to their needs. Ethnic and gender myopias originate in the antipathy, fears, and stereotyping of racist and sexist bigotry. In my judgment the faculty's pedagogical myopia was less a sign of bigotry (positive antipathy) than an imperceptiveness rooted in the social structures of the institutional past. I regret my myopia in all of these situations. It signals not only my socialization in the traditional institutions of society but an insensitivity on my part that cannot and should not be explained simply by the social setting. Insofar as one's sensibility lacks or even suppresses a compassionate alertness to needs, it bespeaks a certain hardness of heart, a certain way of being self-oriented. Thus, it was painful to have my myopia, my pedagogical insensibility, exposed. The protesters thus were, I think, right in confronting the school with its slow pace of pedagogical change. I never liked and strongly resisted the language (accusations of "racism") and saw the Saul Alinsky tactics of the protesters as a kind of overkill.

Academic Activities

I use the term *academic* to describe the everyday activities that my education and "calling" enabled me to pursue: inquiry, teaching, writing, consultations, and lectureships. Throughout my life as a teacher, the primary locations of these activities have been professional and graduate schools (academies). These schools paid my salary, provided teaching opportunities, and granted research leaves. I was forty years old when I joined the faculty of Vanderbilt Divinity School. Thus, my teaching career falls into two major periods: the years at DePauw and Pittsburgh Seminary, and the Vanderbilt years. I had not anticipated how different life would be in the Vanderbilt years. Changed was my relation to the Presbyterian Church (USA). No longer teaching at one of its seminaries as a "theologian of the church," I lost whatever small visibility I had to denominational leaders. The result was that my activities outside my school shifted from denominational events to consultations in the broader setting of theological schools. My consulting trips shifted from the Witherspoon Building in Philadelphia (soon to be replaced by a church center in Louisville) to the Lilly Endowment in Indianapolis, and to projects sponsored by Auburn Seminary or the Association of Theological Schools. A second change had to do with the field-related associations I attended. In my years at Vanderbilt, the primary professional association I attended was not the American Academy of Religion but the Society for Phenomenology and Existential Philosophy. This shift was not prompted by a switch from theology to philosophy. I continued my theological teaching and writing and was eventually active in a small discussion group which had its beginning at Vanderbilt, The Workgroup in Theology. A third change had to do with writing and publication. My years in Greencastle and Pittsburgh were mostly spent in preparation, building historical and other foundations, sharpening concepts, and identifying areas of problematics. My energies were given to the character of the venture of theology, the cognitive foundations, and to ways of settling its disputes and allowing its mysteries to come to discourse. My years at Vanderbilt were years of writing and publication. Thus, I spent my first leave at Vanderbilt writing *Ecclesial Man*, and continued projects of that sort into my retirement.

The three decades at Vanderbilt were stereotypical of the life and career of a professor. They were busy years, and I have little doubt that my insomnia of those years was intensified by a feeling of pressure which never really went away: pressure to be prepared for the next class, the next conference with a graduate student, the upcoming paper at a conference, the next author or text to be studied, the next chapter to be written. This pressure may partly explain why I was content to reside on the margins of professional activities, organizations, and group projects in my field. I confess this marginality with regret. I did not write many book reviews, and rarely shared with theologians scattered over the country (or world) how much their works meant to me, how helpful they were. I began with but soon abandoned a primarily *polemical* (critical, defensive, aggressive) style of working. Only occasionally did I direct sharp criticisms in print to someone's book or essay and regret almost every instance of such as either ego-driven or unfruitful. I wish now that I had taken time to engage, connect with, and express appreciation to my co-workers in the field of theology.

My busy academic life was carried out in many venues: classrooms, leaves, lectureships (in other schools and settings), consultations, and professional societies. Needless to say, teaching in the various degree programs at Vanderbilt was the center of my professional life. (See the essay, "Teaching," in chapter six.) The named *lectureships* are listed in the Curriculum Vita in the Appendix. One of the most enjoyable of these lectureships took place when Memphis Theological Seminary—my daughter, Amy Howe, was a student there at the time—invited my daughter, Wendy Farley, and me to give its annual plenary lectures. There were also many events of teaching and lecturing I have not recorded: to chaplains at Fort Campbell, to a group of interim ministers, pastoral counselors, various churches, and homileticians. Nor is there a record of the many consultations I attended in the 1980s. Almost all of the consultations I did were on the subject of theological education. Connected with these consultations were books and essays I wrote and two books edited with Barbara Wheeler. Some of my fondest academic-personal memories are the many sessions sponsored by the Lilly Endowment (with Bob Lynn) and the Association of Theological Schools (with Leon Pacala). Grants from Lilly and other sources made possible a number of leaves (sabbaticals) over the years. Many of these periods of research and writing took place in my office at the Divinity School. A few took Doris and me (once, the whole family) outside of Nashville. In Freiburg, Germany (a summer), I worked in the Husserl archives reading his unpublished writings on intersubjectivity, anticipating the writing of *Ecclesial Man* (1975). In the late 1980s, I spent a full year on a barrier island off the east coast of Florida writing *Good and Evil* (1990). In the mid-1990's, Doris and I resided at Clare Hall (Cambridge University) where I began writing

Divine Empathy (1996). As to professional societies, one group stood out over all the others in the significance of its projects and in its interpersonal collegiality. The Vanderbilt Five (the theology area) was a close-knit group, ever working to create a solid and even creative program in theology for MDiv and PhD students. Following a suggestion of Walter Harrelson concerning the non-public character of "academic theology," the group invited several theologians from other schools, about fifteen in all, to a meeting at Vanderbilt to discuss the issue. We didn't make much headway on that issue, but we did find a number of topics we needed to address. So began several years of meetings, first at Vanderbilt and later at the Ecumenical Institute at St. John's College in St. Cloud, Minnesota. The group planned, wrote, and published a two-volume work designed for use in introductory courses. Judged by today's standards, the group was vulnerable to sharp criticism. Its membership was mostly men, and its version of the enterprise of theology was more or less traditional. That would change in later years as the group grew in size, became ethnically and in gender diverse, and broadened its understanding of theology as world-changing, liberationist, and trans-academic.

Family Life

In my three decades of employment at Vanderbilt, our children passed through (survived?) adolescence, pursued their college and graduate education, married, and our grandchildren were born. I will not pursue the daunting task of a detailed chronology of those years. I shall instead divide them into two periods: the first from 1969 until the time when the children left home for college, roughly the mid-1970s through the early 1980s, the second from the college era of the children to my retirement. With the exception of Amy, who was seven when we arrived in Nashville, these were the years of our children's adolescence and their middle school and high school years. They were also the years when Doris enrolled in graduate school to pursue a career in social work, and years of intense study and writing for me. In the second period, the children no longer lived at home. They had moved to other cities as they pursued their careers, found mates, created family units.

During the summer prior to our move to Nashville, the family spent several weeks camping through the "wild West." We stopped off in Nashville to visit the Forstmans, hoping to find a house to buy. That search being unsuccessful, we returned to Pittsburgh, hoping our realtor would soon be calling about a house. Hearing nothing, I returned to Nashville to reside there until I could find a house. After only a day or so, the realtor found a house for us in West Meade. I described it to Doris over the phone, and on that basis we decided to purchase it. West Meade was fairly far from Vanderbilt (and everything else), and the house's huge, sloping front yard presented a challenge for grass cutting to both Mark and me. But the house itself was located in a beautiful setting, and soon it was home to everyone in the family.

In my recollection, *the* family event of the 1970s was Doris's discovery of a career natural to her interests and gifts. Glimmerings of what was to come were apparent when she trained for and then taught *Great Books,* and tutored at West End Middle School. Our anticipation of the costs of college for the children had prompted us to discuss her moving into the job force. In my mind, an important issue was what a new kind of life and set of challenges would mean to her. Her decision was a brave one. In her early forties, she faced years of graduate school with its courses in statistics, its field education, its stress over grades, exams, and papers. It was a time of hard work, self-doubts, anxieties, but its positive elements outweighed all of those things: a new circle of friends, a new self-confidence and set of skills, and, for the first time, a career. In spite of her self-doubts, her grades (as I expected) were superb. After two years of graduate study leading to a Master of Social work degree, she accepted a job at Cumberland House, and a year later moved to a second job as staff member, then director, of YWCA's Try-Angle House, a residence for teenage girls who were victims of neglect and abuse. Graduate study had been challenging and stressful, and Try-Angle House was more so. Thus Doris's daily life turned into a constant succession of crises to be handled: hirings and firings, confrontations with staff, judges, bureaucrats, and persistent fatigue. In 1982 Doris's mother, who had for many years resided in a retirement home, died in Louisville at the age of 86.

It should not be necessary to say that life in Nashville differed in a number of ways from anything we had known before. Among other things, it meant new sets of friends at Vanderbilt, our neighborhood, church, Doris's workplace, and my musical groups. Vanderbilt itself was the shared element of a group which included the Scotts (philosophy department), the Rays (he was chaplain to the Presbyterian students), and Bev Asbury (the chaplain for the university). This group of friends purchased sixty or so acres of land in a Hickman County forest bordering on the old Natchez Trace. All of us hoped to either build or rehabilitate some sort of structure on the land. Asbury purchased a house or property abutting the land, and Scott with help built a sizeable cabin. Doris and I had hoped to build a cabin by the small lake we had created, but Doris's work and my summers of writing drastically reduced the time we could spend there. Eventually, we sold our part of the acreage to the others.

Our move to Nashville was life-changing in a positive way for Mark. Through most of his childhood, he tended to lag behind his peers in athletic prowess, and had a struggle with self-image, exacerbated by being highly intelligent, of being nerdy. He began to change this self-image in Pittsburgh, both by taking up wrestling in his school and becoming an accepted member of a group of boys. He arrived at the middle school he attended in Nashville ahead of most of the wrestlers in his weight class, had an outstanding year in which he was undefeated and even unscored on, thus beginning his trek toward a regional championship in Tennessee and a plaque in Hillwood High School's athletes' Hall of Fame. High school classes were easy for him (even math), but not stimulating, and he was elected president of his senior class, delivering a speech at graduation. The downside of his wrestling career was the perpetual diet which kept him at 126 pounds. The diet may have had something to do with his bouts with mononucleosis and histoplasmosis. He decided to attend a college in the state of his birth, New York, and after visits to several New York colleges which had wrestling programs, decided on Colgate. In his high school and college years, he worked in the summers at Baskin-Robbins (which looked to me like a very hard physical job), construction, and a small celebrity-oriented hotel, enabling him to finish college without debts.

Wendy was still in elementary school when we came to Nashville. She took piano lessons, and then discovered the great passion of her teenage years, dance. Her high school curriculum and its teaching offered little that was of interest to her, but a typing course turned out to be useful in later jobs and in her graduate studies. Her social life revolved around two close friends: Liz McGeachy and Randy Smith, but also included (to my great anxiety) occasional scary groups of teens. She was always reflective, living a complicated but mostly non-communicated inner life.

After spending her first three years at West Meade Elementary School, Amy attended Wharton in north Nashville as part of Nashville's busing program for racial distribution among the schools. We never considered private school as a way to avoid this, and she shared the values behind this decision. Wharton was not an easy social environment, but she had her triumphs, including a lead in the musical *Oklahoma*. Like her brother and sister, she went to Hillwood High School, graduating a year early. In my recollection, she was the originator of cheerleading for Hillwood wrestling, and was captain of the team. Wherever we lived, Amy made friends easily: Mary Kennedy (Pittsburgh), Alison Tweedy and others in West Meade, and many High School friends.

With the move to Nashville came a marked change in the family's religious practices. We were not drawn as a family to any particular church in Pittsburgh. In Nashville we searched as a family for a congregation suitable for all of us. I myself would have liked the inter-racial community gathered at Edgehill Methodist, but the three children were less than enthusiastic. Furthermore, it was a great distance from where we lived. Jack and Shirley Forstman introduced us to their congregation, a liberal Disciples of Christ church on West End Avenue, the Vine Street Christian Church. It turned out to be the first congregation in which our whole family was active. I sang in the choir and occasionally taught a Sunday school class. Doris and a friend led a Sunday evening youth group, and Mark was active as a junior deacon. Wendy took confirmation classes and joined the congregation. Amy enjoyed Sunday school. A number of Divinity School students fulfilled their field education requirement by working in the church. The minister, Wayne Bell, reminded us of Doris's father. But this religious "honeymoon" did not turn into a permanent marriage. Wayne Bell became president of a seminary in Lexington, Kentucky. What followed shows how fragile even a strong congregation can be. The church's membership gradually declined in the next decades due primarily to a succession of senior pastors. It has survived and in fact enjoys superb leadership, but has never really recovered from its problematic years. We found the post-Wayne Bell leadership appalling and began to look for another congregation. Wendy's closest friends at the time was Liz McGeachy, the daughter of the newly arrived minister at the very large Presbyterian church near Vine Street Christian. We began attending Sunday morning worship there at her suggestion, and Doris decided to make that her church. But our connection with the church was almost entirely with the McGeachy family and Pat McGeachy resigned as pastor shortly after Doris had become a member. None of the children were ever seriously part of Westminster nor were Doris and I. Vine Street, then, was Mark's last residence in a church congregation as he grew up.

Besides being part of the Vine Street congregation, I was active as a minister in the Nashville area. The "Northern" and "Southern" Presbyterian churches had not as yet merged, and I transferred from Pittsburgh Presbytery to the "Northern" Presbytery of Nashville. I did some teaching at one of the Presbytery's retreats, and in my second year in Nashville accepted (foolishly) an invitation to be the interim minister of a church in Columbia (Westminster). I say "foolishly" because it meant an energy-draining, seven day week and isolation from the family. When the denominations did merge, everything changed. A good percentage of the laity and clergy of the larger, "southern" Presbytery were less than enthusiastic about their new "Northern" and "liberal" colleagues, especially the Divinity School faculty. Several ministers were outspokenly critical of Presbyterian clergy faculty who attended non-Presbyterian churches such as Edgehill or Vine Street. The new Presbytery had little interest in using its non-parish ("academic") clergy for special teaching events. The result of these trends for me was a gradual distancing from both Presbytery and denominational activities. In the next years, my activities as an ordained minister were reduced to a few weddings (family and friends) and very rare instances of preaching. I could have responded to the Presbytery situation in another way, making myself available for the work of the Presbytery. Some of the Divinity School faculty did just this. As it turned out, my primary relation to the Presbytery over the years was my friendships with several of its parish ministers. My self-image, interests, and what gifts I had were pedagogical, and there was no venue for such in the Presbytery. The denominational center was now in Louisville and the old Witherspooners were replaced by a more chastened and cautious generation of educators and administrators. Thus, in the Nashville years, my activities pertaining to ministry took place outside of Presbyterian institutions as I wrote, lectured, and consulted on issues and prospects of theological education.

A second period of our family life developed gradually as the children left home for college, pursued their careers, and fashioned their own families. This transition took place over seven years. In that period, we moved from West Meade to Green Hills. Mark was at Colgate, and Amy and Wendy lived in the new house as they finished their high school years at Hillwood. Doris's graduate work and Try-Angle House job was the center of our first period in Nashville. At the center of our second period were a number of medical issues for Doris: a terrible injury, an arterial blockage, and a debilitating series of surgeries. The injury was a repetition of Amy's Pittsburgh trauma, a severed fingertip requiring surgery. The fingernail was saved but the recovery was long and painful. The blockage turned out to be relatively minor, 50 percent of one artery, and fortunately it has remained that way. The surgeries seemed endless and included a hysterectomy, exploratory surgery for an ovarian cyst, two shoulder surgeries, a knee operation, and two knee replacements. Over the course of a decade, Doris's life was taken up with diagnoses, surgery, physical therapy, and general debilitation from anesthetics and medicines. Fortunately, this era ended, and when it did (after her retirement), her energy returned and she became active in church activities, venues for volunteering, family visits, and the enjoyments of travel.

In the Pittsburgh years, both vocal and instrumental (trumpet) music had gradually became part of my life. When I moved to Nashville, I found new opportunities for both. Although country music was Nashville's national and even international reputation, other musical genres were alive and well in the city: rock, pop, rhythm and blues, jazz, Big Bands, symphony concerts, Broadway musicals. Blair was a pre-college music academy on its way to becoming one of Vanderbilt's professional schools. The Symphony was solid and about to become even better. Theatre Nashville staged musicals, and small chamber groups and jazz trios abounded. Nashville had in fact become one of the three busiest recording centers in the country, and its studios over the years attracted hundreds of Grammys. This musical scene of energy and variety drew me into performance on several instruments: voice, trumpet-flugelhorn, and piano. The Vine Street choir and Theatre Nashville offered the initial opportunity for singing. Shortly after I arrived in Nashville, I learned of the existence of a Big Band composed mostly of non-professional musicians, the Establishment directed by the founder of Blair academy, Dell Sawyer. Sawyer had played trumpet in the Houston Symphony and he eventually played trumpet solos as leader of the band. Many of the players in the band, especially the principals, and sometimes the singers, were first-rate musicians. The band played occasional jazz festivals (Franklin, for instance) but it was primarily a dance band with a busy schedule at country clubs, state parks, schools, and even in other cities. I joined the band as a substitute in the trumpet section, and after purchasing a better trumpet and also a flugelhorn, became fulltime, playing jazz solos that called for improvisation. In order to play the Trust Fund jobs sponsored by the musicians' local, all the members of the band joined the musician's union.

In a very broad sense, jazz was the music of Big Bands, but as an improvisational activity jazz was done in small groups. I played in such a group in Pittsburgh, but I had never really figured out what could and should happen in jazz improvisation. My "improvising" was limited to varying the notes of the melody line of the song. To truly improvise called for a going beyond the melody or song line to play creative variations of the chords and scales. This is what we hear when we listen to vocal improvisations (scat) and the instrumental improvisations of Charlie Parker, Dizzy Gillespie, and Art Tatum, the original giants of bebop jazz. Enter one Lynn Halliday. Lynn arrived in Nashville with a big reputation. In his teenage years, he had played with Maynard Ferguson's band and was (probably jokingly) offered a job by Miles Davis. Another non-musical reputation followed him. He was the "junkie" in the little book about Lenny Bruce, and in Nashville he bitterly complained about the minimum methadone doses available. "I'm a Chicago junkie," he would say. For obvious reasons, his tenor sax was constantly in and out of the lower Broadway pawn shops. He worked at fast food restaurants, and when the sax was on hand blew up a storm in various Nashville jazz combos. For reasons I don't quite understand, we became good friends, and worked out a deal. He was a loyal and enthusiastic reader of the *I Ching* and wanted to know more about "religion." I needed to learn about jazz improvisation. He got the worst of the deal. In our exchanges, he was the real teacher. "Ed, what is all this talk about "the late great planet earth?" "Forget it Lynn, next question." Listening to the way he would develop alternative chords for improvisation, I finally got it, and began to *think* like a jazz musician, using chords and scales. That led to my forming a rehearsal-type jazz group. The players were all beyond me in their adeptness at improvisation, but I did begin to learn some things. In my retirement years, I enjoyed developing my chord-scale skills for piano.

Classical music was my third genre of musical enjoyment. My college vocal training had always been classical rather than pop and was useful through the years for singing in church choirs and other choral groups. After a few years in Nashville, I had the chance to take my trumpet playing in that direction. The change was afforded by the arrival in Nashville of Jack Holland, one of the country's premier symphonic principals on trumpet. He offered free lessons to members of the Establishment and I immediately appeared at his door. Thus began a friendship that lasted until his death a few years later. I worked with him on the rudiments of playing the trumpet properly, and soon tried out for and joined the Blair Symphony Orchestra. In addition, Robert Early, a former student and now close friend, had started a brass chamber group, and he and I were its trumpet section. The group was mostly a weekly rehearsal group, playing for the enjoyment of its members, but occasionally we (bravely) dared to do a public performance. In these years, propped up by Jack Holland's tutoring, I taught trumpet at the W. O. Smith School, newly founded as a way young students of limited financial means could learn to play a musical instrument.

Looking for something musical to do on our Michigan vacations, I took up acoustic guitar, learning how to accompany myself singing ballads, Bossa Nova songs, and even country music, which to my surprise, I learned to like. This minimal prowess was tested in public only once, a performance for the faculty on the occasion of Herman Norton's retirement. I put together a group of songs with several guitarists, with words adapted to the occasion.

In Pittsburgh, George Kehm and I were not only close friends but avid fishermen (fisher persons?), sharing a mutual love of the out-of-doors. When my father visited, he and I often fished for bass in the lakes of Montgomery Belle, where he once caught an eight-pound bass. George and I began our Nashville area fishing in these same lakes, but soon the range of our explorations broadened. George would drive from Pittsburgh in one day with his canoe strapped to the top of his car. We managed to do at least one fishing trip a year, but soon our orientation was as much to explore the wilds as it was to catch fish. Using his canoe, we did wilderness trips from the Adirondacks to the Everglades and places in between. With two other men, we canoed and portaged (mostly portaged) through a chain of lakes in the Adirondacks. We joined a work-oriented Elderhostel on a barrier island off of Corpus Christi, enjoyed a kayaking Elderhostel on another barrier island, and another Elderhostel in the Okefenokee Swamp in southern Georgia. We fished once with a guide in central Florida, and without a guide explored small rivers and hidden lakes in the region. We did an almost two-week canoe trek in the 10,000 Island area of the Western Everglades, camping on Chickies and shell mounds. The primary challenge of this winter-time trip was the mosquitoes. Several times we spent a week with an Adirondacks canoe club which sponsored day trips on small rivers and lakes. Needless to say, I miss this direct way of experiencing nature, its beauties, its challenges, its unpredictabilities.

Doris's twelve years as director of YWCA's Try-Angle House ended rather suddenly. We had an opportunity to spend a year on a barrier island off the east coast of Florida, where I hoped to complete an ambitious writing project. She had the choice of simply taking a leave, thus returning to her position a year later. Although she loved the job, it was not an easy one. Everyday it left her drained of energy as she dealt with crisis after crisis, hired and fired, and interacted with dozens of needy girls. She decided that we should go to Florida and she would not return to her work. The year in Florida was a fruitful one for me, and it included not only finishing the book, but a beautiful setting, many visits from family and friends, and travels with local friends (the Doumas). For Doris the year was both recuperative and boring. Florida was awash with retirees anxious to volunteer for anything, so volunteer opportunities were rare. A few months before we left for Florida, two life-shaping things happened. First, we found the congregation which we had been looking for all our married life, Second Presbyterian Church. The congregation was relatively small, justice oriented, and warmly compassionate. Second, we had planned to retire in the Green Hills house, but as it turned out, a church approached us and a few of our neighbors with an offer to buy our property for its relocation. This happened many months prior to our leaving for Florida. We found a house on Laurel Ridge in Forest Hills almost immediately, but our offer was contingent on whether the church would in fact purchase the property. This took many months, and fortunately for us, the owners of the Laurel Ridge house held it for us. We lived in the new house only two months before leaving for Florida. Returning to Nashville, we became active for the first time in several years in a church congregation. Thus began a new phase of Doris's life, a busy time of church and community activities. Her new activist life began when she was ordained an elder at Second Presbyterian and continued as she took on appointments on Presbytery committees and worked at volunteer activities.

As to our families, my mother died at eighty-one after ten years of reduced health (ischemic incidents) and, after two years of grieving in which he haunted Cave Hill Cemetery where she was buried, my father moved to a retirement residence where he met and married Helen, thus enjoying a number of years of companionship. My brother, Austin, pursued his career in marine biology on the eastern shore of Maryland. His bittersweet life included the death of Lisa in a pony accident and the early death of his wife, Mary Jane, but was enlivened by the eventual marriage of both of his children (Chuck and Laura) and the birth of many grandchildren. We continued occasional visits with my mother's sister, Lillian, and especially her son Wally and his wife Phyl. This family had moved to the west coast of Florida, and includes my cousin Marilyn. Occasional visits have kept us in touch with Bob Nichols, the husband of Ginny, and his sons, David and Jim. We also visit on a fairly regular basis the Walker families gathered around Bardstown and Loretta.

College meant something very different for each of the three children. In one sense, Mark's time at Colgate was the most traditional: one school for four years, employment in the summer, success as a varsity athlete, a tug of war between studies and fraternity frolicking. His early plans for a career in medicine or law gave way to a major in political science. After graduation from Colgate, Mark and his cousin David headed for New York City. David had enrolled in a training program at the Bank of New York, but Mark, still searching for a career interest, arrived in the City without a strategy for entry into a specific work opportunity. As I recall this period, I am not at all happy with my own role in relation to his situation and needs. It was a period of late adolescent alienation between Mark and his family, and often we did not know what was going on. We did of course stay in touch with him but only in superficial ways. I had little self-confidence as a resource or parental guide for career paths or jobs in Manhattan, but I might have offered some general insights into strategies, preparations, and the like. One of his options would have been working on an MBA. Another was a training program in one of the big corporations. This in fact was what he did, at the urging of a college friend. The result was his life-long occupation as an account executive, a career he developed the hard way, building an initial clientele through an ego-crushing tedium of cold calling. I am sure that in his shoes, I would not have been up to that challenge.

It did not take Mark long to develop the expertise required for financial and investment guidance and he soon built up a stable clientele. He remained in New York City for many years, living on the East side, enjoying a circle of friends, dating, and scuba diving in the Caribbean. This stable life in Manhattan was interrupted by a serious health crisis. He didn't learn what was really wrong with his joints, his low energy, for perhaps two years. The diagnosis was Lyme's disease, whose origin was probably a deer tick lurking on a New Jersey golf course. The event changed his life. He had suffered the disease too long for antibiotics to be very effective. Thus, for years his working and even social life was a daily, uphill struggle. Simply to *get* to work was an accomplishment. His dating life was drastically reduced and his plans to someday marry put on hold. Over the years the symptoms abated some, and when he met Dianne, his life changed again, enriched by love, affection, and care for another, and marriage. After a few years of living on Sutton Place in New York City, they left the city for Connecticut, taking up the daily challenge of a long commute but enjoying the tranquility and beauty of a large house in a forested neighborhood.

I think it is true to say that both Wendy and Amy would have profited from postponing college for a year or so. Wendy began her college education as a dance major at a traditional but preppy college in Ohio (Denison), and her first year combined social isolation and loneliness with academic awakenings (to religion). Wendy planned to return to Denison for her second year and was relieved to discover no pressure from her parents to do that. One of her best life decisions was to lay out a year, working for Legal Services of Nashville. Several interests were at work in her search for a non-Denison type of school: social liberalism, non-traditional pedagogies, credit granted for her hours of dance, philosophy as a subject. Antioch College seemed to offer these things, but its liberal self-image and ethos was not only extreme but ideological, and the school itself was on the brink of financial disaster. Wendy's life in the first decades after college was one of great highs and horrendous lows. One of the highs began in her year at Antioch when, on a study break in Oregon, she met Clifford Grabhorn. He was good-looking, counter-cultural, and his awesome intelligence combined technical prowess (e.g., computers) and artistry (pottery). The mutual attraction was immediate and intense, and when it was clear that Antioch was not a viable educational environment, Wendy looked for a school near Clifford, somewhere in the northeast. The University of New Hampshire was the obvious choice, granting her credit for dance and having a fine philosophy department. At the university, Wendy had part-time jobs, struggled with ulcers, and one early morning dazed from medications and sleeplessness totaled her car. In her final year at college, she knew she wanted to do graduate work in the area of religion-philosophy, and her first choice was Vanderbilt. Thus, Wendy and Clifford journeyed to Nashville, where she was enrolled in an MA/PhD program in theology. As I remember it, the years at Vanderbilt were one of the highs of her life. After a rather moribund high school experience and difficult college years dispersed over a variety of schools, jobs, and places of residence, she was introduced to the fascinating mysteries of theology, made close friendships with both her professors and graduate students, and participated in parties, skits, and academic events. It was no surprise to me or her professors that when she finished her program, she was offered a tenure-track position at Emory University and her dissertation was published. Thus began her career as a university teacher and publishing scholar.

Highs and lows also characterized life in Atlanta. The highs include the births of her Emma and Paul, tenure, published books, and growing visibility as a scholar. I will not describe the lows in any detail. They include the growing tension, divorce, and custody battles between Wendy and Clifford, years of migraine headaches in which she was unable to read, and a scary and sad period for Emma as she responded to the situation. But new highs came with love and eventual marriage between Wendy and Maggie, Emma's dramatic recovery, Paul's transition from difficult adolescent years to being a motivated college student, the adoption of a Chinese baby, Yana, and Wendy's recovery from her earlier health issues. Amazingly, throughout even the darkest of the "low" period, Wendy continued to teach and write, and is now busy in the American Association of Religion, attending conferences and in lectureships. Maggie moved quickly from graduate studies at Emory to her chosen profession (financial advice and management), eventually heading her own franchise and company. Emma graduated from Reed college as a chemistry major and presently has a Peace Corps appointment in Mozambique to teach sciences. Paul is doing very well at Georgia State, and Yana pursues music, acting, and many other interests in High School.

Amy's year and a half at Rhodes College was both difficult and serendipitous. She was very young, graduating from high school a year early, and was unlucky in her assigned roommate, a smart but possibly mentally ill person. The serendipity was her linking up with Dave Howe, who would later re-enter the picture as the love of her life and father of her children. Not happy at Rhodes, Amy spent her second year at Appalachian State college, a good fit for her both because of its beautiful setting in the mountains and its program in criminal justice. A personal relationship brought her back to Nashville, where she finished her college work at Vanderbilt. These Vanderbilt years were less than stimulating since, in order to graduate on schedule, she had to spend most of her time taking core courses. The primary subject of her interest in those years was criminal justice, but it was unclear to her what that might mean as a career. During and after her college years, she worked at a variety of jobs in Nashville. In a high-class clothing store (McClures), she was quickly promoted to a first level of managerial position. Then the call came that changed her life and the lives of all of us.

Amy and Dave had dated some at Rhodes, and neither had really expunged the other from their emotional lives. The call was from Dave, who wanted to settle the matter for himself once and for all. The call led to an almost all-night meeting and conversation, then dating, and after nine or so months, marriage in Benton Chapel at Vanderbilt. The rest as they say is "history." They set up housekeeping in Memphis, where Dave worked for Morgan Keegan. In the next years, after several miscarriages, Amy gave birth to Farley (1989), Emily (1991), and Davis (1996). One horrendous event darkened the family's early years, the near death of Emily by drowning in a backyard pool, followed by years of serious health problems. Two events loom large in the Howe family story. The first was a career decision by Amy. As a child Amy had occasionally toyed with the idea of being a minister, an idea which apparently never completely disappeared from her psyche. The family had joined Evergreen Presbyterian Church near Rhodes College, and Amy's ever increasing involvement in the congregation reawakened what seems to be an early "calling." Thus, while she was busy having and tending to babies, she decided to pursue a Master of Divinity degree at Memphis Theological Seminary. It required seven years, and ended in graduation at the top of her class and the recipient of major awards. On graduation, she was ordained as an associate minister at a conservative Presbyterian church in Memphis, Woodlawn, after which she took a position as pastoral associate at Evergreen. The second event was the gradual but striking evolution of Dave's career. His high mathematical intelligence combined with a focus on bonds and other esoterica carried him to ever higher levels of financial success. After earning almost uncountable amounts of money for the companies he worked for (Morgan Keegan, First Tennessee), he formed his own bond–oriented company, thus making possible a pattern of generous giving and a family life of travel and even luxuries.

Retirement

"To be a scholar-teacher, neither guru nor entrepreneur, is to continue the life of study; at best, a scholar-teacher is a virtuoso student."

—PHILIP RIEFF, *FELLOW TEACHERS*

At the time of this writing (2013), I have been retired from Vanderbilt for sixteen years. The year, 1997, was a good time to retire. My TIAA-CREF retirement accumulation was at its peak, and several writing projects needed completion. To continue teaching into my seventies would have stretched these projects into many years. Doris and I were in good health and ready to do some traveling. The *experience* of being retired had its good and bad aspects. On the good side was a sudden quiet, an almost dramatic reduction of both internal and external pressure. Gone were most time-tables, deadlines, class preparations, committee meetings. This is not to say that I experienced my teaching life as tedious, uninteresting, or overwhelmingly stressful. But it did mean that the intensity of work was reduced. On the bad side, with retirement came another kind of quiet, the immediate removal of personal interchange, the flow of talk, humor, and collective projects that mark the everyday life of a school. Even though my daily routine was less pressured, I missed having students and colleagues. It helped to keep in touch both with faculty members (Victor Anderson, Alice Hunt, John McClure, Doug Knight, John Thatamanil) and the emeritus professors, most of whom retired in a period of six or so years. In spite of my antipathy to grading (assigning symbols to levels of performance), I did return to teach an occasional course. Reunions with groups of students from the early decades of my life at Vanderbilt or meetings with individual students have enlivened the retirement years. After I finished the project that was underway, the book *Faith and Beauty*, I settled into a routine. Mornings were given to study or writing, afternoons to exercise, errands, and miscellaneous projects.

"Study and writing" include a fairly wide range of subjects and activities. I have not felt the need to fill my retirement years with academic type publication projects that required intense inquiry. I have written a few things, most of which will never be published. I wrote an occasional children's story for my grandchildren, and a small book of children's poems, *The Magic Window*. In a more somber mood, I wrote *Prayers of an Atheist*. (No, I am not an atheist. The work uses a fictional device—an atheist's compulsion to pray—to explore the complicated issues of atheism.) Although a work of fiction, the piece was a difficult read, and the few publishers who considered it did not see a market for it. Study has been one of retirement's great gifts. I sense that many take degrees and join faculties not simply because they like to teach but because they like to study. All along I anticipated retirement as an opportunity to explore historical periods, genres, literatures, and authors I had previously passed over. Actually, these studies were a broadening of what I had been doing since my high school days. For instance, I had always been absorbed in the "wonder that was Greece" with special focus on philosophy. Now I could study the history, culture, and literature of ancient Greece: the *Argonautica*, *Homeric Hymns*, the *Anabasis*, and many other works of poetry, drama, and comedy. Long before retirement, I had in a non-systematic way worked away at "the Western canon" (Harold Bloom's term), a selected group of the most influential works of Western literature. Over the decades of my life, I had read a good portion of these works, but there were genres of literature (e.g., Norse sagas), individual works (e.g., Castigione's *The Book of the Courtier*, and even authors, e.g., Chrétien de Troyes) that I had yet to read. Thus, throughout the years of my retirement, a primary enjoyment has been discovering or rediscovering the literary treasures of ancient Greece, Rome, the Middle Ages, and the Renaissance. I well realize the ethnocentrism of this enjoyment. There are literary treasures across the globe in Asia, Africa, South America. And who knows? If my life span stretches to 150 years, I will be plucking the fruits from those literary orchards. My morning studies over the last thirteen years have not been restricted to literature. I spent considerable time studying Islam, both because I thought I should know something about it and because I thought it should be taught in church circles. Therefore, I did teach the subject in a number of churches in courses extended over a number of weeks. Retirement was a chance to study some things I always needed to know as a teacher of theology but never could find time for.

One was the history of Christianity from its inception to the Reformation. Like most people in my field, I had worked laboriously on the texts of major authors but not on the vast expanse of historical events, movements, and figures. Thus, I greatly enjoyed reading through a number of works that told the story of early and medieval Christianity. Another several years of study were spent on the New Testament. Teaching a subject may be the best way to learn it, and I did just this, offering courses on the New Testament and the first thousand years of Christian history at Second Presbyterian Church.

As to the out of doors, my fishing and canoeing adventures with George Kehm more or less ceased at the turn of the century. But in my early retirement, I was introduced to a new kind of out of doors activity. Del Sawyer, the Dean of Blair Music School at Vanderbilt and leader of the Establishment, retired about the same time I did. In the years prior to his retirement, he took up sailing as a serious hobby. His initial step was to sail on Percy Priest lake. The next step was ambitious, ocean sailing. He co-owned a boat in Florida with a retired Vanderbilt executive, and soon purchased his own thirty-seven-foot Pearson. He had always been a natural mechanic, a necessary skill for any boat owner, and he proceeded to become a good ocean sailor and to keep his boat in good condition. At this point, he invited me to sail with him on trips up and down the west coast of Florida and beyond. After a few trips, he and his wife Patricia moved to a house on a canal in Cape Coral, and I joined him on trips up and down the west coast to Naples or St. Petersburg, and to the Dry Tortugas off of Key West and the Bahamas and Nassau. I never really became a "sailor" but could assist for him as a second or third crew member. Thus, family, music, travel, literary studies, writing, and sailing have been the pleasurable activities of these retirement years. The low points of the decade have been the deaths of decades-long friends: John Fry, Walter Harrelson, Jack Forstman, deaths which took away parts of my own life.

In the mid 1990s, Doris had recovered from her "decade of surgeries" with a new-found energy, thus took on a variety of volunteer activities. At the urging of Don Beiswenger, she joined the newly formed group, The Living Room, a weekly conversation at a local downtown church with homeless men and women. That enterprise had many spin-off responsibilities: planning retreats at Penuel Ridge (some of which she led) and serving as treasurer of the group. Thus, over the years, she developed friendships with many homeless and formerly homeless people.

On the church front, she was chosen to serve another term as elder at her church and with that came the inevitable committee work. Time-consuming but interesting were her years of service on the Committee on Ministry of the Presbytery and it sub-committees. Thus, she worked as a Presbytery liaison with several churches (she chose the most challenging ones), participated in ordination examinations and interviewed ministers coming into the Presbytery. With all this, it was not only appropriate but overdue that her family, co-workers, friends, even formerly homeless people, celebrated her life and career at Second Presbyterian Church, an event which included food, music, and honorific speeches. Like Doris but in a much more minor way, I did some volunteer work, mainly with Nashville Cares, doing a few things each month for an HIV patient and, in one period of time, his partner.

Adding to the joys of these retirement years have been occasional travels. One of our first was in this country, a huge counter-clockwise circle beginning in Nashville, heading north and west to Oregon, south along the Pacific coast, and back east by the southern route. The purpose was both see the great Western national parks and visit a host of friends. We then took two Elderhostel trips, one to Alaska that included visits to the rapidly disappearing glaciers and cities of the inside passage and a trip to Mount Denali, the other to three of the islands of Hawaii. After these travels in the USA, we turned to Europe, joining Elderhostel tours to Scandinavia, the Cyclades Islands in the Aegean, and Turkey. The main event in our recent years was our move from our house-with-the-view on Laurel Ridge to a retirement complex in Brentwood, Tennessee. The reason for our move was not a health crisis or pressing need but our review of various probable scenarios of the end of life years: the possible need for health care outside the home, being separated from each other because of health problems, the death of one of us leaving the other to cope with things in the isolated situation of a house. Life at the Heritage offered many amenities: trips, parties, events, and the end of house and yard upkeep and daily food preparation. But with the move came two delightful surprises. The first was a group of interesting, compassionate people (teachers, engineers, physicians, scientists) who became close friends. Many had roots in other countries and ethnic groups. The second surprise, mostly for me, had to do with music. For the first time since I was about five years old, I was no longer performing music in a public venue. I assumed that part of my life was over. The surprise came when I discovered that one of the residents, Patsy Kirby, was a "great American songbook" singer. She had enjoyed a brief career decades ago singing in the country clubs and even on TV in Nashville. Our duo (sometimes a trio) began to perform monthly here in a bistro setting, and I performed as a solo pianist in the same venue on another Saturday. We enjoy having what seem to be fans, have recorded a CD, and work hard to expand our repertoire.

The years of retirement for me were busy and eventful years for the family. Mark and Dianne married in a ceremony performed by Amy and me at Union Seminary in New York City, and later moved from Manhattan to enjoy an exurban life in Connecticut. Maggie's clientele and business grew dramatically, making possible the purchase of acreage and building a house on beautiful Orcas Island in Puget Sound. Dianne has retired from her career in radio advertising in Manhattan to become certified (University of Connecticut) as a Master Gardener. Wendy, recovered from her health problems of the 1980s and 1990s, continues to write books, and her reputation as a feminist scholar-theologian has given her an international visibility. Dave's company has had remarkable success and he and Amy continue their exceptionally generous sharing of their wealth, enjoying a beautiful house on Pickwick Lake, frequent visits to northwestern sky slopes, New York City, Europe, and the Caribbean. Amy's position as pastoral associate at Evergreen has abated, and Evergreen itself is nearing its end. At the time of this writing, Farley has married and is enrolled in Emory law school. Emily is considering development work in a non-profit corporation and eventual graduate work in child and adolescent psychology. Davis is in High School, on the swim team, and is just beginning to look at colleges.

FOUR

Opinions

"Pardon my existence.
    No, that's not quite right.
Pardon my non-existence,
    my not being there or here,
    my emptiness
    my non-availability.
No, that's not quite right either.
Pardons carry a heavy load
    hiding the measurements of the insecure,
    sagging with accusations.
Understand my existence and my non-existence,
    and if you can, add a pinch of love."

        —EDWARD FARLEY

O ne of the aims of this memoir is to make myself better known to my family and to connect them with a past, a time in history, a cultural setting with which they might want to be familiar. In these final chapters, I present some reflections on a variety of matters that will both extend what they know about me and offer a picture of what is going on at the beginning of the twenty-first century. These thoughts, in other words, are my take on things, some having to do with general themes that show where I am coming from, some addressing what is happening now in our society. Altogether, these thoughts express how I experience and interpret the world, thus people, institutions, and trends. The reflections make no attempt at a self psychoanalysis, an impossible undertaking. But much of myself is revealed in them, so that to read them is to know me better.

These thoughts are not so much arguments as confessions. "Here is the way I see it," is their tone. They are not meant to educate, convince, or change the reader's opinions. One thing I regret about these opinions and confessions is their tangled discourse or "philosophical" style. For this reason, I fear that they may not communicate very well, especially to those whose take on things is very different from mine. I have tried to avoid an abstract and dense style of writing but without much success. Like the characters whom a novelist creates, the thoughts take on a life of their own; they make their own demands, call out for certain words, develop in their own directions as implications open up and meanings are clarified. The essays in this present chapter are major themes of my world view: the Poetic (my general way of experiencing the world), Knowing, Individuals and Relations, Words, The Tragic, and the Ethical.

The Poetic

"More strange than true. I never may believe
These anticke fables, nor these Fairy toyes.
Lovers and mad men have such seething braines,
Such shaping phantasies, that apprehend more
Than coole reason ever comprehends.
The Lunatick, the Lover, and the Poet
Are of imagination all compact."

—SHAKESPEARE, *MIDSUMMERS NIGHT DREAM*

"…poetry has to do with reality in that concrete and individual aspect of it which the mind can never tackle altogether on its own terms, with matter that is foreign and alien in a way in which abstract systems, ideas in which we detect themselves, can never be."

—WALLACE STEVENS, *OPUS POSTHUMOUS*

A "worldview" has to do with the values, commitments, loyalties at work in a person's interpretation of the world. Its contents are assumptions (sometimes, insights) about "how things (in general) work," what the person is up against, threatened by, delighted in. A person's worldview becomes apparent when the person has to deal with the various situations of life, makes crucial decisions, develops patterns or styles of life. A worldview treats of things the person takes seriously as "real," important, evil, beautiful. The interpretations I offer are inevitably idiosyncratic and personal, but some of them are shared with others. Thus they enrich relations between friends, colleagues, and family members. When I probe what orients me in most situations, I discover a very general but persisting way of responding to things. Of course, I may be wrong about this, and people who know me in ways I cannot know myself may dispute it. For example, I am aware of the typical ways Doris responds to the situations of her life, namely by way of an interest in, a heartfelt empathy for, and emotional perceptiveness of other human beings. I think she would agree. Similarly, my relatives and friends will have their version of my typical responses to things.

I might best describe my worldview by first saying what it is not. Some people who know me well might describe my most prominent feature as kind of dour intellectuality, a Faustian hunger to know things, a "reality" obsession to understand whatever presents itself. I would not dispute this. But whatever cognitive obsession constitutes my karma arises (I think) from a deeper, broader, emotional orientation than simply curiosity or a passion for clarification. In my self-awareness, this orientation is more a matter of feelings and emotions than of ratiocination. I say this because of what it excludes or opposes. For whatever reason, I have always been suspicious of abstractions, even the abstract quality of cognition or knowing. "Knowing" of course has multiple meanings, but even the specific act of perceiving and identifying a specific thing ("That is a red tail hawk flying by") is an abstracting act. I am aware that I experience, apprehend, understand, know, or put in words only a tiny fragment of the contents that constitute that event. I fail to perceive the red tail hawk in its total make-up, its constant nano-second changes, it's almost infinite relationships to what is nearest to it or to the space-time of the universe. Nor do I apprehend in any specific or direct way what is the red tail hawk's flow of perception and experience. I can only guess at that. For this reason, all experiencing (specific sense perceptions, the specific scientific probings of experiment) of anything actual necessarily leaves out, fails to know, most of its subject's contents: in other words its very concreteness. I say "abstract" because concretely there is always a "more" to what we perceive, think, know, or speak. (This was a theme of one of my poems for children.) There are those individuals, even schools of thought that reject the notion that to know is to abstract. For these approaches, what we "know" is the "reality itself," captured in the experiment, the test, the logical implication, the nouns, verbs, and adjectives of language. My own orientation or worldview differs from this. I see such orientations as reductive and pre- or extra-cognitive. The very act of reducing what is concrete to what is known or experienced or researched is a pre-knowing or extra-knowing attitude, unable to justify itself by its own methods of knowing. Such is the door I would open to my own worldview, a door of suspicion or resistance to any and all cognitive reductions. I should clarify that I am not a cognitive skeptic. I do think we know things, a lot of things in fact. I simply see knowledge not only as perspectival and ever changing, but seriously limited when compared to the actual events or entities.

If actual things in their totality and constant change always slip by our most intense efforts to know them and capture them in words, this very occurrence of concreteness invites one into a way of being in, living in, and interpreting the world. My worldview begins here, with certain general features of the world and world-experience left over from one's failed or at least limited cognition. I say this for several reasons. First, our knowing (experience) is always partial (abstract), always running to catch something whose constant process or change can never be caught. Second, to reduce anything to what language (or knowing) can express is not only a cognitive mistake but may be a kind of *violation* of that thing, a refusal to recognize it as itself, a deprivation of its being. Third, all the actual things—planets, cells, molecules and atoms—have a certain impenetrability. They do in a way show themselves to us, yield something of their make-up, but at the same time they retain their secrets. They are always combinations of discerned contents and mysteries. The mystery only deepens when we attempt to grasp and replicate in language the actual responses (in some cases experiences) of the thing to what impinges on it, its life from its own perspective.

Many of you who are now reading these words may recognize that what I am talking about is not utterly idiosyncratic, "subjective," or speculative. In my opinion, all human beings, however confident they are in their knowing and however reductive they are in their ways of talking, are aware that language never actually reproduces, embodies, or replicates anything, that they never know anything (not even themselves) in its completeness, its total details, its own specific flow of experience. Perusing the records of past historical eras with their cultures and languages, we sense that a certain awe has attended the experience of discovery (knowledge) and its limitation by the concrete. The more Plato (through his literary device, Socrates) probes the world to understand it, the closer he gets to its ordered structure (the *eidoi*), the more his text uses metaphor and even myth. In early Greece (and also many other peoples), a new genre of writing appeared in such writers as Archilochus and Sappho, which did not simply record the stories of gods and goddesses but used language to express the mysteries of concreteness, for instance love. This use of language (in Greece, iambic poetry) would always be a failure if the aim were to clone or replicate the actual concrete thing. Things keep their secrets even from the poets. But poets see this failure as itself something to be incorporated into language as they try to voice the emotional intensity of their experience of things, the world, and other human beings. Poetic language cannot replicate the concrete, but it can so clothe itself in metaphor, that the hearer (or reader) might re-experience things in their concreteness. In its narrow sense, poetry means units of discourse (usually for hearing) that employ non-prose devices (rhyme, meter, accent, metaphors) to evoke the concrete. In a broader sense, any writing (novel, short story, prayer, even "academic" essays) that would do this has a poetic character. Looked at in this way, poetry's very meaning is a *therapeia* for the overconfident abstractions of knowing.

My worldview, my so-called intellectualism, is primarily a poetic perspective on things. Thus, my orientation and even vocation is closely bound up with those we call poets (not simply versifiers), and other writers who labor to keep the world open and mysterious. At the same time, my orientation to things is closely attuned to and appreciatively involved with common sense, formal scholarship, scientific, and pragmatic knowing. I am not an anti-scientific romantic but an anti-reductionist "realist." Negatively speaking, my "poetic" stance is a resistance to reduction and a restlessness about the inevitably abstracting character of knowing, experiencing, and language. Positively, it is a fascination with actual (and active) things as they go about their business and with their impenetrable ways of experiencing and responding to things.

Two final comments. I have little doubt that my discomfort with abstraction and reduction and my attunement to the concrete is why I found phenomenological philosophers (yes, even Edmund Husserl) useful. The attraction was not to a neo-transcendental, post-Kantian probing of the possibilities and conditions of experience (knowledge) or to what would appear to be a new essentialism. It was to a method, a kind of philosophical electron microscope, which when turned on, exposed things in their elusive complexity. For me, phenomenological analysis was always a journey into mystery, an adventure in the concrete. Also, because I experience things as incomplete, partial, relational, and in passage (in other words, poetically), I see the world and its things as a kind of surface, offering something yet to be explored, and also something that resists exploration. Here arises a kind of skepticism about surfaces and an endless curiosity about their depths, and an aesthetic enjoyment of the ever unfolding quality, complexity, and variety of things.

Knowing

"It may be said with some plausibility that there is an abecedarian ignorance
that comes before knowledge, and another, doctoral ignorance
that comes after knowledge: an ignorance that knowledge creates
and engenders, just as it undoes and destroys the first."

—MICHAEL MONTAIGNE, *Essays*

My everyday responses to life situations (interpretations, styles of talk, decisions) are never simply logical applications of my worldview. Poetic mystery is, however, my general emotional orientation, and is a kind of matrix (a primordial *Gaia* or Earth Mother), or to change the metaphor, a fountain from which flows many streams. I shall mention only a few of these ways poetic mystery shapes various aspects of my life: knowing, individuals and relations, words (labels, categories), the tragic, and the ethical.

I labeled these scribblings about my life convictions, values, worldview as opinions rather than contentions or arguments. This is not to say they have no basis whatsoever, that I am either skeptical about or indifferent to their "truth" or reality status. Even if they do not sound like factual claims or logical derivations, they have their roots in practices of reflection. I do in other words have reasons for what I say about poetic mystery, relations, the tragic, the ethical, and words, and I do find that at least some other people have similar intuitions. The fact that these "intuitions" or convictions might be shared also by other people raises the issue of their cognitive status, whether in some way they are rooted in experience, apprehension, or knowing. Questions about what is and is not known and the very character of knowing have been a central concern of mine most of my life, certainly since adolescence, and, given my vocation and area of teaching, they have been the bread and butter of my work. I will not at this point visit my own writings to dredge up a history of my struggle with these issues. I only want to make one rather obvious point, a notion not commonly held in the specialty fields of academia. I include this point because it is an important part of my take on things, and like my other convictions, is spawned in the matrix of poetic mystery.

This being the case, I will use the word *knowing* as the inclusive term for a whole set of cognitive activities: experience, perception, apprehension, research, reflection, proof, understanding, and interpretation. This one point is that we human beings "know" the "way things are" in a variety of ways. To put it negatively, "knowing" is not one thing but a rather broad set of activities which takes many forms. What these activities have in common is that when they occur, something about "the way things are" is disclosed. While my own preoccupation has always been more with actual things than formal structures of logic and mathematics, I acknowledge that "the way things are" can have to do with both the actual and the formal. In a certain sense geometry, statistics, calculus, symbolic logic, and lattice theory struggle with the way (formal) things are. The mathematicians are subject to certain necessities or outcomes that they themselves do not control. But in what follows, the focus is on the ways actual things (a vague term I realize) are apprehended.

Two rather obvious features of knowing show why it occurs in many types of activity and genres of language: its constant adaptation to the variety of known things, and its occurrence in degrees. First, our activities of knowing or grasping what discloses itself cannot be simply one thing because the things to be known are themselves so many kinds of things, and thus evoke or require different kinds of acts to apprehend them. Apprehending or understanding a Euclidean rule of geometry and deriving other rules from that is a different sort of act from recognizing a species of bird sitting on the limb of a tree, a recognition which itself has multiple sources of hearing the bird song, observing behavior, or visually identifying shapes and colors. Apprehending how a narrative or story unfolds (the plot, conflicts, surprises, resolutions, etc.) is yet another kind of cognitive activity, and awareness of the devices of a narrative (humor, tragic structure, tropes, metaphors) is again a complicated act, not simply a following of the sequences of the story. Perceiving another's responses, moods, or intentions by way of that person's face, comportment, and speech is itself a distinctive situation of apprehending. Different from all of the above is a long, gradual assembling of data and repeated experiments with that data having to do with cancer cells. In all of these examples, knowing takes place in the sense of an act or activity in which there is a disclosure of "the way things are." These many activities take place constantly as a human being sorts out, prepares for, and pursues various undertakings of everyday life. Some of these activities take place in brief situations and involve spontaneous reactions: for instance two people conversing with each other. Some are deliberate, drawn out, and oriented to linguistic precision and appropriate evidence. I do think that to limit disclosure, apprehension, and knowing to one of these modes is a mistake, something Whitehead called "the fallacy of misplaced concreteness." Such a narrowing has the character not of something proved but of something stipulated, something that itself is not the result of knowing, demonstration, or science but brought to it as a kind of attitude.

At this point, both a cautionary and laudatory appraisal of science and the sciences are in order. My cautionary word is that knowing is something broader than science in the sense of research, discovery, experiment, and the like. I can see why the individuals whose life work is given to research and the society that profits from such would be prone to regard science and knowing as synonymous. The activities we call "scientific" are awesomely complex and marvelously successful in uncovering "the way things are." These activities call for special gifts of memory, language, calculation, and imagination. I have only two comments to make. I note, first, that every specific science, even the sub-specialties of a science, and even the cognitive challenges of very specific projects vary from each other and give rise to different procedures, the reason being that there are no identities in nature, the field of what is actual. Identities are a phenomenon of human discourse and are more a way of talking than a way of being of such things as the particle, the cell, the molecule.

This is why the history of the sciences is a history of revisions, corrections, dead-ends, controversies, new methods, and mergers of methods (cf. biochemistry). But to limit knowing to this history or some phase of it or to a group of specialized methods would undermine science itself. This is because every researcher working on a specific project must be capable of multiple types of apprehension simply to make her or his way in the everyday world and conduct an inquiry: thus, acts of perception, memories of previous testing, using language, grasping formal (mathematical) entities, imagining possibilities.

The laudatory word is my own paean to the sciences. I am clearly a "rationalist" in the eyes of some movements in our present society. I mean by this that while the types of knowing are varied, ever correlative to what is researched, they more or less are what we consult when we would grasp "how a thing is." Thus, while the geologists and paleontologists may be wrong in their construction of continental drift and plate tectonics, they are the ones to consult on that set of puzzles. That is because there is some appropriate fit between that selected field of phenomena (mountain ranges, ages of the earth, etc.) and what they do to study such. What I am not open to (as a "rationalist") is some alternate construction based not on geological evidence but on something else: a biblical text, a legend, an ancient tradition or author. The same would hold for the social sciences such as history. If the "field of phenomena" is the historical past, I know of no other methods of apprehending that past than very detailed, critical, linguistic, archaeological, work. I resist determining the phases of early or late manuscripts, the authorship of ancient works, or the meaning of ancient terms by some other method than historical work: for instance, an institution's authority, a community's a tradition, or a long-held theory of some sort.

A personal aside. For me, the Enlightenment names a period to which we owe a great deal and a literature to be taken seriously. As an era and a literature, the Enlightenment is subject to all sorts of criticisms. At the same time, the Enlightenment has left us with a double legacy which to ignore opens doors to superstition, bigotry, and anti-intellectualism: the rationalist principle that evidences (not traditions and authority) determine scientific and scholarly knowing, and, the principles and traditions of human equality and rights. Because of this double legacy, recent assaults on the "Enlightenment" make me nervous. According to one anti-Enlightenment view (primarily religious, pious, authoritarian), the Enlightenment was the victory of human autonomy over revelation, the dominance of reason over sacred scripture. At work in this dismissal is a tendency to allow something besides historical work (or scientific research) to determine what in fact are historical matters: dates, meanings, authorship, textual authenticity. Another general dismissal or discreditation of the Enlightenment, the postmodern, sees the Enlightenment as tarred with the brush of chauvinism, sexism, and the like. While it is the case that in spite of the Enlightenment's broadening of the space, topics, and methods of knowing and its political philosophies of human rights, the old male-over-female and Caucasian-over-slave hierarchies and oppressions were very much in place in the Enlightenment period. Thus the phrase from Orwell's *Animal Farm* would well describe those societies: "All men are equal, but some [males, whites] are more equal than others." But a new and radical principle did because part of the self-understanding of European peoples and the New World at that time, the principle of human rights, and this principle did create new societal structures. Thus, the seed had been planted from which grew vigorous efforts having to do with human rights and equality. The result was world-changing: new sciences, a new jurisprudence, new forms of government, non-self-absolutizing ways of being religious. Thus, because of the Enlightenment's notion of the autonomy of evidences (thus, the sciences, social science, research) over authority and the emerging rights of all human beings, I am very much an offspring and defender of the Enlightenment.

A second reason why knowing is inclusive of multiple kinds of apprehensions and exists in the form of multiple genres, methods, and acts is the "degree" character of any and all activities of knowing. To know something is always "to a degree," which is why all acts of knowing carry with them a long train of qualifications. I know "insofar as," "until something corrects me in the future," "from my own and ever-changing perspective," "in the setting of my culture, age, gender." We know any actual thing always in some degree of abstraction. However specifically and intensely we perceive something, we still miss most of its contents, which themselves take place in a flow of constant change in the particle world, and which sustain multiple relations to local and even distant environments. Such contents constitute what a fingernail or crystal or a cell are in their actuality. Knowing an actual thing takes place in the flow of events in the everyday world and the flow of brain activities of the knower. Almost all such knowing, the everyday perceptions of human beings, have to do with disclosures that are not linguistically registered or expressed.

A shape or color is briefly registered as one walks along a street. An object may be identified but only in a certain degree of precision. No grammatical entity (verb, noun, adjective) merely clones or exhaustively expresses any concrete, actual entity. Most of the knowing of everyday life is utile, serving our interests and our needs. We must "know" (apprehend) many things simply to find our way about, cook a meal, drive a car, or converse with someone else. This is why even knowing that is precise and overwhelmingly supported by repeated experience occurs in degrees of abstraction, of certainty, of exposure, of linguistic accuracy. Accordingly, when I review my own "knowing," my research, writing, and teaching over the decades, I realize that it has always had a paradoxical character. The more I came to "know," the more my knowing broadened and deepened, the more I experienced a not-knowing. As precision, quantity, and explanations accumulated, I became increasingly aware of my fallibility, cognitive limitations, and the persisting mystery of things.

These comments on knowing describe my own ambiguous attitude toward the convictions of my worldview. This take on things (hopefully) has some rootage in my own knowing, that is, apprehensions of things. At some level, then, it would seem that my reflections have a basis; and that means they take their cues from everyday life disclosures. Even if they have some roots in disclosures, they are also abstract, partial, correctable, and in process. But to the extent that they emerge from disclosures, they are not simply hypotheses or theories. They have a dim rootage in "the way things are."

Individuals and Relations

"It is a fact that we who have gone through the age of individualism,
that is, the separation of the person from its natural connex,
can no longer find our way back to the original life of community."

　　—MARTIN BUBER, "COMMUNITY," 1919

"As a sensuous body meets sensuous body,
each finds itself under the demand of the other's singularity."

　　—CHARLES SCOTT, (ON LEVINAS), THE LIVES OF THINGS,
2003

A third "worldview" topic has to do with a common sense assumption about what constitutes our world. The way we speak about things in the world, our grammar so to speak, tends to separate *things* (entities, specific items, objects) and *relations* (the ways things are constituted by their own systems and their enmeshment with and dependence on their environment). What is obvious is that things and relations are, as ways of speaking, handy abstractions. No individual thing exists apart from internal and external relations and relations themselves have no "existence" apart from things differentiated from each other in an environment. Thus we tend to be uneasy about all absolute distinctions, all discourses of separation, especially when frozen into worldviews. All actual things have internal and external relations and depend for their existence and welfare on large, complex environments. This holds for everything from galaxies to cells to quarks. In the case of human beings, they are related to a biosphere, an already formed history and culture, and to each other. My own convictions about the sociality or relationality of human beings are strewn throughout most of my writings. There I have argued, using especially Jewish continental philosophers, that the "interhuman" as a condition and a constituent of every human individual, is "always and already there" as the human being develops language, convictions, individual traits. This inter-relationality, this way human beings live from and in relation to each other, is not reducible simply to the ways they are members of organized entities such as societies and institutions, socialized so to speak. Ethnic, sexual, familial and cultural socialization are of crucial importance but they do not constitute or exhaust what makes human beings relational. To think this way is to risk reducing the human being to external explanations (one of the ways and models of knowing) and to an effect of preceding quantifiable causes. I see human relation in a broader way, as the manner in which the very being of human beings is constituted by intimate human entanglements, a kind of ongoing interaction of shared emotion. Here we have the strange, but also elusive, relations of friends, parent to child, nuclear families, brother-sister, units of a dangerous or rigorous undertaking (a football team, the Navy Seals), and these relations tend to be structured by emotions of dependence, resistance, loyalty, manipulation, even stylized indifference, romantic love, jealousy, affection.

This inevitability and primacy of the relational (environment, social, institutional, and interpersonal) may prompt us to be wary of views that isolate the individual and empty it of its dependencies, its history, its culture. One result of such isolation (individualism) is a certain simplistic moralism that is unable to apprehend and acknowledge the many ways human beings are victims and that forgets that human folly, brutishness, and pathological syndromes have settings in genetics, cultural eras and movements, and even ethnic traditions. Yet *individuals* in the sense of differentiable entities in the universe are never reducible to their relations, settings, or another individual entity. I limit my comments here to human individuals. However much human individuals are enmeshed in, related to other things, dependent on their environment, or socialized and influenced, they are centers of certain self-aware ways of experiencing that acts on and responds to the world, and however much their features and behaviors resemble those of others, their concrete flow of experiences are unique to that individual. This uniqueness is not simply "free will" but the unreplicable details of location, setting, and embodiment (the organic, cellular, and molecular systems) that constitute the individual. The active, responsive life of any individual (the actual practices, flow of experiences) is never simply a clone or repetition of any other individual. In general and even at the sub-particle level of things, there are no exact replications in nature, not even when living things are cloned from DNA. No single individual simply repeats the life of any other individual, nor does an individual have direct knowledge of the concrete experiencing of any other individual. With this notion is born another skepticism on my part, one which resists the reduction of individuals to their relations, to their "socialization" to the totality of influences on them, and sees them as simply effects or products of their family, DNA, local environment, or cerebral structure. Thus, I have always been skeptical of essentializing "explanations" that reduce human beings to mere structures and ignores their uniqueness, temporality, and complexity (concreteness). By reducing what is explained to internal and external constituents and/or influences, such explanations empty the individual of its integrity, creativity, and self-transcendence, the things that make it an individual. The human being of such explanations is a mere a collection of its internal and external constituents and/or influences. Views of this sort have seemed to me to be meta-scientific, a pre-cognitive and philosophical set of convictions, a kind of credo, whose origin is not and cannot be research, demonstration, knowledge.

I conclude then that both individuals and relations are in themselves and in their separation abstractions. Both abstractions spawn views that empty the human being (and other things too) of a concreteness that is ever relational, changing, and individual. In both abstractions, the ethical tends to disappear. In the reduction of things to their *relations*, it disappears into causal explanations (e.g., Marxist Stalinism); in the reduction to an *individual*, it disappears into a relationless autonomy.

Words

"Taffeta phrases, silken terms precise,
Figures pedantical; these summer-flies
Have blown me full of maggot ostentation:
I do foreswear them;"

—SHAKESPEARE, *LOVE'S LABOURS LOST*

"And it is not always face,
Clothes, or fortune, or the youth:
But the language, and the truth."

—BEN JONSON, "A CELEBRATION OF CHARIS
IN TEN LYRIC PIECES (I)"

It goes without saying that to experience the world poetically, as surface and depth, will shape one's attitude about how language works. It may come as a surprise to some that my skeptical side extends to words. I say this because I am by trade a wordsmith, one who writes, researches, teaches: activities that force me to constantly clarify meanings, sort things out, attend to grammar. As a wordsmith I combine two seemingly incompatible things, a low tolerance of ambiguity and a high tolerance for mystery. A low tolerance for ambiguity does seem to clash with a poetic sensibility. And sorting out functions, meanings, referents, and features does have to do with surfaces. But as soon as I say this, I realize that distinguishing things, sorting things out as one speaks or writes, is an inescapable feature of living in the situations of everyday life. If we didn't do these things, we would find ourselves shopping for groceries at a hardware store and driving someone else's car off the lot. If we did not use words in a fairly precise way, we would have trouble cooking a meal or crossing a busy street. The utile living of everyday life fiercely demands clarity, and we pay a high price if we settle for confusion and ambiguity. So we live and move and have our being amidst the surfaces: conducting our lives by means of labels, categories, grammar. To think about things, at least as we human beings are accustomed to doing, we use words.

At the same time, I am aware that the poetic depth of things constantly engenders a skepticism about words, a perpetual discontentment with labels, categories, names, as they are used both by individuals like myself and by groups, movements, schools, and marketers to press their cause and exercise influence. Words have built-in limitations simply because even in their most specific settings, both usages and meanings are abstractions, and as such they cannot and do not replicate (even if they are used to express or communicate) the actual event, the specific individual, the temporal process. To speak, to use words, is of course itself a concrete event, but the concrete event itself is never simply reproduced in words. What words can do is evoke, remind, refer to, correct, express emotion, command. All general terms for people in groups (nations, ethnic groups, classes, language groups) are at best benignly reductive. That is, they collect into a single identity a vast complex of times, places, behaviors, and individual variations, no one of which exactly reproduces or embodies the identity. Words and grammar are benignly reductive in several ways. As verbal entities, they are unable to contain the contents of their references, the trillions of ever-changing events and constituents of even a single human being: the cells, DNA molecules, atomic events in the nucleus of the atoms, the "mental processes," the flow of emotions. They cannot directly describe even a single human being's ever-changing world experience and responses. They cannot express the multiple relations going on between individuals in a class of things, or the relation of the selected group to everything else in the universe.

As individuals and groups use them, words are not simply innocent or neutral limitations, but are potential instruments of influence, manipulation, threat, status, and social power. And these possible deployments of language evoke from us a more radical skepticism, aware not just of the limitation but the potential violative power of words. When fear and antipathy become institutionalized or embodied in social movements, they find expression in words that are not just abstract and benignly reductive but, in a tacit way, violent. In the world of the sexist, all words for "women" (or "men") have subtle, poisonous connotations of flaw, weakness, pollution. In the world of racists, even the politically correct words (black, African-American, Latin, white) have connotations of incapability or threat. History is full of these ethnocentric words of exclusive, hierarchical management, and potential violence: *barbaroi*, Jew, pagan (*paynim*), Untouchable.

So far I have dwelt on the ambiguity, limitation, and toxic possibilities of words in their everyday world (surface) functions. But it is misleading to link words and the surface too closely. As expressions of what is actual, words are inevitably abstract, but then so are human speech, knowing, and perception as they select, limit, focus, and suppress. I confess at this point another relation I have to words, one of enjoyment and wonder. This relation is possible because words not only are of the surface but also of the depths and they can be used to undermine themselves, to qualify, correct, explore, imply. They can be used in service of the "more" in things. Another way of saying this is that they, like portraits, designs, bodily movements (dance), musical sounds, and constructed structures, can be used in service of beauty, and in their own way, they themselves can be beautiful. And when we immerse ourselves in the written words of poets, story-tellers, novelists, and many others, we discover that writers can work a kind of magic with words. They can so expose the word's abstract character, so use words against themselves setting up paradoxes and tropes, that a trace of the depth glimmers.

"For Orpheus' lute was strung from poets sinews,
Whose golden touch could soften steel and stones,
Make tigers tame and huge leviathans
Forsake unsounded deeps to dance on sands.

—SHAKESPEARE, *Two Gentlemen from Verona*

Need I say more?

The Tragic

"This thing all things devours:
Birds, beasts, trees, flowers;
Gnaws iron, bites steel;
Grinds hard things to meal;
Slays kings, ruins town.
And beats high mountains down.

—J.R.R.TOLKIEN, *THE HOBBIT*, 1937

I am trying in these brief, reflective vignettes to express my "take" on a few very general ways of thinking about the world. Poetic mystery is the matrix and possibly the coherence of these themes. To experience the world poetically is, I think, to experience it tragically. The tragic, as I am using the term, seems to be present in the poetic (literary, religious, dramatic) visions of all the great civilizations from Egypt and Sumer to the present. The exception may be the postmodern, if in fact there is such an epoch of civilization.

I use the term, *tragic*, in a very specific sense. The tragic is not simply another word for "bad things happen," a word for mishaps that injure, spread disease, or end life. The tragic names something structural, built into the way the world works. Tersely expressed, it means that whatever human beings (or other entities) experience as stable, beautiful, life-enhancing, fulfilling, necessarily and inevitably carries with it limitations, vulnerabilities, risks, and outcomes that conflict with, undermine, and even end what is valued and enjoyed. Furthermore, the "higher" or more complex is the experiencing entity, the more intense is the fulfillment or accomplishment (as for instance made possible by the human brain), the more intense is the risk and suffering that comes with it. Hence, the tragic always has an element of irony about it. It is the courageous hero (Oedipus), the passionate lovers (Juliet, Romeo) who undergo the most intense sufferings. The worldviews, narratives, and literatures of ancient and modern people all have versions of the tragic element of world working. The Trickster figure in Native American lore is an example. Other examples are the tragic dramas of ancient Greece, of Shakespeare, or more recently the stories of Kafka ("The Burrow"). In these worldviews and stories, to enjoy life at all is to experience the interdependence between one's accomplishments and fulfilled desires and the contingencies that frustrate or even end them.

For me at least, to experience the world in this way and to make that experience part of one's world view is not to be "pessimistic." Pessimism describes not so much a worldview or world interpretation as the enduring emotional tone or syndrome of an individual who is more preoccupied with the bad things that might happen than with life's stabilities, opportunities, and enjoyments. If a person's worldview is primarily dark ("pessimistic"), this means that the person has transformed this emotional tone into a metaphor for a general world structure. Like everyone else I regret, resist, and work to avoid "bad things that might happen." At the same time, I affirm and even enjoy the tragic structure of the world. Without it, there would be no world at all. All actual entities in the world (atoms, cells, planets, and plants) can exist in their life situations, thus dealing with various challenges and threats posed by living in fragile environments, only if they can select among possibilities. No species, no individuals, would ever come about on the world scene, much less survive very long, if there were no contingencies. For any entity, every second or nano-second of existence contains novelties and thus constitutes a new situation that never before existed. To live cannot mean, in a literal sense, repetition, nor are there any exact repetitions in nature. Actual existing things are not geometric or algebraic structures but entities in the flow or passage of temporal process. In a world of this sort, contingencies, conflicts, competitions, accidents, and endings are simply built in. They are the conditions of survival and well being, both for groups (e.g., species) and individuals. Thus species compete for space and galaxies gobble up other galaxies. A world of this sort mixes stability and instability in every second of its processing. Accomplishments, benefits, successes take place in situations of danger, competition and passing away. "The tragic" then names both what we are up against and what we are given: existence, self-making, inheritance, spaces of possibility.

The Ethical

"The I before the Other is infinitely responsible. The Other is the poor, the destitute, and nothing about the Strange can be indifferent to it."

—EMMANUEL LEVINAS, *PROPER NAMES*

"Ah, nothing doth the world with mischief fill,
But want of feeling one another's ill."

—CHRISTOPHER MARLOWE AND GEORGE CHAPMAN,
HERO AND LEANDER

To include "ethics" or the ethical in this memoir surely invites suspicions of being moralistic, or self-righteous. Perhaps such notions do apply to me, but like almost everyone else, I resist them as exhaustive self-descriptions. Yet I must include the ethical because it is an aspect of my poetic or aesthetic orientation to the ever-changing depth and mystery, the inner responses, relations, and creative impulses of things. In other words, I experience this poetic orientation as also an ethical orientation. To acknowledge the "reality" or actuality of something at all is to perceive it as located on its own space, struggling to survive and even enjoying its environment, as it lives a life of its own. It also means being aware of the thing's inaccessibility to one's attempts to know it and its resistance to manipulation. To acknowledge another thing's "reality" also means to be aware of the network in which that thing lives, a situation in which the things in that network are both attracted (dependent on) and in competition with each other. It seems evident that all things are dependent on their local and cosmic network for their very origin and continued existence, and in their specific setting interact with other entities that resemble themselves. To the degree that we human beings live "poetically," attracted to the stability, harmony, novelty, and beauty of things about us, we tend to develop not only accustomed dependences on other things but appreciation for them, even to the point of desire that others survive and, like us, enjoy life. And with this appreciation and attraction comes a certain sensibility to the vulnerability of other things.

Ethics and the ethical, as I use these terms, have to do with behavior and feelings toward other things that reflect this desire for their welfare and well-being. In its broadest sense, there seems to be an ethical dimension in the life of animals. Thus, I do not find it particularly helpful to reduce or explain all non-human behavior as the outcome of "instincts." Something of the ethical is apparent when families or groups look out for each other in a kind of mutual enjoyment. The ethical is apparent in broader ways as ethnic, tribal, or linguistic groups and their individuals cooperate and work for each member's welfare. Once an ethical orientation is at work, a further broadening is possible toward the non-human world and inclusive of the world itself. In human societies, it would appear that the root of this orientation is the "poetic" acknowledgment of the "reality," rights, needs, and self-orientations of anything that exists.

My tragic orientation prompts me to recall that we human beings live among threatening, dangerous, even violent groups and individuals. I only want to affirm another tendency (the ethical) at work in living things. I am not proposing a casuistry, a moral code, or my own or anyone else's specific version of moral obligations or taboos. But human beings over the world do seek their own, their tribe's, their nation's welfare, try to avoid dangerous situations, and if they are able, strive to tame microbe-based diseases. In other words, an ethical orientation is part of the mix of the many behaviors and dispositions that seem to oppose it. And it goes without saying that non-ethical or anti-ethical orientations (pragmatic, rapacious, cruel, manipulative, piratical, abusive) can be primary orientations in individuals, their organizations and societies, and historical movements that compete with and suppress the ethical.

I will not try to make the case that the ethical *should* be the primary or preferred way human beings relate to the world. For me there is something primary and defining about a poetic orientation and its ethical component, and something not primary and defining by mere conflict, competition, domination, quantification, and manipulation. To say this may be simply a self-serving idealization on my part. Can one know one's own primary orientation to things? Surely such varies in our life situations, perhaps even our life stages. And it is evident, I think, that we human beings are very good at fooling ourselves about our strengths and weaknesses, our virtues and flaws. My only point is that I sense about myself some way in which my general poetic orientation to things in their integrity, beauty, and novelty carries with it a kind of empathy for them, a desire for the welfare of entities, groups, environments that are broader than simply myself and my immediate setting. I realize that such an observation will seem a bit comic, measured by my behavior. Although I have always been involved in promoting the welfare of friends and family, and occasionally of those beyond these circles, I have never been an activist: that is, active in political, community causes. Why this is so, given the ethical component of my relation to things, is not easy to for me to understand. It is related, I am sure, to my ratiocinative orientation, which makes me leery of certainties, suspicious of the language and agendas of political programs. Is this a result of my overwhelming sense of vocation, a resistance to what would compromise it? I simply do not know.

FIVE

Confessions

Life In the Academy

"Alack, so sly they are, these scholars old,
I can't make out what doctrine I should hold."

—CHAUCER, *TROILUS AND CRESSIDA*

From the age of eighteeen (1949) to my retirement, the primary setting of my life and activities outside the home was some sort of post-high school academic institution: a college, university, or seminary. I worked in these institutions first in college and as a graduate student but mostly as a teacher. In the essays of this chapter, I reflect on several aspects of my life in these settings: my initial attraction to being a teacher (vocation), the setting itself (schools), the challenges of writing and teaching.

Vocation

GOOD ANGEL: "O Faustus, lay that damned book aside,
And gaze not on it lest it tempt thy soul,
And reap God's heavy wrath upon thy head.
Read, read the scriptures: that is blasphemy."

BAD ANGEL: "Go forward, Faustus, in that famous art
Wherein all nature's treasury is contain'd.
Be thou on earth as Jove is in the sky,
Lord and commander of these elements."

—Christopher Marlowe, Doctor Faustus

One of my high school friends at one of our reunions commented that I was the most "blessed" person he knew. I think he had in mind my history of good health, the long duration of a great marriage, and my good fortune in finding a lifelong, self-fulfilling vocation. "Vocation" may have a hollow ring for the postmoderns of the present generation. The concept not only has vague religious roots; it flies in the face of the "real world." For a growing number in our society, the pressing problem is simply to find the wherewithal to survive, to stay off the streets or out of institutions. For many others, it is deemed great fortune to find work that pays more than a minimum wage and is at least tolerable. Regular life-sustaining work of any kind is a great gift. A goodly number of our society settle into a "career," an enduring, fairly stable work environment requiring training and skill. I always assumed I would have a career, something I prepared for and that might fit my tastes and abilities. But I grew up in a relatively conservative Protestant congregation, and the issue of "career," especially a clerical one, was often thought of in terms of "calling," finding one's divinely appointed life's work. I never made much of this, although it was part of my childhood and adolescent worldview. But I did have a kind of secularized notion of vocation: something stronger than simply "career." I hoped in a half-conscious way that what I ended up doing would be personally self-fulfilling. In other words, I hoped there might be a connection between the environment and challenges of my work, whatever abilities I had, and my aesthetic and personal needs. In this sense I sought a "vocation."

In early adolescence, I had identified three options for a career: music, ministry, and "something else" (which meant a job in the business world). For whatever reason, the "professions" of law, medicine, and engineering were never part of my envisioned future. It turned out that the decision would be between (ordained) ministry and music. Both of these areas of life and work had begun to define my person so that when I left high school for college, they were my two main options. There were early signs that music would not be my vocation. I had some success early on as an instrumentalist and singer, but was never drawn to the kind of single-minded discipline necessary for making a living singing or playing an instrument. Doing what was necessary to master an instrument or voice and spending my life refining that mastery was unthinkable to me. In late high school and early college, my musical option was composition. I think that such a thing could have been a "vocation." If I had pursued that option, I would have done the necessary graduate work and sought a position in music theory or composition in a music school, using that as a base for a life of composing classical music. Satisfying as that would have been, it would have pushed aside a much more intensive interest which was beginning to emerge.

At the end of my freshman year in college, I chose "religion" and ordained ministry as my future work, thus becoming a pre-ministerial student. Although this decision did set me on a course toward seminary study, pastoral ministry would not be my "vocation." When I consider the factors in my move toward ministry and religion, I realize my mother had a significant role in resolving the matter. I do not recall any overt pressure on her part. On the other hand, before I was born, she had lost a daughter due to a pre-natal fall, and my birth was for her a personal, religious event, a special gift of some sort interpreted by way of certain stories or events in the Bible. Furthermore, the highest echelons of people in her social world were ministers. They embodied and acted out what she could only dream of: education, church vocation, positions of authority and responsibility. Being aware of how she felt about this was a kind of push in that direction. I never felt it as a fate, but it did place ministry before me as something to consider.

Although my seminary studies were oriented toward the parish ministry, something else haunted my dreams and fantasies. From late childhood on, I had a kind of waking dream, little more than an image. It was probably planted in my subconscious by some story or book I had read. The image was that of a tower or upper story room in a large house. In that room, surrounded by books, I worked at some mysterious project. The image carried with it no subject, no content of study. I had no strong conscious desire for such a thing, only the image. It was not strong enough to draw me toward serious study in high school (I wish it had), or prepare me for a life of scholarship in college. But in my third and final year of college, I began to wonder about teaching. My intellectual self-confidence was fairly high in one-on-one conversations with others but low when I considered the institutional hurdles that lay ahead. These were the early signs of what eventually became a vocation: that is, a lifelong practice of teaching and intellectual exploration. More specifically, career or vocation meant the chance to explore and clarify a set of questions in the company of others joined in the enterprise of learning. I can at this point say that to discover this and have the chance to pursue it was a gift of a sort, a kind of luck or good fortune. Many human beings are fortunate to find work at all, much less a career in which their abilities match their job opportunity. I did find a career, but an added benefit was that I eventually was paid to do what I would have wanted to do anyway. I did end up doing something toward which I had been drifting for many years.

In a general way, higher education turned out to be the natural environment for my enthusiasms and abilities. But I had one special qualification for doing the sort of thing demanded by the puzzles of philosophy and theology. It was not intelligence. Although I have had a good measure of analytic-verbal ability, I have always been surrounded by people who were more intelligent than I am. Although my memory was at one time very good, it was nothing like the awesome recall of a polymath, or a linguist. But something else was in the mix of my qualifications for study, inquiry, and teaching, namely a very active imagination, and with that, a certain kind of creativity. This was the capacity to envision possibilities, options, alternative notions based on a certain empathy with the life and character of other things. I am not suggesting at this point that other human beings or scholars lack imagination. Imagination is a necessary skill simply to get along in the world and to some extent is a feature of all knowing (scientific, practical, poetic). But I sense in my own case that it is the imagination that constituted a rather distinctive empowerment, and later on, a way of thinking.

Becoming aware of the specific route to my vocation did not happen all at once. Early on I knew I would have to find my way through graduate school and locate a position somewhere in an institution of higher education. But my understanding of my vocation did change over time. In the beginning my initial style of intellectual work, perhaps a residue of graduate work, was polemical, analytic, aggressively pressing a point. In most cases, this style served the aims of clarification rather than the ego-needs of winning (I am not sure of that). And in the early years of my teaching, my study was largely recuperative and preparatory, filling in the enormous gaps (linguistic, historical, textual) of my college, seminary, and graduate school education. I studied world religions, ancient and modern philosophies, and began the long trek across centuries of Christian texts and languages. But I knew in my years at DePauw University and Pittsburgh Theological Seminary that something else awaited me, that these recuperative studies were not an end but a means, an assemblage of tools, a forming of perspective, method, issues. In this period I began to form a picture of the way centuries of texts posed massive and complex issues, problems, and insights (as well as a lot of nonsense). In that period, I began to move away from tool gathering and had a glimpse of another horizon. One step toward this was the year I spent (at great cost to my family) in Basel, Switzerland. That year was also a tool-building year; helped by studies in Latin. More important, it was a year of learning to think. Every day in the Basel library, with pen in hand, I would pose an issue, examine the many possible meanings of the terms used, formulate a variety of possible answers, examine the assumptions behind each one, relate them to each other, consider the coherence of the claim, and search for evidence for or against the claim at every level I could think of. These inquiries were not for publication, and none of them ever saw print. But there was a payoff. I began to experience what a disciplined, imaginatively posed, argued sequence of inquiry involved. The year also had another result. Orthodoxy (Protestant) and neo-orthodoxy were set aside as viable frameworks. I did not have to read Schleiermacher, Tillich, or Whitehead to arrive at this negative conclusion. It gradually emerged in my daily attempts to unravel various theological issues as well as the character and grounds of theology itself.

A second step toward critical-imaginative and constructive theological work took place by means of another year of study, a sabbatical at Pittsburgh Theological Seminary, in which I read through Edmund Husserl's *Ideen I* and *Logische Unterssuchungen*, and similar texts. Again, not a line of publication ensued. I was still gathering tools, in this case, a kind of philosophical electron microscope. And when I looked through it, what appeared was the intentional structure of meaning, and that opened up vast new worlds of contents. The year was not just another step of a journey but a breakthrough and a turn in a different direction. I realized how much I had failed to grasp the enterprise, grounds, methods of theology. My fairly sophisticated version of theological thinking

had been individualistic (Cartesian?). It abstracted the individual's experiences, faith, self, and knowing from the matrix of those things. This
matrix was not simply "sociality" or social influences or institutions but
the structural interrelations between human beings (intersubjectivity).
With that year behind me, and the paradigm of the interhuman in hand,
I was ready to write *Ecclesial Man*, the initial critical-imaginative journey
into the lands beyond orthodoxy and neo-orthodoxy, in other words, the
landscape of my vocation. This of course was only the beginning of a
vocation that included teaching, research, and writing, subjects which I
discuss in other essays.

Schools

"More especially, it may now be declared that Professor Teufelsdröckh's
acquirements, patience of research, philosophic, and even poetic vigour,
are here made indisputably manifest, and unhappily no less his proxility
and tortuosity and manifold ineptitude."

—THOMAS CARLYLE, *SARTOR RESARTUS*

For about four decades, I taught in three quite different post-high school
educational institutions: an undergraduate department of philosophy
and religion, a professional school (Seminary), and the Divinity School
of a university. I have given an account of these schools in Chapters 3 and
4 and supplemented that with a short essay on teaching. In this essay, I
offer a few general impressions of my life as a professor in these educational milieus. Because of my experience in only a few schools and in a
specific stretch of time in American history, I hesitate to generalize about
"American higher education." I do offer a few comments of this sort, but
they are highly impressionistic. As one would expect, my experience was
a mixture of satisfactions and frustrations. With only a few exceptions, I
greatly enjoyed my colleagues, some of whom became close friends. In
some cases, I admired and made friends with school administrators: Russell Compton at DePauw University, Gordon Jackson at Pittsburgh Seminary, Walter Harrelson and other deans of Vanderbilt Divinity School.

There is now a huge literature—there seems to be a "huge literature" on almost everything, probably one on the hyoid bone in Nean-
derthals—on the failures and flaws of American higher education. This

literature varies much in quality, some studies amounting to little more than tirades with little factual inquiry behind them. There also seem to be recurring myths about professors and universities. Perhaps there is a solid core of fact behind these myths, but for the most part, they are not confirmed by my own experience. One of the myths is that the tenure system has produced professors who, after obtaining tenure, go into a kind of semi-retirement, recycling for the rest of their life their dissertation research and initial courses. In my experience, almost all of my colleagues at DePauw Pittsbugh Seminary, and Vanderbilt were solid, hard-working scholars dedicated to the challenges of teaching. These teachers, my colleagues, varied widely in how they taught, conducted scholarly research, and wrote for publication. Some published very little, others kept editors busy preparing their works for publication, and some wrote the occasional article or book. In my view, this variation is as it should be. Given the number of professors for whom publishing is required for tenure, there is already a surfeit of published works in almost every field. If all professors published many books over their lifetimes, the surfeit would be a flood. I would not be enthusiastic about professors, especially those guiding PhD research projects, who make little attempt to keep up with the advances in their field, or have little interest in doing any research themselves. Post-high school professors need not be researcher-publishers but they should be researcher-thinkers who keep up with their field. Perhaps there is a grain of truth in the fairly widespread notion that professors obtain tenure and then go into semi-retirement. But I knew almost no professors of that sort.

A second myth portrays the typical professor as more a researcher than a teacher. This stereotype calls for a close examination of different types of schools and different academic fields. A few "big reputation" professors in major universities are primarily researchers, and in fact are appointed to be just that. Perhaps professors who have research appointments in prestigious fields do have a different relation to teaching than the typical teacher in a small college or in most fields of a university. In the three schools where I taught, I had no colleagues whose focus was on research/writing at the expense of teaching. (There were, of course, some who were not very good at teaching.) The myth may be a generalization of a situation found in some schools in which tight budgets, huge classes, and technology together create a certain type of professor, one who is an occasional lecturer or online presence assisted by a host of graduate assistants. An offshoot of this system is the hiring of adjunct or part-time teachers to handle face-to-face teaching, do grading, teach unpopular courses. Online education, a new way of taking courses and obtaining a degree, may replace the professor as a face-to-face teacher and dialogue partner with a Skype presence. My experience is too narrow (three schools) and too epochal (the 1960s–1990s) to count much when I say that my colleagues and those I knew in other fields were not so research oriented that they were indifferent to teaching.

When I consider the general issue of how professors relate to or pursue the challenge of teaching, I do find a kind of confirmation of the myth. What is confirmed is not that professors eschew teaching because they are researchers but that they do not give the act of teaching and the challenge of teaching much thought. Professors do not typically read the literature (a "huge literature" of course) on pedagogy and teaching. What attracts and preoccupies them is their specialty field and the challenge of grasping, communicating, explaining its subject. What it means to "teach," how to go about it, are things most of them pick up in their graduate school years. A professor may even have the self-image of a "serious teacher" but not attend reflectively to teaching as itself an intellectual content to be researched or a skill to be developed.

I strongly suspect that something else is at work in the trend (if there is one) toward the pedagogically inept research professor. There is something in the milieu of the university, something in the way the university works, the system so to speak, which makes it difficult for teachers to focus on teaching. That something is not the professor's subject or field but the "new complexity" of postmodern institutions and life (see chapter 7). Most major American institutions have undergone extensive bureaucratization in recent decades. In the universities, everything has grown in numbers and complexity: staffs (e.g., library, development, publication, student life) and administration (central office, graduate school, department, special operations, athletics). What it takes for a modern university to survive and function resembles the organization and operations of a corporation or government, a kudzu-like growth of accountants, lawyers, public relations people, fundraisers, editors, marketers, computer experts, engineers, and builders. Every unit of the university (the professional schools, athletics, libraries) requires a large staff of specialists. One would think that this complex of specialists would release faculty for teaching and research, and in a way it does. But something else has happened to draw faculty away from teaching and study. Sometime in the twentieth century, faculties became disillusioned with the authoritarian structures of the preceding era and underwent a democratization. The result was to draw faculty into many school operations: publications, editorial boards, tenure and promotion, athletic, and student life committees, recruitment, graduation ceremony planning. Within a department or school, an enormous amount of time is spent on committees that consult, evaluate, and report on the micro-details of education. My suspicion is that, in many cases, what competes with teaching is not so much research as the obligations created by the new complexity. Faculty members complain about their "committee work" but would never dream of reducing their bureaucratic obligations. In one university I know (one of the most prestigious), a significant percentage of senior faculty time is spent on faculty reviews and the securing of new faculty. In sum the mushrooming complexity of bureaucracy plus the democratization of faculty roles are in the mix of things that compete for the faculty member's time.

One set of criticisms of universities originating from political and other types of conservatism complain about the liberal bias of the college faculties, the tendency of faculties to align with Democrats rather than Republicans on a number of issues. As far as I know, this generalization is fairly accurate. (It probably does not hold for hundreds of conservative religious colleges or for certain professional schools—management, engineering, medicine, possibly law—in the university.) But I am curious about several things. I would like to see the exact data, the nose count, how it applies to different areas in the universities. More important, I would like to see a study that turns up how much partisan loyalty is actually verbalized in the classroom or makes a difference in teaching, both for conservative and liberal faculty. Does the "liberal university" mean that there is a widespread political ideology at work in how English, sociology, biology are taught? There is, I think, a kind of liberalism that is almost unavoidable in an institution of research and learning, something that goes back to Socrates. The issues, the subjects of research, the trends of the fields, the selection of methods, the determination of evidence are not settled by tradition, authority, or ideology but by peer-reviewed debate and in national or even global exchanges. Researchers of course have their viewpoints, their angles on things, and as evidence accumulates, their commitments. But in the ethos of the university, any and all issues are open to review, criticism, testing, and retesting. In my experience, another kind of liberalism is definitely manifest in departments of religion and divinity schools. These faculties tend to fall on the liberal side on debates over oppressive or dehumanizing societal trends. The reigning ethos of these schools or departments does tend to oppose movements that reduce or deny basic rights to selected groups, thus, concerns about sexism, racism, and homophobia. Included in this ethos is also an antipathy to the kind of religious fervor, be it Muslim, Roman Catholic, or Protestant, which is self-absolutizing to the point of violence and persecution, closed off to any and all other religious faiths. If any of these issues become matters of public debate, legal options, or matters faced by the government, the theological faculties I know will take the liberal side: for instance, on the Vietnam war, the civil rights movement, women's suffrage, and sexual identity. It is, I think, the case that the divinity school faculty members are liberal on these issues. What I am unaware of is teaching that introduces into the classroom the partisan conflicts that resound in elections and government bodies. If such things have to do with civil rights or gender unfairness, perhaps so. A recent study which asked whether college students change their political commitments as a result of their college experience concluded there was little or no change. This confirms my suspicion that, however "liberal" they are, professors of history, English, biology, or sociology do not bring partisan politics into the classroom. Of course there are always exceptions to whatever seems to be a prevailing trend of behavior. I do hope that the experience of a university education does influence students in a "liberal," direction so that they are more critical of what is mythical, rumored, assertional, more aware of their own biases, more flexible and open to change and to other viewpoints. I would also hope it would push them in the direction of moral or civil rights liberalism and arouse them to oppose dehumanizing societal movements and powers. Whether it does affect students in these ways I do not know.

Altogether, the many books on higher education springing up like mushrooms in recent years have the character of jeremiads about administrators, the non-tenure track class of teachers, the cost of education, the new bureaucracy, the pedagogically indifferent faculties, the small effect of its education on students, the Leviathan of athletics, the non-academic core curriculums. If even some of this is accurate, American higher education appears to be in serious trouble: financially, pedagogically, organizationally. I do not have much to say about most of these jeremiads,

mind can piece by piece grasp and express in language. If they are soft reductionists, teachers will impart what they know but alert their students to what is left out. If they are ideological reductionists, they will be quite certain that what they know and teach is identical with the concrete thing itself. The result is not only cognitive inflexibility but aggressive competition with other interpreters, perspectives, and even fields. At the very heart of every act of teaching is this challenge and task posed by the abstract character of knowing and teaching. How can one teach without closing the world down and turning students into cognitive ideologues? How can one teach what one knows passionately, honestly, accurately without reduction, without claiming too much, without sealing reality off into words, types, causes, explanations? In a popular and superficial sense, postmodern societies are relativistic, scientifically oriented, relatively free from older authoritarian and tradition-bound eras. Perhaps so. But with liberated education may come a new naiveté, a new reductionism, content to identify "the real" with the utile information needed by governments, institutions, and industries. Education is expected to deliver what society needs (products) and schools do take up the task. If the problem of the abstract and the concrete did become an element in current pedagogy, higher education would, I think, be drastically altered.

The reduction of the "real," the ever-changing complexity of the actual to what is known, spoken, researched and applied, affects our schools, faculties, and pedagogy in a variety of ways. One of them is the new hierarchy of fields. In the European Middle Ages, when universities first came into existence, the hierarchy of the areas of learning and teaching was self-evident. Since God and heavenly things were the origin and acme of the universe, a reigning causality presided over by an authoritative and hierarchical institution, the knowledge of such things was the highest knowledge. Theology presided over the sciences as their queen. Close to theology would be the knowledge of the formal structure of things: metaphysics, mathematics, and music. Below this fell studies of the universe itself (astronomy), and finally sciences of changing things: nature, animals. This structure has not entirely disappeared. At the apex of university learning and research are the sciences, which combine sophisticated mathematics with experimental verification: quantum physics, astrophysics, chemistry. Close to such sciences in rigor and methodological complexity are biology, biochemistry, physiology, and the like. Below this group in the hierarchy would be the social sciences: history, economics, political science, sociology, psychology, anthropology, communication theory. These sciences are burdened with the messiness, the elusiveness of historical process. From the viewpoint of the mountaintop sciences (physics, etc.), the social sciences are "softer," and the result is that social scientists work very hard to emulate the top stratum of university sciences, developing sophisticated mathematical and statistical methods of inquiry. At the bottom of the hierarchy is a group of studies which are hardly sciences at all (although they would insist they are fields of scholarship) and therefore have the status of interlopers, visitors to the party thrown by the university. They are a bit like a disheveled and somewhat clueless homeless person who wanders into a mayor's fund-raising event. They are the humanities: philosophy, religion, arts, literature. Sensing that their *raison d'etre* in the university is problematic, their topic elusive, their "methods" puzzling, they do their best to imitate the methods of the fields in the strata above them. Thus they use the historical, contextual, even empirical methods of the social sciences, to study literature, religion, or how language works. Accordingly, philosophers become scholars of the history of philosophy. Religious scholars become ethnographers and linguists of Asia, Africa, or Polynesia. Literature professors do biographical, historical-contextual research. Of course there are many exceptions to these generalizations. But the cognitive hierarchy and the imitation of higher stratum fields by lower fields does seem to be a feature of the modern university.

To describe the new hierarchy is not necessarily to attribute reductionism to individual physicists, anthropologists, or historians. Among faculty members, physicists may be those most aware of the non-identity between what is actual and what is known. The new hierarchy like the old hierarchy is a structure of prestige, hegemony, and influence. In the Middle Ages, the church, the monarchy, and the barons were in a three-way power struggle. Theology at the top of the cognitive hierarchy reflected not only what was valued most (heaven, salvation, the mediating hierarchy) but something of great societal power. Eventually, all three claimants to power were replaced by something else. In a similar way the new hierarchy of studies mirrors what the society most relies on for its economic, military and other securities, namely sciences having to do with the management of physical resources, front-line technological know-how, industrial competitiveness, military sophistication, medical systems. In such a society, we would expect physics, chemistry, and biology, each with their engineering offshoots, to be the fields society depends on the most. Their scientist/teachers earn the most from their research grants and from university salaries.

A second effect of the reduction of what is actual to what is known (spoke, applied, used) is what might be called the new "fields." Departments and areas of teaching are only one of a number of things which constitute a university. Some observers even argue that pedagogy and degree-oriented learning is marginal to other activities such as bureaucratic complexity, sports, leisure and social organizations. But areas of teaching/learning organized into "fields" (cognitive-methodological specialties) have not disappeared. Without fields there are no faculties, pedagogies, classes, grades, degrees: in other words, colleges, universities, and professional schools as they presently exist. The modern university teacher knows this and to some degree is committed to an institution constituted by a variety of fields. At the same time, fields have a double character. On the one hand they are designated areas of inquiry, learning, and teaching whose contents are organized by a paradigm of some sort: thus, "history," "communications," "religion." On the other hand, a field is an institutional (e.g., political) entity formed by specialists educated in specific graduate programs who are dependent on the good will of a variety of trans-field figures and on the broader policies of the university, which determine budgets, library resources, size of graduate departments. As a subject-paradigm area and as a political unity, the fields of university are a bit like medieval fiefdoms or urban wards. The paradigms that draw the boundaries of the subject are important to maintain. How is the total complex of fields related to the actual world of events and constituents? The relation is not unlike how a two-dimensional map (with states, counties, cities) is related to an actual geographical area. The map fixes and draws boundaries of what is in fact in constant motion, events of emerging novelties, changing interrelated complexes. In the best of academic worlds, teachers/learners know the difference and are not averse to crossing or blurring the boundaries of their areas (fields) of location. But the social system of graduate school specialties, precise and efficacious (but narrow) expertise, and inter- or intra-field competition invites teachers to absolutize their paradigms and methods. The result is a way of teaching that so identifies the specialist's knowing (methods) with what is actual that the professor's field becomes a paradigm for all knowing. With this move, teaching/learning takes on an ideological, almost propagandistic character. At best the field-based university professor is aware of the perspectival, abstract, and map-like character of the specialty field and is open to trans-field influences. At worst, the professor is an ideologist of a "school" of thought, a method, a movement. One might argue that such a situation, even its ideological element, is in the long run positive and fruitful. Close, intense inquiry in cognitive areas is what yields discovery and new knowledge. Furthermore, paradigm battles between perspectives (fields) may have a pluralizing affect on students who visit the various territories on the map. Perhaps that is a sufficient rationale for a university to organize itself into intellectually aggressive and even competitive fields. But I still worry about the matter. One result of the arrangement is that education means compiling in the student's memory a variety of relatively isolated compartments that altogether constitute what is actual or "real."

A third effect, and possibly also a cause, of the reduction of the actual to knowing, method, and language has to do with tenure. I am not sure just how tenure originated in the history of universities. I think that its primary rationale had to do with academic freedom. Teaching-based, open-ended research or inquiry is surely undermined if it is subject to the ideological monitoring of religious, political, or cultural groups. Tenure gives the teacher a degree of freedom from such monitoring. It says, in effect, let the best research available be the basis of what you teach and you will not be fired by a Board of Trustees, dean, or department chair pressed by ideologies at work in the broader culture. A tenured faculty is more or less cognitively independent and not subject to the culture wars, party politics, or groups whose traditions or agendas are threatened by the new discoveries. For this reason, I would be very worried if state legislatures, donors, and other powers removed tenure from the universities.

Perhaps the following problem is limited to large research-oriented universities. I am not sure. Tenure policies and criteria have created fairly isolated departmental fiefdoms—there are exceptions of course—and specialists who occupy very narrow territories on the map of fields. Typically, the newly hired faculty member must be tenured or let go after seven years. The criteria that measure scholarly expertise do vary from school to school, and even from one field to another. There are other tenure criteria (teaching, contribution to the life of the university) but they tend to be marginal when compared to academic prowess measured by books, articles and scholarly reputation. In some universities, the teacher can receive tenure only by research projects of national or international significance. The professor has seven years to become a nationally recognized scientist or scholar. One can imagine how these beginning teachers spend those seven years. They must continue the specialized focus that began with their college major and continued through graduate school, and they must carve out a cognitive area narrow enough to break new ground and render the professor visible in the field. The result is an exceedingly competent researcher of wide repute in a narrow sector of a field. Thus the tenured professor may not only be clueless about other fields, but is only minimally informed about his or her own field. I realize this account is a caricature, a worst (or best, depending on your viewpoint) case scenario. It is an observable trend in research universities. The teachers in such universities are embodiments of a cognitive abstraction, their research area. Narrowed by years of preparation for tenure, they are hardly aware of the abstract character of their knowing and teaching, nor are they concerned with other paradigms of knowing beyond their research. They are research specialists but not intellectuals. The distinction is, I think, important. Intellectuals, be they researchers (scholar/teachers) or non-researchers, are able to grasp and articulate the general structures and trends of human life and the flow of issues and problems of their time and culture. It may be a bit ironical that most intellectuals exist outside of research universities, and many intellectuals in this sense may not even be highly educated. Returning to the tenure issue, in the best of possible academic worlds, the first years of a new faculty member should be a kind of *therapeia* and correction for the years of focused inquiry. One would not expect new faculty members to abandon their specialized research, the excitements of their projects, but one would hope that in the early years of teaching, a broadening is possible.

At this point, I offer what is only a speculation. I wonder if the pressure toward specialized academic accomplishment might be responsible for a kind of early burnout for many faculty, a loss of interest in what they do. I also wonder about what sort of education students experience when those who facilitate their learning are specialists but not intellectuals. Might that have something to do with the complaint that a university education has the character of exposure to various compartments of knowing but lacks the Socratic element of pressing beneath and beyond the patterns of knowing and thinking that specialized knowing cannot reach? In other words, do students experience not only the awesome technical mastery of the specialist but the passion of the intellectual? To utter such a utopian notion calls of course for endless qualifications. The enormous variation of schools, faculties, and fields in the country may undermine or blur the point. There are, of course, schools which grant tenure on other bases than accomplished research. There may even be schools which expect tenured faculty to be "intellectuals," in touch with issues over a wide spectrum. (I do not know of any.) But in the universities I am familiar with, the trend is in the other direction. Tenure policies, field organization, awards for research altogether promote the notion that "reality" coincides with the cognitive yield of research.

Writing

"But worse was to come. For once the disease of reading has laid hold on the system it weakens it so that it falls an easy prey to the scourge which dwells in the inkpot and festers in the quill. The wretch takes to writing."

—Virginia Woolf, *Orlando*

"Why did I write? What sin to me unknown
Dipped me in ink, my parents or my own?"

—Alexander Pope, "Why Did I Write?"

My vocation, that is, a lifelong undertaking involving a fit between my deepest interests and capabilities and the activities of teaching and research, did not initially include writing. Most of my college teachers were not authors and did not plan to be. In high school and college, I never thought much about writing and publishing as something that might be part of teaching. In those years, I did write school papers, the occasional poem, letters, sermons. Eventually, in graduate school, I had to write serious research papers and a dissertation that, to my surprise, was published by Westminster Press. In those early years, I wrote at the bidding of editor friends two series of adult Christian education materials, one of which was published as a book by Westminster. Without being very aware of it, I was preparing for what would eventually be an ambitious program of published writings. I spent much of the seven or so years after graduate school trying to extend what had been a minimal exposure to the major texts of Western philosophy and theology. When I had the chance to spend a year in Europe, I spent a significant part of every day in the Basel University library writing. This writing was simply a recording of an open-ended dialectical thinking on issues that puzzled me. It was exploratory writing and had no relation to any publishing plans. (Given the pressure to publish major pieces of research prior to tenure, such a venture would not be possible for young professors today.) It was only in my years at Pittsburgh and my initial attempts by way of continental philosophy (phenomenology) to uncover how theology might be done that I realized a publishable project might be ahead. At that time, *writing* became part of the way I understood my vocation.

I am not sure why writing merged with my self-understanding as a teacher. I had no notion of trying to emulate the well-known published theologians of the day. Many of my colleagues were good scholars and skilled teachers whose pattern was to labor over many years on an occasional essay or book. Such a pattern is, I think, the normal one for university professors. Typical college or graduate school professors maintain a balance between an ongoing and rigorous program of research, keeping up with the field, and even pushing its horizons, and teaching based on those activities. My own writing plans emerged along with and possibly the result of a vision of how certain fundamental problems might be solved. If I could work them out, then I might write something for publication. Such was my attitude about writing. The initial fruit of this vision was the oddly titled *Ecclesial Man*, published in my early years at Vanderbilt.

Unfortunately, writing itself as a distinctive activity and challenge did not get my attention in these years. The reason (apart from plain obtuseness) was that my primary challenge was to understand and utilize a daunting, difficult set of texts (Husserlian phenomenology). When I used this framework as a tool to explore certain theological problems, my consciousness and writing style became Teutonic and jingoistic. Thus, the onset of my writing established my reputation in theological circles —I don't think the philosophers agree—as an obscure, difficult, and poor writer. When I look back on these works, I concur. If I revised *Ecclesial Man* now, I would probably simplify, alter, shorten almost every sentence. I have no plans to pursue such an arduous task since there would be a minimal readership and certainly no publisher. When I did revise one of my earlier published essays, I changed about eighty percent of the writing. And I have been properly chided by close friends to get some help in writing. I take less seriously complaints that my writing is "obscure." I may be wrong on this, but I see behind some of these complaints a long American and even Protestant antipathy to the use of philosophy and thus to philosophical styles of writing and thinking in theology. This mix of piety, biblicism, and pragmatism insists on theological writing which is accessible, immediately relevant ("applicable"), religious in tone, Bible-centered, and perhaps even marketable. There may be in these complaints an anti-German element. One theologian friend of my generation whose roots were in German scholarship was so frequently caricatured by reviewers and critics that he simply abandoned his writing projects. Not many analytic or even process theologians, however technical are their works, are faulted for their writing. I do think that the works of my later years (*Divine Empathy, Deep Symbols, Faith and Beauty*) are more accessible, and some reviewers have even praised the writing itself.

Certain built-in tensions, even contradictions, are part of writing whose setting is a community of teachers of religious and theological subjects. In the university, the projects of knowing have no pre-set limits. The chemist, the archaeologist and the Egyptologist have no choice but to push beyond any present horizon of what is known, using whatever tools and materials are appropriate, however difficult, esoteric, and technical they are. Religious scholars or at least theologians are caught between two communities and two sets of expectations. They resist the role and reputation of the "popularizer" who compromises the rigors of evidence and precision of cognitive inquiry. At the same time, theologians who embrace these esoterica have a bad conscience. This is because something about the subject itself (the human condition, suffering, human evil, liberation) has to do with a just society and with personal transformation, solace, and meaning. Accordingly, they resist the role and image of the isolated, irrelevant and ivory tower pedant. Religious academics are thus caught between commitment to an uncompromising but not very accessible rigor of inquiry and the articulation of world changing or personal transforming insights. Traditional pietists and recent generations of feminist, liberation, and black theologians have strongly pressed for the transformational function of writing, and have embodied the paradoxes and strains of combining rigor and accessibility.

My own writing has been largely of the esoteric type but has included, if not popularized, at least non-technical pieces. My own "bad conscience" tracks both sides: my lack of rigor and my inaccessable style. But all writers in the humanities and perhaps even in the social sciences face a second, never really solvable contradiction and task. The contradiction is that the subject is, in a necessary way, about an ever changing, ever inter-relational entity or complex, and writing itself cannot capture, reproduce, clone, replicate this complex thing, be it a historical text, a person's life, a political movement, a social trend. This is why, with the possible exception of mathematics, statistics, and formal logic—note that I say "possible"—all writing is in some sense metaphorical. An inaccessible and mysterious depth ever lurks in and behind the grammar, tropes, and clauses of writing. In the case of "religion" and theology, to write is at least in part a poetic task. This means more than simply the deployment of metaphors. In everyday talk, we say, "He is as strong as an oak." Writers sensitive to the poetic element in language cannot be content with the simple use of metaphors. Another step must be taken, a use of metaphor that undermines itself, that expresses its own inadequacy by hinting at the mystery behind it. Frost's poem "Stopping by Woods on a Snowy Evening" does more than offer a simile to the reader. It invites the reader to contemplate a whole set of mysteries: decisions, options, even death. Writing too is a struggle between the inevitable abstraction of knowing and the poetic mystery of the concrete. At this point too, I have a bad conscience. Even though the poetic is my worldview, I have never very successfully written of theological matters in a way that both displays and hides, expresses and at the same time cancels insights.

Before leaving the subject of writing, I should say something about my published and unpublished works. I am not proud of some of the titles of these works, some of which are my own mistakes, some the publishers'. I wanted to entitle my dissertation *The Most High*, using the common device of an initial metaphor and a descriptive subtitle. Westminster Press wanted a descriptive title, thus, *The Transcendence of God* (1960). This work studied the theme of God's transcendence in several mid-twentieth-century philosophers of religion and theologians. *Requiem for a Lost Piety* was my title, and, unfortunately, Westminster Press went along with it. It was both inaccurate and misleadingly negative. This small book had been a series of adult Sunday School lessons for *Crossroads* whose editor, Dennis Shoemaker, was a friend. It attempted to undermine traditional notions of "Christian life" and ethics and offered an alternate way of understanding such things. *Ecclesial Man: A Social Phenomenology of*

Faith and Reality (1975) was the first of two volumes on whether faith is grounded in any reality at all and on theological method. It used Husserlian and social phenomenology to explore the ways human interrelations (community) might embody and mediate insights into things. The title was disastrous. For reasons I shall not elaborate, Fortress Press took almost four years to bring the book to publication. The book was given its title at the beginning of the process. By 1975 a consensus had arisen that "man" could no longer be used as a general term for human being. It seemed as if the author and press were simply thumbing their nose at the feminists. The result was that the book was simply ignored by a large percentage of potential readers. Even if "man" had been a legitimate term, the title was a poor one to describe what the book was about. *Ecclesial Reflection: An Anatomy of Theological Method* (1982) was also my title and not a good one. The term *reflection* did indicate my notion of what theologians did, but it was misleading to many. The work, a sequel to *Ecclesial Man*, moved beyond the "reality problem" of faith to the specific ways theologians make judgments and arrive at some conclusions. Much of the work was an archaeology of the "house of authority," a centuries-long way the grounds and norms of theology were understood, and it included a critique of the traditional ways of grounding doctrines, beliefs, confessions, theologies in institutional and textual authorities. *Theologia: The Fragmentation and Unity of Theological Education* (1985) was my title, and I still think that the Latin title helped jolt the readers into an awareness of the ambiguity of the English term *theology* and called forth an older and very different meaning. The book offered a deconstructive history of the concept, theology *(theologia),* which grounded the standard fourfold way of organizing theological (clergy) education, and explored "theology" as a term for a very different genre of activity. *The Fragility of Knowledge* (1988) collected a number of essays that reflected the new and broader way of understanding theology as an undertaking of churches and the Christian community. *Good and Evil: Interpreting a Human Conditon* (1990) continued the series of books that began with *Ecclesial Man* and moved beyond issues of grounding and method. The subtitle was at least accurate, but the title was unfortunate, a binary title in an anti-binary era, sounding like a work in theodicy. The content was a tripartite analysis of human beings in history: their tragi-comic, bio-social features, the social-individual distortions of such, and the reparation of the distortions. *Divine Empathy: A Theology of God* (1996) probably should have been called simply, *A Theology of God*, but even that is problematic due to the ill-fated connotations of the term, *theology*. *Deep Symbols: Their Postmodern Effacement and Reclamation* (1996) was my title and another mistake. Technically, what was at issue were not so much "symbols" but certain deep, almost lost values at work in the deep recesses of the institutions and communities of Western societies. I had preferred *Words of Power*, but a number of works were already published using that title. The work records a rather superficial encounter with postmodernism and deconstruction, and explores whether the winds of the postmodern have blown away every vestige of value, meaning, law, or even "reality" itself. *Faith and Beauty: A Theological Aesthetic* (2000) would not be an accurate title for those who define the aesthetic as the realm of the arts. The work corrects and supplements my early works, which tend to ignore the aesthetic dimension of the experience, nature, culture, language, religion. "Beauty" is the work's theme, and it locates and utilizes a departure from the "great theory of beauty" of ancient Greece in the works of Jonathan Edwards. In the case of *Practicing Gospel: Unconventional Thoughts about the Church's Ministry* (2005), the problem is with the subtitle. The title, "practicing good news," is okay, odd as it is. Some editor at Westminster John Knox changed "ministries" into "ministry," a word which suggests that pastors are the book's primary subject. But only some of the essays (e.g., on preaching) specifically have to do with clergy tasks. I had the good fortunate to co-edit a collection of essays with my friend, Barbara Wheeler: *Shifting Boundaries: a Contextual Approach to the Structure of Theological Education* (1991). I co-edited a second collection with Thomas Long to honor the work of David Buttrick: *Preaching as a Theological Task: World, Gospel, Structure* (1991).

Nachlass, a German term, refers to a writer's literary legacy or estate, including unpublished works, papers, lectures. Given sufficient fame (cf. Edmund Husserl), the author's unpublished writings may be assembled, edited, and published by loyal followers. If I include file drawers of notes and lectures, my *Nachlass* is large. My handwritten pieces would not be decipherable, even by codebreakers, and my typing is not much better. These materials functioned to help me organize, remember, interpret, and teach. Neither the lectures nor the study notes are publishable. There are, however, three book-length works that are theoretically publishable, even if in the opinion of publishers they are not marketable and would attract no significant readership. All three books were written in my retirement years and are the following.

Teaching What is Unteachable: The Concrete and the Abstract in Religious and Theological Pedagogy is a serious academic work. I have pursued its publication in only a minimal way. The two publishing houses that have looked at it do not see its heavy dose of philosophy and its theme of pedagogy as attractive to a readership. My own authorial egocentrism may be what prompts me to place a higher value on the work than it deserves. The reasons for this are several. It is a serious and extensive analysis of a single problem at the very heart of the act of teaching, and as far as I know, no other author has been concerned with this problem. Because it includes the teaching of "religion" (cf. religious studies), it struggles with the recent trend that places the idea or category of religion in doubt, and offers a theory of religion that, hopefully, is not derived from or dependent on a theological point of view. Further, because it also addresses theological pedagogy, it continues my career-long analyses of theological education, taking former projects to another level. I recognized at the start that such a work would have difficulty finding a publisher. Teaching (pedagogy) is, paradoxically, only a distant interest for university teachers and graduate students. Their primary motivation, activity, rewards, and reputation have to do with research in their own specialty field. In addition, *Teaching What is Unteachable* is written by one whose specialty is in theology, hence the "religious" element in the work would be of little interest to scholars of religions. Finally, the work proceeds by way of philosophical analyses. Analyses of this sort were required by the problem and subject of the work, but in many circles, there is a low tolerance for philosophy. These things are what make the work unmarketable, so at the present it remains on my computer.

The following piece of writing sounds like a popular work, potentially attractive to a significant body of readers, but in fact it too turns out to be a rather dense (although not technical) analysis. *Prayers of an Atheist*—no, I am not an atheist—is a work of fiction, a record of prayers by a person obsessed with speaking to God but who knows God is a figment of the imagination. The prayers record his struggle with the issue of his own atheism. As the story unfolds, it has an outcome, but it is not conversion from disbelief or atheism. In my judgment, the work would be useful in college classes of philosophy of religion or even an introduction to religion. A handful of publishers and even a reputable agency do not think so.

The third unpublished work is *The Magic Window: Verses for Children Young and Old*. It collects fifty short poems I have written for children on a variety of subjects. No publisher or agent has seen them. I think that they are publishable, especially if illustrated by a good artist. But I also see the futility of simply sending such a manuscript to an overworked children's editor who sees fifty such manuscripts a day, and to date, I have not discovered even a route to an agent. So I have not pursued the matter.

Teaching

"It was the worst lecture I ever heard.
What had I done to deserve this cadaverous parade of sounds?
What cleverness brought about this ability
   to kill words simply by using them,
   to render soporific the exuberance of things?
What horrible things has the topic done to deserve this interment?
What amount of learning did it take to steal from verbs,
   adjectives, nouns their wildness?
What strange loquacity obtained the power
   to empty words of their mystery,
   to imprison them in cells of definition,
   to reduce them to their references?
How was it possible to empty the words of their play, their whimsy,
   their battles with each other?
How was the lecturer able to enlist words designed for awakening,
   summoning, evoking in the service of anesthetics?
It was the worst lecture I ever heard.
Unfortunately, it was my own."

—EDWARD FARLEY

For about forty years (from 1957), my primary work was teaching in theological schools or universities. In 1957 I finished graduate school in New York City and took a position at DePauw University, where I taught a variety of subjects: world religions, ancient and modern philosophy, various Christian themes, selected authors. Prior to 1957 I had done a little college level teaching (University of Louisville, Tusculum College).The students I taught over many years varied in age, gender, and level of education and included college freshmen, seminarians, students on track to be professors. While my own graduate studies in a special area prepared me for a teaching career, they did not include the study of or reflection on teaching itself. This lacuna remains typical of programs of graduate education. Teaching goes on, but not the teaching of teaching. It was assumed that "good" or at least competent teaching would ensue from doing what one's teachers did, from the studies that prepared one to be a scholar, and from one's personality and creativity. A fixed tradition of teaching more or less determined the pedagogies in place in the humanities programs of graduate schools and was passed on to each new generation of teachers. This tradition included both policies of degree-granting institutions and practices taking place in a classroom: thus, course organization, assignments, testing the students accomplishments by examinations and essays, and rating those accomplishments by grading. In the college I attended, teaching was solid and competent in the fields of history, languages, and natural sciences, and highly varied in other areas. The variation was probably because of the shaky or undeveloped state of such fields as literature, philosophy, and the social sciences. In my seminary and graduate school, teaching was primarily lecturing and, for the most part was competent. In the case of Reinhold Niebuhr and Paul Tillich, it was much more than that.

Throughout the many decades of my teaching, I more or less imitated the teaching of my teachers without much critical reflection on what best enabled learning or what characterized good teaching. At the same time, "education" as a phenomenon of our culture, something carried out in schools and by faculties, preoccupied me from the beginning. From the late 1970s on, I questioned whether theology could be restricted to an academic elite, something pursued only by academics or clergy. At that time, I began to address issues of pedagogy in adult church education. My criticisms targeted the prevailing notion (still in place today, with few exceptions) that education in the religious community meant "nurturing." (The catch-word today is "spiritual formation.") Since everything a religious community does can be described as having that aim, "nurturing" turns out to be a rationale for not pursuing education oriented to learning. Eventually, in mid-career, my interest in education shifted to my own institutional setting, and I began to examine the assumptions behind the curricular structure of theological education. In a set of writings, I probed the historical origins and primary concepts behind the standard (four-fold) organization of teaching fields in Protestant theological seminaries.

The "education" of these writings was institutional and curricular and did not include the actual activity of teaching. Accordingly, my career-long interest in church and theological education had little effect on my own classroom activity. Not being able to observe my own teaching, I have little to say about it. I think I did my best teaching (facilitating learning) in the small seminar, focused on very specific issues or texts. I never really figured out how successfully to teach the required, large-class introduction to theology. I was probably helpful to some students as they worked through their research projects. Some apparently experienced me as a "good teacher"; others did not. What follows is my present take on teaching as an activity, focusing on the primary challenge teachers confront when they would facilitate learning. My comments are rooted in and shaped by the specific settings and events of my life experience, thus, the degree-oriented education of American colleges and graduate schools, with special focus on the Humanities area. Thus, I do not assume these comments will pertain to tribal societies, Asian cultures, skills (dancing, cooking), or science and mathematics.

To pose the question of what teaching/learning is all about is to face a crossroads. Does one attempt a factual, empirical account of what goes on in universities or an idealizing, critical-imaginative analysis of what is possible or desireable? As to the former, what characterizes one type of teaching/learning is the ethos and institutions centered in credentials. We are told that, with certain exceptions, credentials are the main concern of both students and state-sponsored education. Teaching/learning, therefore, is a doorway to higher salaried jobs. This of course is disputed like just about everything else in current publications about higher education. I shall not include credential education in the following remarks. While I do worry about narrow ways of understanding liberal arts education, I have no objections to education as a track toward a specific career. In fact one of my main criticisms of pre-college public school education is the virtual absence in city and county school systems of classes on specific life-skills, crafts, and industrial arts.

Two primary motifs arise when I think about "what I do" as a teacher, one transparent and observable, the other elusive and vague. Another way to put it is to say that teaching/learning has a subject and a (trans) subject, and both together constitute the aims of the teacher and the student. The first aim is utile. What happens in the classroom is a worthwhile activity because it prepares the student for expertise (and credentials) in certain future situations. A broader way of understanding the future reference of education would include the next level of schooling. The elementary school teacher prepares students for middle school; the high school teacher prepares them for college. The college major gets them ready for post-college professional or research-oriented studies. Here we have the initial or primary aim of education: learning needed for some future activity or life-situation.

But there is a second, more elusive aim of education. In its most profound sense, education has to do with certain ways human beings travel a road toward a kind of freedom, transcendence, openness, even creativeness. It has to do, in other words, with what human beings are and what they become. This aim has a flesh and blood embodiment in an ancient text, the firestorm stirred up by an ugly and generally unpopular man (Socrates). A single issue was at the center of the disputes between Socrates (and his disciple, Plato) and the professional teachers of the day. Is teaching simply a utility for an elite class of young men who need rhetorical skills to exercise power in the *polis* or is it a process by which human beings are opened up to the very nature of things, which nature (*phusis, eidos*) has to do with the deepest needs of both each person and the society? For Socrates-Plato, the educated person will not simply make pretty and politically manipulative speeches, but will constantly probe how things work, what things are, what differentiates one thing from another, and therefore what a "good" society is. These are issues which concern human beings living together in society: power, good, justice, beauty. Such questions open up structures, processes, types, functions, varieties, meanings. There are those interpreters of Plato who dismiss this issue because it promotes "essentialism," "idealism," and other mistakes. But education in the Socratic sense rescues the human being from the slavery of mere bias, the cynical wielding of power, the slothful indifference to the ways of the world. Yes, the teacher and the student should together work hard to facilitate a learning that survives the pedagogical activity itself. But goaded by the second aim, which has roots in certain convictions about what a liberated, productive, pleasurable life is, their inquiries, studies, teaching will take place under a Socratic vision of the possibility of discerning, engaging, and acting on the world as it comes forth or is manifest in its complexity, change, and patterns.

In my judgment, every subject of teaching can embody the second aim. The teachers of the sciences struggle with how the world works and in doing so open themselves to correction and new discovery. Those who study history find themselves confronted with an inexhaustible story of violence and blood, conflict, brutality, and courage. Those who study poetry and literature engage texts and authors who probe a concreteness that eludes analysis and explanation. All of these areas of learning can function as a Socratic opening up of "the way things are," the structures and processes of things in their depth and horizon. Such education continues the Socratic not the Sophist side of the old conflict. Like the first aim, the orientation of the second aim is the future of the student, but this future is not simply gaining needed credentials but obtaining a certain freedom. Credentials education quite properly focuses on what is useful and relevant for the future, but without the second aim, education loses its "soul." I would think that without some vision of human life and potentiality, teachers as facilitators of the utile learning would easily burn out. The traditional stereotype of soul-less education is the old-timey Victorian enforcer of rote and memorization. The new stereotype is the teacher as preparer for examinations. I suspect, however, that most teachers do teach from a vision and from aims that are broader than their subject and their specialty, concerned in some way with what marks human life as moribund or violent, and with what opens it to beauty, compassion, and excitement.

If these comments on the general aims of teaching/learning are cogent or make sense, they provide some clues about what teaching is and the challenges it poses. They are guided by the conviction that most learning occurs from self-teaching, self-education brought about by persistent study, focus, and inquiry. The teacher functions as a stimulus, guide, and resource, to facilitate that self-learning. These activities begin prior to and outside the classroom. A successful course of study depends to a great degree on how clearly the teacher grasps the steps or phases of understanding required by a subject. Crucial then is the selection of topics, texts, examinations, papers, discussions. Traditionally, these things take place in face-to-face situations of a classroom. This typical setting is apparently being partially replaced by online education classes (in the university) of hundreds of students, and tutors displayed on a large computer monitor.

It is self-evident that in order for teachers to successfully carry out these functions (pre-classroom and in class), so as to facilitate learning, they must have sufficient knowledge of the subject. What is not so self-evident is their need for a certain behavioral-emotional skill. In order to properly plan a course of study or teaching event, even a tutoring session with a student, the teacher must be attuned to the particular situation, capacities, interests, and even educational history of the one being taught. This "trait" or capability is a mixture of empathy and imagination. The teacher must be able to so empathize with the students' emotional readiness (or resistance) and their phase or level of understanding that he or she can set the students on the appropriate path to learning. At the beginning, the teacher must engage the students, draw them to the subject, and begin with the steps proper to both the subject and the students' situation. A group of students or an individual student may be indifferent, resentful, or highly motivated and excited by the challenges of a difficult subject. Lacking empathy and imagination, the teacher is ill-equipped to facilitate learning in both long-term courses of study and even one-on-one tutorials. The principle holds even for informal and non-classroom teaching/learning. To teach someone how to play the piano or use a saber saw, the teacher must intuit what the pupil knows and doesn't know, what the motivation is. I would guess that when students praise their teachers as "good teachers," what they most often have in mind is only partly the teacher's function as an explainer or communicator of information. The "good teacher" is one who has worked hard to frame the steps of study appropriately and who intuits the specific needs and situation of the students. This empathy/imagination is something that guides all the activities of the teacher: the preparation, the seminar session, the lecture, the assignment, the face-to-face interchange. Accordingly, it is often the case that as a scholar or scientist of wide reputation, the teacher has an awesome knowledge of the subject at hand yet is a "poor teacher," that is, facilitator of learning. The reason may be that the teacher's primary capability and focus is simply cognitive, dominated by the complexities of the subject, the result being a myopia about what the students are up against as they face the challenge of the subject. Lacking empathy and imagination, the "famous scholar" may be clueless about what facilitating the learning of the subject requires.

Empathy and imagination are needed and appropriate for all the situations and levels of teaching, necessary if the teacher hopes to engage the students' "deep curiosities," their possible fascination with the depths of world processes, history, human beings, the mysteries and novelties just now unfolding, the multiple types and genres of things, and the different modes in which they can be known, experienced, and studied. At this point, the empathy/imagination of the teacher engages (by way of the subject) the empathy/imagination of the student. Ideally, in a teaching-learning event, students and teacher together experience the novelty and complexity of things and develop insights that are new to them.

When I describe teaching/learning in these ways I risk a kind of idealization, a kind of how-to manual easily put into practice. But most teachers know that the success of teaching/learning varies with the situation and the capabilities of teachers and students. They sense that teaching/learning has a deep, even tragic character. By "tragic" I mean the tension, failures, compromises that come with any and all ventures. These things follow even the "great teacher" into the classroom. Perhaps the primary tension that is never simply solved by methods, good intents, or awesome research is the maladjustment between the demands of the subject or material and the huge variety of personal situations and capabilities of the students. Another tension, less visible and apparent to thought, is always already there in the teaching situation because what is *known* (by scientists, scholars, researchers, textbook authors) is inevitably and always an *abstraction*. This is because to know something is to focus on it, draw it out of its context, out of the flow of things, and to freeze it in the grammar of a language, thus pushing into the background the trillions of events, particles, cells, which constitute it. Knowing and the language and tools of knowing never replicate any actual totality, process, or relation. If teaching's subject is, in various senses, what the teacher knows (or, as in a practice such as dancing or swimming, knows how), then there is an unclosable gap between the known of teaching and the concreteness of what actually is, including the concreteness of the teacher and the student. Thus the teacher and the students never simply "know"; they interpret, select, restate, search for words, apply, and many other things. However well they know their subject and however oriented by empathy/imagination, they cannot avoid this disjunction, maladjustment, non-replicability between their (known) subject and what is actual. The challenge of this "tragic," that is, limited character of knowing, is to teach without reducing the world to the known. Somehow, teachers must find a way to "keep the world open," to remind themselves and their students that what is learned and known is never a mere clone, an equivalent, of what is actually happening in world process.

When I apply these comments on the act of teaching to myself, I can see many ways I could have been a better teacher. I do think that I had a certain empathy/imagination in framing the teaching/learning events of the course, the classroom, the tutoring, but I can make no special claims for success at this point. I think I was a competent teacher in my planning, lecturing, and classroom engagements. But my limitation, even failure, as a teacher was my inability to attract the unmotivated student to the subject, to stir the cauldron of the student's interests so as to arouse fascination and excitement. This leads to my final topic, the challenges of teaching in the area of religion (theology).

"Religion" (religious studies) and theological studies are general terms for areas and departments in schools of teaching. They do not name specific areas of expertise such as Indology, Islamism, New Testament studies. My own area has been "theology," although I do disagree with those colleagues in theology who think that "religion" can be excluded from that.

I have written a chapter on these matters in the unpublished work, *Teaching What is Unteachable.* I may be wrong when I say that the teaching/learning that takes place in historical, scientific, humanistic, and social scientific specialities has a fairly undisputed and defined content or subject, and that their teachers have a fairly clear notion about the foundations, methods, and content of what must be grasped before something else is taken up. Focused experimental activities may render the subjects of teaching in the sciences relatively unambiguous, which may be why the scientists, perhaps also the mathematicians, are perpetually tempted to think that what is actual is identical with what research uncovers. In the social sciences (whose researchers ever lust for the clarity and methodological precision of physics, chemistry, and biology), things get a little muddier, and disputes arise over the very subject and therefore over research methods. They get muddier in the humanities, literature, and religion. In my area, theology, there have been disputes since the Middles Ages over just what the enterprise is, and these disputes are still with us. Even the very genre of theology, as well as the sort of "knowing" it might lay claim to, are disputed. Thus, a teacher of theology tends to wander in a forest of proposals or versions of what the subject is. I have made my own forays into that jungle and will not repeat them. One sign of the non-consensus about theology as a subject is that most dissertations in the field are textual-historical studies, even as mine was in the 1950s. Judged from these dissertations, theology appears to be a kind of historical-textual description with a dollop of criticism thrown in. This resolution of the ambiguity of theology reappears in the classroom. Thus, theology's subject tends to be past and present texts, and the pursuit of theology is the interpretation of these texts. If there is a "theological thinking," it tends to be a thinking from, against, or for what is written in a text. This ambiguity of theology greets every new teacher of theology, and presents a challenge about the clarity of the subject itself.

SIX

Confessions

Interests and Enjoyments

"The stars have not dealt me the worst they could do:
My pleasures are plenty, my troubles are two.
But oh, my troubles they reave me of rest,
The brains in my head and the heart in my breast."

—A. E. HOUSMAN XVII

The following pieces, altogether, express the interests, feelings, and spheres of activity of my life from childhood to the present. Some of these themes are, of course, more important (as life-shaping) than others. These essays, I am sure, will repeat some material treated in Chapters 2 through 5. For instance, it would not be possible to tell the story of my adolescence and leave out music, nature, or friends. It should not be necessary to say that these pieces do not by any means record all the aspects of my life which are important.

Idiosyncracies

"The other self, the antiself or the antithetical self, as one may choose to name it, comes but to those who are no longer deceived, whose passion is reality."

—EDMUND WILSON, *AXEL'S CASTLE*

In this chapter, I distinguish between "idiosyncrasies" and more life-shaping commitments and activities. Most of my idiosyncrasies, my various interests, enjoyments, biases, and even self-identity, are trivial compared to such things as nature, religion, or music. Sports or house repair would not rank as important to me as reading. I begin this account of my idiosyncrasies with what is most general, my own peculiar self-identity and my relations to family, friends, and even ethnic groups. It is not only natural but inevitable that one's birth, DNA, nature, gender, education, acculturation in a specific historical era and culture will form what might be called a regional self-identity, and that self-identity will show itself through strong emotional attachments, loyalties, antipathies, and preferences. In my case, that regional self-identity would include being a male, American, Christian (Protestant), middle class, and many other things. Given such things, it seems strange to me as I look back on my early years that I rarely if ever felt a negative antipathy to people of other races, or gender, or cultures. I was of course shaped by the racism of my era, region, family, and culture. Not growing up in the epoch of racial integration, mine was a racism of distance or separation from the black community. No one I knew in my early years had friendships with blacks. Blacks were not present as peers in my school, church, places of work, musical events, parks, and places of amusement. But for some odd reason, I saw these "distant" blacks as different but never as genetically inferior. Thus, I never developed a racial self-identity constituted by strong emotions of fear or antipathy, and ways of thinking that presupposed strong negative stereotypes. Kentucky as a state had Jim Crow laws, but in Louisville there were no back-of-the-bus laws as in the Deep South. I am told that a grandmotherly black woman (born as a slave)—a stereotypical memory I realize—attached to the house of my great grandmother in New Castle, Kentucky was a "mother" to me in my infancy-toddler years. I don't remember her, but I have always wondered if that relation undermined the development of racist antipathies. In childhood I not only sensed a strong emotional antipathy to blacks in my father's talk and feelings, but felt there was something wrong about it, a kind of weakness or fear.

Something similar characterized my self-identity in relation to women. Sexist generalizations about women were common in the talk of some male members of my larger family and their friends. While I did have a strong sense of being a boy, a male, this self-identity didn't create the kind of emotions that prompted that kind of talk. The same holds for my relation to my own nation, state, cultural region, high school, college. In my adult years, I realized that, while I was ever appreciative of my country's history, rooted for its success in its wars, competitions, and internal crises, I was never very much attracted to "patriotism" in any strong sense. "My country right or wrong" never made a bit of sense to me. This meant that my sense of belonging was to something larger, something that included other languages, cultures, histories, customs. Thus, I never really became a "Southerner." Louisville itself, although located on the southern shore of the Ohio and thus south of the Mason-Dixon line, was never a "Southern" city.

I don't really have an explanation for this trans-ethnic, low regional self-identity. As far as I know, it was not moral self-consciousness. In fact I became self-conscious of it only as I remembered certain childhood feelings or lack of them. Was its origin a kind of early rationalist suspicion about unproven generalizations about others? I doubt it. Was it the effect of my early reading of children's books on other cultures (*Heidi, Pinocchio, Robin Hood*)? Was it an intuition of the flawed dynamics of a self-identity formed by exaggerated valuations of one's place and setting? To reflect on my very early low regional self-identity is not to claim I am without prejudices, or that my antipathies never rise to silly generalizations about groups. I am plenty capable of that sort of thing, even if I am, at the same time, leery and rueful about it. But the targets of my prejudices are not women, minorities, ethnic groups, nations. On an intellectual level, I can observe and generalize about group traits and tendencies. But for whatever reason, these observations are always tempered by another set of generalizations, the traits all people seem to have in common as creatures of feeling, contexts, tragedy, enjoyments, and a variety of things that make them unique, unrepeatable, irreducible to generalized traits.

Frustrations, Irritations, and Prejudices

I take up now what my family and friends already know about me as they (amusedly) observe my peeves and prejudices. They may in fact suspect that I have edited out what is most visible and public. To "confess" is always a risk, since confession both reveals and suppresses. I shall take the risk, aware that this account of my foibles and personal tendencies is filtered through my subjectivity, pride, and tendency to minimize them. Some of these peeves and criticisms might have a kind of rationale or justification. The biased person always thinks so. I shall make no attempt to provide them with an objective grounding. Many of my peeves are more or less inevitable given my worldview, my reading, my life vocation. Some arise because of my vocation, or at least because of what was required to prepare for it and practice it. They express, in other words, the wonky values and negativities of an elderly professor. Such antipathies reveal my place and role in the culture wars, especially as they have to do with religion. Some of these peeves are fruits of my biochemistry, gender, and class, and no doubt express the low tolerance of certain kinds of things by a retired and aging professional.

Does my placement on one side or another of these cultural differences reveal me as an elitist? Yes it does. The elite stratum of every nation-state, society, or social grouping I know about may have a hereditary or DNA factor, but it also originates in whatever social processes make possible levels of understanding, literacy, skill. In Medieval society, there was a small elite group associated with the court or barons of fiefs or with the guilds and merchants. These elite members of society possessed power, skill, noble birth, sometimes literacy. Edwin Markham's poem, "The Man with the Hoe," depicts the pathos and cultural impoverishment of the non-elite. As to the meaning of elite in a modern or postmodern society, the matter is far from clear. In a minimum sense, those who can read and write are "elite" (earn more money, enjoy a more stable life, have more power) than those who cannot. In narrower senses, the postmodern elite are those with wealth, significant comfort, politico-cultural power, and those who have access to and are equipped to appreciate and pursue the "higher arts." Measured by such criteria, many college graduates may not qualify as the society's elite. However we settle these ambiguities of meaning, I belong to the cultured elite in various ways. *Elitism*, a term used in critical-moral analysis, is another matter. Am I an elitist, one whose worldview is elitism? I probably am at the emotional level. That is, I have a certain gut-level scorn of the cultural barbarian, the anti-intellectual. I hope that is not the case at the intellectual level. That is, I do not celebrate a society whose laws and dynamics are designed to protect and advance the elite and keep the non-elite in their place.

As I review my various peeves and antipathies, I find that they fall roughly into two types: spontaneous irritations and personal reactions, and, antipathies rooted in some way in my general value system. I see the former as more trivial than the latter. My incapacity to tolerate small frustrations, a trait shared with my father, has always been a public (or at least familial) phenomenon. I react in excessive fashion (like the paranoid sensitive to a slight offense or discerned slight) to minor mishaps, especially those that delay some ongoing project: a traffic tie-up, a broken tool. My family remembers the loud and profane dramas that attended my adorning the Christmas tree with lights. Fortunately, the volatility of my reactions was in direct proportion to the triviality of the event. The smaller the louder. Such is my "impatience," a personality syndrome or trait of character. I mention it because it is partially responsible for a number of frustrations and peeves. Along with my "impatience" I think I have a deeper equilibrium, a kind of acceptance or being at ease with the tragic character of the world and even with my own flaws. This may be why my reaction to seriously threatening events is different from my trivial frustrations: that is, an injury, a ceiling collapse, a car wreck. In those situations, I tend toward stoic quietness and analysis of what the event calls for.

There are a few recurring life situations that tend to trigger my impatience. Waiting, standing around, is difficult for me. These are not the situations of expected or scheduled waiting, as in a doctor's office (unless it goes on for hours) but the unexpected waiting that disrupts plans. Unlike the Dalai Lama and those who are at ease with all life situations, I do not "wait" very well. Nor do I manage my psyche very well in traffic situations. I do enjoy driving, but not on packed city streets or amidst the truck-filled Interstate traffic of my retirement years. I experience those situations as boring, frustrating challenges to be completed as soon as possible. My impatience also shows up when I take on a project that I do not enjoy and therefore rush to finish it in order to do what I really want to do, thus putting additional stress on myself and others. This "rushing through" can be my way of handling a major project (moving into a new house) or a trivial task (transposing a piece of music into another key).

This behavior may symptomize a kind sickness, an incapacity to restfully pursue everyday life tasks, and calls for the time-oriented therapeutic one associates with Buddhism.

Besides impatience as a personality syndrome, I also tend (on the spectrum of neurotic behavior) more toward order than messiness. There are of course rational reasons for an ordering (organizing) of one's projects, time, and spaces. Keeping things in order contributes to efficiency. I suspect my low tolerance of disorder or messiness has some relation to my impatience or "rushing through" things to be done. In the myths and philosophies of ancient Greece, the ordering of the world (creation) by the gods and goddesses was an activity of beautification. In that view, chaos (messiness) was not as such beautiful. It was a cauldron of conflicting powers, and a transition from chaos into differentiation and harmony had to take place for there to be a world at all, or for anything to exist at all. I agree, and see the experience of an ordered environment as an experience of beauty. Ordering can of course become so exaggerated and compulsive that it signals neurosis (or whatever pathology we want to label it). Thus I also would offer a defense for the messy side of things. It does seem to be the case that messiness (non-order, non-organization) is a necessary condition of and even component of creativity. Whatever is actual is never simply a structure or pattern. Thus, even the human activity of ordering is both a preservation and a creativity. It is also a way of existing in time, a way of living, choosing, planning, preserving, altering.

In addition to frustrations that come with everyday life, I have a deeper set of antipathies which, at their strongest, become prejudices. These critical responses are the negative side of what I value, appreciate, enjoy. There is nothing unusual here. All human beings (and for that matter, all life forms) have positive and negative tastes, preferring some things and avoiding others. Many of my typically negative responses are idiosyncratic, rooted in the sort of person I became over the years and having to do with my biochemistry, education, family-structure, and my academic and pedagogical setting. This is not to say that such things simply "explain" or "cause" my critical responses, but they are a kind of predisposing background. I offer no formal analysis here but rather a miscellany of items, mostly minor, and some even trivial. These preferences and antipathies have changed some with age. Many were, in fact, present in some form in my youth and young adulthood, but a few things that evoke humor, disgust, derision have surfaced in recent decades.

I realize that many of the things I oppose or deride have their own rationale and place in our society and are what others prefer, enjoy, and defend. The following comments are not intended as rational assessments submitted to a debate club but as descriptions of my gut-level responses. If there are justifications for my preferences and antipathies (ethical, worldview), they are set forth in a minimum way in chapters 4 and 7. At present, I am only "confessing."

One set of mostly minor irritations originated with in the popular culture of the twenty-first century, namely, the fusion of technology, entertainment, and the marketing of products. A byproduct of this fusion, probably accidental, is a culture (or subculture, or strand of culture) that resembles an autistic child. This subculture cannot endure, it seems, inactivity, quietness, pauses. Since I myself am caught up in this, I include myself as part of this fusion. In this autistic culture, every moment, every event must be filled, usually with the help of the new devices of communication and self-entertainment. For many of us, it seems, what it takes to distract and gratify is what is larger, louder, explosive. In the new popular culture, more is better. I experienced the following in a musical concert I attended this year. Almost instantly after the intermission began, the rows of the theater were lit up with hundreds of tiny lights as people continued to amuse themselves by texting, playing games, retrieving information. We have produced it seems a culture where one's everyday life requires constant stimulation of sounds, information flow, a staged entertainment, even an advertising event. Thus we have the sing-along, drum-accompanied entertainments of Sunday morning religion, the half-time competitions of eight-year-olds at basketball games. It is as if the only tolerable and even legitimate state or content of consciousness is a device-enabled entertainment. Thus, the only way a human being can be "religious," entertained, experience meaningful work, be creative is by means of the devices which offer pictures, sounds, communications, and small bits of information. The point is not that our society is reducible to this three-fold fusion, but that it is prominent enough to evoke from me resistance, irritation, regret. Perhaps I exaggerate. Perhaps our (non)culture is not like this, and I am simply abstracting a segment of it and missing all sorts of important things. But this is what I experience as everyday or popular (non)culture, and the experience is mostly a negative one.

At one time, the initial shaper of everyday life by the fusion of technology (devices), entertainment, and marketing (industry) was television. (That seems to have been replaced by portable devices.) Television, the device of the aged, offers entertainment of a sort. For me it is more an irritant than a pleasure. I realize that without its incessant, noisy marketing, sports and a few other things I enjoy would not be available. Nevertheless, I experience most of the visual-audible manipulations of the television screen not simply as trivial, silly, or boring, but as an assault, an actual psychic pain.

Similarly, I experience the following three cultural phenomena in varying degrees of discomfort. The call-in talk show has been around for many decades. Its primary venue may still be radio. Small rural and urban radio stations air sports, music, religion, politics. I am not sure why I am repelled by even a minute or two of these shows. Certain primetime hosts are clever and entertaining and I can be drawn into their interviews. But for the most part, I experience call-in shows as boring, loony, rabid, even when many callers are informed, sincere, or needy. A second repelling offering of techno-entertainment has to do with violence, a noir genre of drama. I admit that my disconnection with this genre has grown with aging. Except for the sit-coms and Hallmark sentimentalism, much of TV fiction has to do with violence: a parade of corpses, tortures, detailed autopsies, amputations, explosions. Surely both Hollywood and the television industry would move toward bankruptcy if the pyrotechnic engineers ever went on strike. I can bear the short-term incident and the cartoon violence of adventure movies (Batman, Indiana Jones). I find the violence offered by gifted and serious writers and directors intolerable.

The third irritation is evoked by certain kinds of music. I have never enjoyed, for whatever reason, the two-beat hotel band music of the 1920s and after, polka music, and "Hawaiian" music of the ukulele and steel guitar. I have enjoyed, without understanding it very well, many of the songs and performers of rock music from the 1960s on and also the folk music of those eras. Within the broad genre of rock music, there are types of music I find painful. I shall not spell that out in detail. In classical music, I am not drawn to the non-lyrical, atonal compositions of Schoenberg or to what appears to be computer generated music. And while I enjoy opera in general, I must confess that its non-aria aspect, the use of music to stage conversations between characters, is not very satisfying. Showing my age, I am not an enthusiast about most of the songs which win Oscars for Hollywood movies nor for the recent type of Broadway musical in which the songs are written only for their function on stage and almost never survive to be heard or enjoyed in other venues than the performance itself. For instance, the musically sophisticated *Cats* and also *Chorus Line* each produced only one song to be reperformed.

I have a number of antipathies and prejudices that have to do with "types" persons functioning as public performers: the radio or television preacher, the salesperson, the slick or bigoted politician, the religious fanatic. But what gives rise to these antipathies are not individual human beings but types (abstractions), and they often appear as stereotypes in novels, sit-coms, and dramas. (I am aware that I myself as a "professor" and an academic am a type, and that type evokes both antipathy and comic stereotyping from Hollywood, comedians, and others.) There are types, functions, groups, and trends in "religion" which evoke strong prejudice on my part, but I have dealt with that elsewhere in this memoir. Similarly, the academy (higher education, the university) as a lifelong work environment is replete with types that evoke stereotyping, humor, and negative reaction.

Crafts, Repairs, and Other Impossibilities

"I presume you know, since I've told you, that my distrust and hatred of vehicles in motion is partly based on my plerophory that their apparent submission to control is illusory and that they may at their pleasure, sooner or later, act on whim."

—REX STOUT, *SOME BURIED CAESAR*, 1939

Cognitive psychologists have filled the journals with research on various types of intelligence. The basic point has been around since Adam and Eve. Individual human beings are better (smarter) at some things than others. Groups of human beings show proficiency in some areas of doing and knowing but not others. Whatever smarts I possess have to do with specific kinds of insight and understanding. Unfortunately, the spatial and kinetic arts of building, repairing, and tinkering is not one of them. There are probably socio-cultural factors at work here. The Italians seem to be pretty good opera goers but do not build machinery as well as the Germans. (The Germans seem to be good at almost everything.) But I suspect that very good mechanics, mathematicians, and engineers have some specialized genes and brain structures that bestow on them certain interests and capacities. In this respect my patriarchal and matri-archal DNA are very different. The Walker family DNA of my maternal grandfather and my mother is artistic, word-sensitive, and intuitive. The Farley family males were good with machinery. My paternal grandfather invented a towel-dispenser, now commonly used in public places, which, lacking another kind of intelligence, he sold for a pittance. One of his sons was a successful printer and a grandson a well-known Louisville architect. My father was a "natural mechanic," able to build or repair almost anything. To us wordsmiths and aesthetes, a natural mechanic seems like a seer who wields magic powers. The "natural mechanic" seems to grasp instantly the structure, function, and relation of the parts of machines, and intuits the steps necessary for dismantling, rebuilding, and repair. My father, therefore, could build houses, do refined cabinet making, repair auto engines. He did these things all of his life and was available to his neighbors and friends when they needed him. I probably owe my non-mechanical orientation both to the Walker DNA and to an Oedipal relation to my father: that is, a childhood and adolescence that was overwhelmed by a father who could construct or repair anything. He was disappointed in me early on, and in middle school threatened to pull me out of music (the band) because I did not do very well in shop. But he probably knew all along that he had a "Walker" on his hands, a philosopher-musician, and therefore a hopeless case. Thus, he made no effort to teach me anything about tools, wood, paints, or how things work. My father was only the first of many people I later knew, friends and relatives, who were very fine builders, repairers, mechanics: John Fry, Del Sawyer, Jodi Combs, Harry Douma, and many others. I envied their expertise but never was attracted to mechanical-spatial puzzles as intellectual challenges. I never made the effort to know much about such things or spend time working on them.

Although mechanically challenged, I could not utterly avoid the puzzling world of things needing repair and maintenance. When my fa-ther came to visit, what he liked to do best was to work on our house and I learned a lot by working with him. And I used this knowledge when I (grudgingly) had to repair, build, paint, install. The more I could do these things out of doors, the better I liked it. Design, landscaping, and garden-ing were activities I enjoyed. I did successfully finish a few (very few) craft projects. In my first years of teaching, I built a dyna-kit amplifier and pre-amp (the latter with the help of a friend). Of course I didn't have to actually *know* anything about electronics to do this, only match colors, wires, shapes, and do hundreds of soldering connections. But that was an exception. My typical mood when faced with a repair was disinterest and frustration, a mood that set up my overreactions when things went wrong. Thus, for the most part, the Walker, not the Farley DNA won out. My Walker side prompted my self-identification with the fictional detective, Nero Wolfe, who was convinced that "machines act on whim." The best account I have read of a machine acting on whim was a hilarious passage in Steinbeck's Log from *The Sea of Cortez*, which recorded the crew's endless struggles with a maleficent boat motor. So to my mechanical friends and family, my parting words are that I envy you, but I must make do with my books, words, musical phrases and sounds, and the living beauties of nature.

Enjoyments, Satisfactions, Gratifications

"Crown me with roses while I live,
Now your wines and ointments give,
After death I nothing crave,
Let me alive my pleasures have:
All are Stoics in the grave."

—ABRAHAM CROWLEY "THE EPICURE"

If peeves, frustrations, and antipathies were my only idiosyncrasies, the everyday tone of my life would be negative, a Three Stooges-like struggle always ending in defeat. In spite of the fact that I come across (to some) as morose, brooding, and internalized, my experience of things is almost the opposite. I would guess this is the case with most people. However much they face obstacles and entertain antipathies, the ongoing mood of their daily lives is not a constant flow of mishaps, conflicts, disappointments, frustrations. Devastating illness and grief aside, most people enjoy their bodily activities of breathing, seeing, hearing, walking, eating, conversing, and experiencing the happenings and situations of daily life. I go into more detail on this matter in a my essays on poetics, music, nature, books where I discuss the my enjoyments and satisfactions.

In spite of my rather grim assessments of the present time and situation of postmodern culture in chapter 7, I take pleasure in many of the things most of us now take for granted. These include the political and cultural changes that opened the workplace, schools, and government to those who were once racial or domestic slaves. These changes continue as the nation grumpily moves toward granting full rights and status to gays and lesbians. Because of these changes, ours is a more humane era. What has not changed is the growing, grinding poverty of a huge portion of the country.

Most of my specific satisfactions are not distinctive or private but the sorts of things most people enjoy. I have always enjoyed the out of doors, sweat-inducing physical work, and the kind of tiredness that comes with its cessation. I enjoy the kind of travel that introduces me to the environments, artifacts, and ways of life of other cultures and places. As to food and drink, I must confess that I am not a knowledgeable fan of *haute cuisine*. I very much enjoy the food of other cultures, but it tends not to be the creations of chef schools. The Mexican, Asian, and Italian food I enjoy is probably some version of that culture's everyday food. Thus, my palate welcomes everyday cooking more than the artistically crafted cuisine of chefs. I also find pleasure in simply learning new things. These "new things" tend not to be the factoids or info bits delivered instantly by a machine but patterns, processes, novelties that have to do with the way the world works, a historical era, animal life. My enjoyment of them comes both with actual experiences of them and learning about them through study or conversation. The few things I mention here are only a selection, a glimpse into what I find enjoyable in life.

I include sports among my idiosyncrasies because I don't know where else to discuss the topic. Some readers of these pieces will be surprised that sports or athletic competition is a theme of my life experience. Like most adult males and many females, I have a modicum of spectator interest in football and basketball, enough to follow in a casual way a few selected teams, most of which are local. In my adolescent and young adult years, I was not a jock, a successful or varsity competitor in school sports. At the same time, I would be suppressing an important aspect of my life if I omitted the topic. I should say at the outset that what I have in mind here is, technically, not simply sports (competitive, physical games) but something broader, the effortful deployment of the body in fishing, canoeing, hiking, even yard work.

There was a time when I was a successful competitor in my age group at physical games, namely childhood and pre-adolescent youth.

When I was ten to twelve years old, I had enough natural coordination to be fairly good at football and other physical games. At age ten I won two rather large prizes competing in games at a park event, one of them after breaking a toe in a false start of a sack race. Every fall I looked forward to football in backyards, schoolyards, parks, an activity that carried with it occasional minor injuries. No referees, huge trophies, no fancy uniforms, no screaming parents: just pick-up games between young kids. When I was eight, I could hardly wait to learn to swim, and in that year, the YMCA pool made it possible. In those years, some sort of physical activity (football, swimming, bicycle riding, hiking) was very much a part of my daily life. I had hoped this would continue in high school varsity sports, but in middle school I was disappointed when I realized that I would not have the size for a career in football. I was neither big nor fast, and good physical coordination was not enough. But even in high school and college, I was active in non-varsity sports: tennis, swimming, hiking, two-person volleyball, touch football, fraternity basketball. Reflecting on my relation to competitive sports, I do not think I had the intense competitive drive required for first-rate athletes. I was always competitive to a degree, but in competitive sports, I lacked the intensity I sensed in my father-in-law (Dewey Kimbel) and my son, Mark, both of whom were superb prizewinning athletes. Eventually, my competitiveness did show itself, and I myself was my primary rival as I tried to penetrate the abstruse issues of theology and philosophy.

In a broader sense than competitive sports, physical activities continued all my life. One period of my life required a cessation of such things, namely my graduate school education (six years) and my early years of teaching. With this exception, I have always engaged in activities which mobilized and hardened the body: exercise, hiking, canoeing, gardening, a few sports. I liked the feeling of being physically tired from strenuous activities. In my first year of teaching, a whole set of physical activities was ended forever by an injury due to playing one-on-one basketball. I made a sharp cut for the basket and ruptured an Achilles tendon, an injury that ended tennis, handball, and basketball. But it did not end jogging, vigorous walking (which I still do), or the rigors of backpacking and canoeing. The one out of doors competitive sport available to me was golf, a game I "enjoyed" occasionally in graduate school and in the years at DePauw and in Pittsburgh. I place "enjoy" in quotation marks because it was a love-hate relation to a game which I never had sufficient time to develop. To play the game competitively requires an enormous amount of time. The pressures of writing, study, and teaching finally brought that to an end. Physical activity in the out of doors, especially the wilderness, has always been an ongoing pleasure, a part of who I am. My friendship with George Kehm made this possible over many years, thus we fished and canoed in lakes, streams, and swamps throughout the Eastern part of the country. I associate my physical activities with different friends: basketball and touch football (Dan Hunt), tennis (my father-in-law, Dewey Kimbel), golf (Dennis Shoemaker, Lynn Hinds), handball (Don Hartsock), outdoor canoeing and camping (George Kehm).

On Reading

"Some fools display a wealth of wit
Who hide behind the books and Writ,
Think they're striped and famous sages
When they have thumbed a volume's pages."

—SEBASTIAN BRANDT, *SHIP OF FOOLS*

"What a place to be in is an old library! It seems as though all the souls of
all the writers, that have bequeathed their labours to these Bodleians,
were reposing here, as in some dormitory, or middle state. . . .
I seem to inhale learning, walking amid their foliage."

—CHARLES LAMB, *THE ESSAYS OF ELIA*

I have a hard time imagining what it is like to be a child or young person growing up in the late twentieth and early twenty-first centuries. Like my grandchildren, I live in a high-tech world that abounds with sophisti-cated electronic toys, movies, and TV shows with endless pyrotechnical displays, and a constant visual and auditory bombardment of marketing events. I observe but do not really know what it means to be a child or adolescent in today's subcultures, schools, and families. There are obvious advantages. Dentistry is relatively painless (unlike that of my childhood). A lot of new medicines immunize us, ease our pains, and sometimes cure us. Techno-amusements require and promote a special set of skills, possibly a new kind of intelligence. Being an "old person" from another era, I don't envy those who are growing up in the "brave new world" (cf. Aldous Huxley's novel). I don't want to idealize the era and place of my growing up. All times and places have their dark secrets, their idolatries, their social structures that exclude, oppress, and dehumanize. The social world of my time and place was anti-Semitic, racist, sexist, homophobic, with few roles for women outside the home. Only in rare instances did women or minorities attend graduate school, teach, research, practice law, medicine, or ministry, or become senators. Those dark episodes of our past have not, of course, disappeared, but our society is now vastly different. There are always new targets for human fear and anger, religious and ethnocentric prejudice, and now that the "communists" are no longer the monsters in our closets, we have illegals, Muslims, gays and lesbians, and an ever-growing population of poor people. And to grow up in one of these groups means a low probability of education, status, power, or political success. But there are reasons why I don't envy the childhood and adolescence of those who are accustomed to good schools, jobs in the offing, and affluence. Their social worlds, subcultures, even families have their own deprivations. What I have in mind is a difference between the 1930s–1950s and the 1990s–2000s on the matter of books, reading, and the enjoyment of written texts. I realize my account of this may be quite wrong. Statistics about reading habits and book buying and a comparison of habits between the earlier period and the present one may not support my generalization. Harold Bloom (*The Western Canon*) voices the suspicion when he says that "deep reading" is rare, and even those who read are more oriented to quick amusement than reflective encounter. My sense is that television, technological devices (toys), constant intercommunication, and instant information retrieval have replaced the book and the leisure-time enjoyment of books. Although I envy the technological prowess the young of our generation take for granted, I would not trade it for that great gift that my generation gave me, the presence of books as "what there was to do" in the evenings. Perhaps the Kindle and its kind will replace the codex, the leafed book. I see that as a trivial change when compared to the displacement of aesthetic or deep reading by technologically enabled amusements. Such a comment marks me as a technophobic old Luddite, but I am grateful that books and reading were a big part of my childhood and adolescence.

It is probably a foolish undertaking to try to identify the things that have exercised influence on me, shaped whatever preferences and values

I have, pushed me in one direction rather than another. Most of this shaping took place beneath or at the edge of my awareness. The overwhelming power of present experience tends to render our recollections dim, filtered, even suppressed, hence we are only marginally conscious of the deep reaches of ourselves. But for what it's worth, I will try to recall a few highlights of my early reading that made my subsequent life something different from what it otherwise would have been. My primary influences were surely not books but people, events, cultural trends. But I do think I am a different person because of the stories, poems, and novels I read in my early years. It may seem odd to say this, but the most influential works were probably not literary gems. I did read through the canon of children's classics, and some of those books were significant events in my life: thus, *Pinocchio, Heidi, Gulliver's Travels, Robinson Crusoe, Tom Sawyer,* and *A Child's Garden of Verses.* This last book was my first encounter with the magic world of poetry. That may be why when I was still a child, the first thing I would do after being seated in the pew on Sunday morning was to read the poem printed in the bulletin. And in early adolescence, I was given a collection of poems (which I still have), *One Hundred and One Famous Poems,* a work I practically memorized. But many of the books that pushed me in a certain direction did not have the status of "literature." Their influence was two-fold. They opened up new worlds (forest, ocean shore, animals, other cultures, even careers), and, they formed lifelong orientations, interests, appreciations. The following stand out in my memory. *The Bobbsey Twins* books were about a very young brother and sister whose adventures took place in different environments. Hurlbut's *Stories of the Bible* collected narratives from Genesis to Revelation. I read it cover to cover twice. That is because, at eight years old, I spent part of a winter as a refugee on a relative's farm and Hurlbut was one of two books in the house. The house was unheated, uninhabited by other children (except for my one year old brother), and I had nothing to do. So I read Hurlbut.

In my adolescent years, I was deeply impressed by two novels by a Methodist minister, Lloyd Douglas. The first volume of the story, *Magnificent Obsession,* told of the transformation of a wealthy young loser from an egocentric playboy to a gifted and compassionate neurosurgeon. *Doctor Hudson's Secret Journal* described what human life would be like if a person helped others in all sorts of way without anyone else knowing about it. Another writer I read in adolescence was Max Brand, famous later as an author of Westerns. One series of novels had a special effect on me. Their central character was a young hospital intern (Doctor Kildare) who was utterly absorbed in his work. Those books conveyed to me for the first time the idea or ideal of *arete* (excellence, competence) obtained by a determined and disciplined labor. I read many other books in this period that, I am sure, had their effects, but these do not stand out in memory. In high school I moved into the unheated attic of our house, and read every night into the late hours. This reading included Cooper's Leather Stocking novels. I later enjoyed Mark Twain's very funny essay on Cooper's "Indians," the works of H. G. Wells, Jules Verne, Conan Doyle, and many others.

As to the books of my adult years, I resist the temptation to fill these pages with hundreds of book titles, a sleep-inducing thing to do. I do want to mention some of the main genres of literature I have enjoyed and a few examples of each. I shall omit altogether the reading and studying I did in connection with my vocation, teaching, and writing: works in mostly Western philosophy and religion.

I have always enjoyed many genres of books: history and culture, fiction, science, natural history, poetry. From the Book of Psalms to Vassar Miller, poets have had a place in my library since I was very young. While I do collect the writings of individual poets, I also enjoy anthologies: Untermeyer, the Oxford volumes, Amis, Norton, Keillor, and many others. An anthology is useful because it is a way of discovering new poets and because it often contains the best and most representative works of the selected poet. I constantly revisit the garden of poets of my library. I do have my favorites: Shakespeare (sonnets), Dante, Yeats, G. M. Hopkins, Emily Dickinson, E. A. Robinson, Walter de la Mare, Wendell Berry. As to religious poets, besides Dante and George Herbert, I am always shaken by the dark poetry of Vassar Miller and R. S. Thomas (first collection).

Like most readers, I enjoy many genres of prose fiction: fantasy, science fiction, mysteries, novels, epics. For reasons that escape me, I have never spent much time on short stories, although I have a few favorites. In my young adult years, I read a number of science fiction novels. Jules Verne was one of my childhood authors, and from him I moved to Asimov, Clark, and other writers of the 1950s and 1960s. Later, I returned, thanks to my son, Mark, to Weber's Honor Harrington series. As to fantasy, I am in a large company when I place Tolkien at the center of that canon. He is probably the only fantasy writer who was a world class scholar in the Medieval roots of fantasy: that is, Beowulf, the Norse sagas, Teutonic and Celtic (Welsh, Irish) tales, all read in the original language. I tend not to read the innumerable imitators of Tolkien. I do enjoy writers such as Ursula Le Guin who developed a rather profound theory of magic, language, evil and the like. I must confess that Lewis Carroll's two Alice books leave me on the outside looking in. The author was a mathematician and word-puzzle freak who filled the text with countless subtle verbal oddities. I think there is more in these works than simply a collection of puzzles, but so far (I still work at it), it has eluded me. The elusive feature seems to have to do with a series of jokes and caricatures on famous people (or types) of his day.

I have always enjoyed detective stories. This reading has of course been highly selective, since a new detective novel seems to appear every hour of every day. I am not particularly drawn to those novels whose primary focus is the intellectual problem of identifying the criminal on the basis of various clues. The lure of the detective story for me is primarily the outrageous eccentricity of the detective himself: for instance, Sherlock Holmes, Father Brown, Hercules Poirot, Nero Wolfe, Lord Peter Wimsey, Frost. The setting of the story is another lure, which is why I enjoy the Anna Pigeon series of Nevada Barr set in national parks and Tony Hillerman's detective novels about Navaho detectives solving crimes in the four corners area of the Southwest. Rex Stout's Nero Wolfe stories are my favorite reads in this genre because of the humor, eccentric characters, Manhattan setting, and sharp writing. It is the setting or region that draws me to "regional novels." My all time favorite work of this sort is Marjorie Rawlings' *Cross Creek*, although its genre is memoir, not fiction. This is why I enjoy all of the Nevada Barr novels, and also Carl Hiaasen's very funny novels set in the Florida Everglades. The ocean is another favorite setting, thus I have greatly enjoyed both older (Verne, C.S.Forester, Melville, Stevenson) and more recent (Patrick O'Brien) authors.

Although I have spent years reading in these genres, I have found a deeper pleasure in my lifelong love affair with the "Western canon" (H. Bloom). In Bloom's work of that title, the Western canon is his list of authors whose significance was both intrinsic and because the author exercised influence on the subsequent history of literature. In his view the very center of the canon is Shakespeare. I do think that the books of the Western canon have marked me in a number of ways. Most superficially, they have passed on to me the histories and cultures of different peoples and periods in a way that reading history books and religious and philosophical texts could not. But they have also imprinted me in a deeper way. More important, there are reasons why these books (from Homer to Melville) have survived their times, are translated, and continue to be read. It has something to do with the authors' ability to feel, experience, have insights into the events and peoples of their times, and find a way to express those insights. Displayed in these works is the human phenomenon in the way it varies, takes distinctive shape, eludes generalizations. Paradoxically, it is this concreteness or specificity that fascinates readers, whether they are contemporaries of the author or live in later epochs. In this textually experienced human phenomenon, we meet specific instances of pathos, evil, humor, eccentricity, bad luck, serendipity, courage, dying and death. As far as I can tell, we do not encounter the human phenomenon in the car chases, one-night stands, pyrotechnics, and super heroes of television, computer games, best-selling popular novels, and most movies. No poet or fiction writer can actually replicate human concreteness in words. But great authors work hard to mediate the concrete (or their insights into it) by metaphors that connect the imagination to the concreteness they experience. In this deeper imprinting, these works correct my constant tendency to reduce the world to my abstract knowing, awaken my own concreteness to myself, and open me to the pathetic and courageous story of the human comedy.

I continue even now to track down works I have missed in the Western canon and to revisit texts and authors from ancient Greece through the nineteenth century. I am not sure why ancient Greece has always fascinated me more than its successor, ancient Rome. What beckons me are not just the writings of Plato and Aristotle and their ilk but the rich complex of myth, cosmology, history, humor (Aristophanes), politics (democracy), drama. In ancient Greece, we have mythographers (Hesiod, Apollonius), scientists (heliocentrists like Aristarchus), poets (Sapho), demythologizers (Plato, Epicurus), dialecticians (Socrates), comic writers, artists and architects, politicians, historians, tragedians (Euripides, et al.), military strategists, inventors. What fascinates me is the elusive unity of the whole thing, and over the years I have worked out my own version of that unity. I will not put you, the reader, to sleep by an account of my theory. It has something to do with the way several culture-wide concepts function together to embody and express the life and culture of the *polis* or city state: *paideia* (acculturation), education), *arete* (excellence), *kallos* (beauty), *eidos* (the characteristic structure of anything), *episteme* (knowing). For me the author who took a step beyond simply telling the stories or assembling the myths (mythography) to a demythologized, semi-rational world structure that laid the groundwork for Plato and the "forms" was Hesiod.

I have not avoided Roman literature completely, and in recent years have read the major historians (Livy, Caesar, Tacitus, Lucan, Suetonius) as well as secondary histories of Rome. My favorite authors are Ovid (*Metamorphoses*), Petronious (*Satyricon*), Cicero, Lucretius, and Apuleius. Like ancient Greek authors and often imitating them, the Romans produced a variety of literary genres (satires, odes, novels [of a sort], works in cosmology and science, learned essays).

While I sporadically dipped into Medieval and Renaissance literature over the decades, I did not make it a major project of study until late in my retirement years. At that time I read most of the major works of European peoples between 1400 and 1700. I always had favorite authors (Dante, Chaucer, Langland), but the more ambitious project opened up to me the many genres of the period: French Fabliaux, Pastorelles, Books of Beasts, fables, knight errantry epics, Arthurian cycles, collections of stories, Norse sagas, Celtic hero stories (the *Tain*, and the *Mabinogian*), and unclassifiable sorts of writings such as *The Ship of Fools*). As we would expect, a different "Middle Ages" makes its appearance in these genres than what we learn reading the philosophers, theologians, and encyclopedists. They give us a glimpse of the "medieval panorama" of people in their everyday settings: shepherds and shepherdesses, animals, women military leaders, knights, Viking chieftains, lusty friars, pilgrims, and many others. The genres paint a picture of what people feared, enjoyed, made fun of, celebrated. As to the Renaissance period (earlier in Italy, later in England), I was intrigued to discover a genre of works by authors from difference times and places who are usually not placed together. Each work is written either for or having in mind the author's sovereign (Prince, King): *The Courtier* (Castiglioni), *The Prince* (Machiavelli), "On the Diginity of Human Beings" (Pico), *The Lusiads* (Comaes), and *Utopia* (More). I was also delighted to encounter the intelligence and wisdom of Montaigne.

Since my youth I have, like so many others, enjoyed the King Arthur stories. In the 1940s, these stories were for us what *The Lord of the Rings*, or the Harry Potter novels were for a later generation. Only later did I have occasion to get to know the many contributing streams of texts from which the Arthur cycle of stories originated. Elements of the stories are found in the *Mabinogian* (Wales).The figure of Arthur, originally a sixth-century chieftain, was given content by the mostly fictional work of Geoffrey of Monmouth, *The History of the Lives of the Kings of England*. The literary Arthur and the Arthurian "myth" and cycle ranges over both Medieval and Renaissance periods, but is the creation of Chretien deTroyes and the anonymous French author of a multi-volume work, *Lancelot*. This French cycle of stories returns to England in Mallory's *Morte D'Arthur* (sixteenth century). Judged by literary standards, the great works of this cycle are those of Chretien and Mallory.

Returning to the Western canon, there are for me a few brightly shining stars of the literary sky, and they are the one's one would expect: Homer, Virgil, Dante, Chaucer, Shakespeare, Spenser, Milton, Cervantes, Goethe. Although I have read with various levels of enjoyment most of the major authors of the Western canon, there are some works I have not been able to penetrate or appreciate, although I haven't given up on them. They include Joyce's *Ulysses*, the *Cantos* of Ezra Pound, and the works of Tolstoy. For sheer pleasure I reread every few years Marjorie Rawling's *Cross Creek* and Dickens's *Bleak House*.

Music

*"So Margaret sang her sisters home
In their marriage mirth;
Sang free birds out of the sky,
        Beasts along the earth,
Sang up fishes of the deep—
        All breathing things that move
        Sang from far and sang from near
To her lovely love."*

—CHRISTINA ROSSETTI, "MAIDEN SONG"

Each essay in this chapter is about some area of my life experience, topics such as religion, teaching, or nature. Paramount among these areas is music. In this piece, I will try to avoid too much repetition in my account of how music became part of my life in childhood and grew in importance in adolescence. Rather, I will instead offer a few reflections on music and what it means to me.

Both the enjoyment and the ability to perform music were gifts to me from my genetic inheritance and my cultural and family setting. My musical "ear," in no way that of a prodigy or even a highly gifted performer, was fairly refined. I made the highest score in my college on the Seashore test. This may explain my early childhood delight in music as I heard my mother and aunt sing and the carols ringing forth at Christmas. Music, then, was part of my world before I even remember it, and performing (singing) began when I was five.

The music I enjoyed and performed ranged over several genres: church choral, classical, Big Band, pop or Tin Pan Alley, folk, jazz. That these genres were available to me was a gift of both my family and my era. As to my family, my mother had a similar love and talent for music, and her tastes included almost everything. My mother sang in the church choir, carted me around to various places to sing solos before I began school, and eventually took me to concerts of the Louisville Symphony Orchestra. The one type of music I do not remember hearing was country or bluegrass music. This is a little odd since that would have been the music my maternal grandfather played on his violin in and around Loretta, Kentucky, and the music of my mother's childhood. The broad musical tastes of my mother says something about her, but it also says something about the 1930s and 1940s. The following comments no doubt reveal a "good old days" perspective of an elderly person.

For some reason, there seems to be a greater partitioning of musical genres in American society than I experienced when I was young. We are told that 2 percent of the population can tolerate classical music, and I would guess a smaller percentage of the young. In most American cities, the symphony orchestras are hard pressed for patrons and verge on bankruptcy. Of course there have always been differences of musical taste based on age, class, ethnicity, and regions. But the several genres of music I grew up with were all rooted in the same basic tonality of Western music. That tonality was present in church hymns, the lyrical symphonies of Russian composers, Broadway musicals, movies, and popular music. In the 1940s, a number of "Your Hit Parade" songs were pop versions of the romantic/lyrical works of classical composers. To sing the hymns of Sunday morning and listen to the choirs was to enter a world going back many centuries. Brass band concerts and their soloists played music linked to classical composers. The musical scores of Hollywood movies often incorporated classical (Romantic) works. There are of course exceptions to these generalizations. Country music did exist, and bluegrass had found its way out of the rural hamlets and mountains. In the 1930s the radio and its high antennas spread country music throughout the land. The black community and its churches had created a distinctive music from the time of slave songs (spirituals) and was now giving birth to a new Afro-Cuban genre (jazz). This was the era of American *apartheid* and spirituals and New Orleans jazz were only just now becoming part of the repertoire of white musicians. It was also in the period of the 1940s that Appalachian music was discovered (John Jacob Niles), paving the way for the folk music movement (Burl Ives, Joan Baez). The main point is that while there were very different genres of music, some of them more or less isolated from the mainstream, to grow up in that era was to be exposed to and enjoy a whole range of genres. Teenagers would dance to the music of the Big Bands on the weekends and listen to Debussy's "Clair de Lune" on their radios at night. If they grew up in churches, listened to high school bands, or went to the movies, they could hear the works of classical composers. This was the background, I think, of my mother's love of many kinds of music and also of mine.

Something of the sort does exist today. We all know families where the children enjoy, study, and perform both classical and popular music, thus are attuned to various musical genres. Both mainline and conservative congregations welcome a variety of musical genres, and church choirs still perform organ-based choral music. The Christmas carols are still around. Folk music has come on strong over the decades, appealing to a wider group of listeners than ever before. But trends and events of the broader culture and its subcultures have more or less partitioned the taste for and experience of music for much of the population, isolating the listeners of classical and popular music from each other. The result of this partitioning is that many young people typically do not grow up exposed to, learning about and enjoying a wide range of musical genres. A number of cultural events and trends contributed to this partitioning. The most general trend is the new "two Americas" (see chapter 7). In older times, "two Americas" meant several things: the division between the Anglo-Saxon peoples of the American Eastern seaboard and the

French and Spanish competing for a new world foothold, the separation between a free citizenry and the slave population, plus the reservation-located Native Americans. The new "two Americas" is economic, racial, and class-like: a separation of educated, affluent, exurban people from impoverished Latin, black, and white inner city people. Musically, the young and the not-so-young may divide into "two Americas." Some isolation of musical taste along class and other lines has always been around. In the era of my youth, the European-tonal music (pop, classical, etc.) was the music of the white population and was separated from folk music and the music of the black community. But once the "two Americas" had emerged, the small remnant of classical, Broadway, and folk music resided in the exurban classes and various genres of non-classical music resounds in the inner city. Several genres bridge the "two Americas:" rock, country-western, bluegrass, the praise music of the Evangelicals.

The second trend took place in the 1950s and 1960s, the cultural alienation of adolescents and post-adolescents from the "adult world," an event which created for the young particular styles of dress, ways of talking, and a distinctive music. The continuity of popular and folk music with European classical music continued in the Beatles who had deep roots in the classical tradition. Even in the case of Elvis Presley and Buddy Holly when rock was being born, the tonal music and basic song structure reflected European and Western music. So began the music of the new adolescent and young adult subculture, a cultural phenomenon of arena-size concerts, turned up amplifiers, a new kind of dancing, cult-like stars, costumes and stage extravaganzas. The new music was of course not an absolute break with the past. Many of these features were present in the Sinatra era. But coupled with the self-conscious subcultures of adolescence and antipathy to the adult world, the new music was experienced in a cultural partition, a space closed off from the great classical composers, Broadway, and even jazz. It became possible to grow up in a culture indifferent to, perhaps hostile toward, other genres. From the end of World War II to the present, there continued to be individuals who experienced music in broad, multi-genre ways, but this became rarer once we entered the age of rock. One sign of the narrowed musical orientation is the low tolerance (I am sympathetic) by youth and young adults of traditional church music and the introduction of rock music genres into the Sunday morning events of Evangelical Protestant churches.

Oriented to a variety of music genres from my youth, I especially liked the early rock (the Beatles) and the folk music of the 1960s and 1970s. I have never been able to really enjoy the singers who seem to be screaming, decibels that promote hearing loss, and lyrics of extreme violence. When I played guitar (for myself), I enjoyed playing and singing many traditional country music songs, but my interest began to wane with the fusion of Rock and country. As to other genres, my musical tastes were fairly divided early on between classical music and the popular music of the day. My income source as a teenager was popular (Big Band) music and trumpet was my instrument. But the symphony orchestra, choruses, and concert pianists always yielded a deeper satisfaction. Eventually, I became fascinated with improvisational music (jazz). There was something natural about this since I had been experimenting with chords and melodies on the piano for years. "Jazz" is itself a term for a number of genres (Dixieland, ragtime, bebop, Bossa Nova, progressive), and that is due no doubt to the many streams that brought it about. I had enjoyed listening to jazz in the long years of graduate study and in my early years of teaching, and I was a fan of the great progressive jazz musicians of the day such as Charlie Parker, Art Tatum, and such bands as those of Stan Kenton and Duke Ellington. It was only in the Pittsburgh years that I made some feeble efforts to do improvisational jazz on the trumpet, playing with a sextet of friends. (The trombone-piano player was the primary jazz musician in the group.) When I moved to Nashville, I joined a Big Band and did improvisational solos in the trumpet section, but it was only when I formed my own jazz group that I began to feel at home in the genre. I eventually began to experiment on the piano with the chords, progressions, standard works of jazz, and ended up playing piano and keyboard on a regular basis. In the Nashville period, I continued performing many genres of music: vocal (Broadway musicals), church choirs, the Vanderbilt (Blair) Symphony Orchestra and a brass septet (trumpet), and on vacation, guitar. A music lover or musician can be related to music in many different ways: as a listener, an interpreter (conductor), performer of notational music, improviser, composer. My relation to music has been more that of a performer than listener. I have never (unfortunately) been able to enjoy music as a background to my study and writing and envy those who can. Thus, I have only a very selective knowledge and appreciation for the great repertoire of Western and non-Western music. What has given me the most musical satisfaction has been performing in groups and improvising and interpreting music in my home.

Nature

"This is my letter to the world
That never wrote to me—
The simple news that Nature told
With tender majesty."

—EMILY DICKINSON

" 'Tis sweet to see the evening star appear'
'Tis sweet to listen as the night-winds creep
From leaf to leaf; 'tis sweet to view on high
The rainbow, based on ocean, span the sky."

—LORD BYRON, *DON JUAN*

For some postmoderns, "nature" is an old-timey if not forgotten word. A frequent topic of eighteenth- and nineteenth-century poets and writers (cf. R. W. Emerson), the word has roots in ancient Greek (*phusis*) and Latin (*natura*). It has a variety of meanings in both languages and also in English. I use it as a general term for the biosphere, the setting and realm of living things and their environments. In this sense, we can say that human beings are part of nature, and its physical structure and its flora and fauna enrich the places where human beings live. In these "confessions," I have tried to identify some important strands of my life experience, things that have constantly preoccupied me: music, teaching, books. This life portrait would surely be incomplete if I had nothing to say about nature. A panorama of scenes or events remains with me to this day: a distant and faint spouting of a migrating humpback whale off the coast of Oregon, the springtime sound of an alligator's roar in the Okefenokee Swamp, a cottonmouth water moccasin striking at my fishing rod as I tried to retrieve my lure from a tree, a shrimp boat seeming to float in space on a dark night in the Gulf of Mexico, the incredible song of a Rose Breasted Grossbeak in the backyard, a hawk attacking (unsuccessfully) a pheasant in the forest behind our house, a coyote asleep by a tree a few yards from our driveway, clouds of mosquitoes making themselves uninvited mealtime guests in the Everglades, a single loon calling on a lake in the Adirondacks. Nature then has inscribed itself on my remembered experiences. The fascination began early, when in childhood I accompanied by parents to the ocean, farms, and rivers and as I read *A Child's Garden of Verses* and various books about jungles, animals, and forests. Over the course of my life, I spent countless days in places flush with living things interacting with each other (and it some cases with me). I do then have a certain fascination (awe, appreciation, curiosity) about nature. What gave birth to that curiosity? My first guess is that it comes with being human, a life-form born in the midst of, dependent on, and constantly interacting with nature. But there are also some specific roots of my fascination. One of these would be my family. My father, an urban soul, found by means of fishing a way to enjoy beautiful places, and occasionally he would put that into words. My mother, a "country girl," was throughout her life a nature romantic who would react to a single blooming plant with high emotions. For her the seasons, the avian visitors in her yard, the scenes of a vacation trip had a kind of holiness about them. A second root was the good fortune of my birth into a family whose maternal side resided in rural Kentucky: farm people, river people, small town people. Thus, from birth on, I spent many summers and one winter on a farm or in a house in a small town on the Kentucky River. The city where I lived was of course not devoid of nature. Louisville too was a "river town," but because of its size, buildings, streets, and large population, nature was a less obtrusive part of everyday life. On the farm and on the river, there it was in "all its juice and joy" (Hopkins). So, from my early years, I was hooked on nature. I could never be away from it very long without experiencing a kind of impoverishment. My fascination with nature has prompted me to read widely in ornithology, oceanography, herpetology and other sciences.

Much of the story of nature in my life is told in chapter 2. Here is a brief summary. My regular visits to the farm at New Castle and the Kentucky River at Gratz gave me access to water, gardens, farm animals. From early on, my father took me with him fishing, first as a seven- or eight-year-old observer and then as one who fished with him. In my early teens, the bicycle period of my life, a friend and I pedaled to the Ohio River each spring and foolishly plunged into the icy waters off of an oil barge. In my middle teens, I spent four summers as a counselor in a YMCA camp on the Ohio River, living in a cabin, and pursuing adventures in caves, on the river, and in the forest. At college I linked up with a pre-med biology major and each spring we collected various species of central Kentucky snakes that I would sometimes bring home to my brother. (My mother's ecstatic love of nature was severely tested by this appalling behavior of her sons.) In Seminary I served two rural churches where I sometimes helped in the farm work. My years of graduate study in New York City and my early years of teaching marked a break in nature adventures. When I moved to Pittsburgh, a new phase opened up. We lived in a house on a cul de sac whose rear windows opened on to the treetops, and for the first time, I could observe, even study birds. Spring and fall in western Pennsylvania was a time and place of many migrating species, and many avian species visited our backyard trees. Moving to Pittsburgh was serendipitous in another way. On the faculty was a colleague in theology (George Kehm) who like me was a passionate outdoors lover, piscator, and camper. Eventually, he volunteered as a Nature Conservative activist and monitor of an assigned area. Thus began forty years or so of fishing, wilderness canoeing, and camping. We portaged from lake to lake in the Adirondack mountains, camped on Chickies and shell mounds in the Everglades, and explored multiple rivers, lakes, and ponds in various states. Besides my adventures with George, our family at one time did occasional camping, with one long trip to the West and the Rockies. In my retirement, I was lucky when a musician friend (Del Sawyer, founding dean of Blair School of Music) decided to become a serious ocean sailor in his retirement, the result being a number of trips with him off of the west coast of Florida to the Bahamas and other places.

My relation to nature and the out of doors is that of an urbanite, and that prompts me to reflect on the variety of ways postmoderns (most are urbanites) are related to nature. Some are estranged, even repulsed by much of what nature offers. Many are simply oblivious, and nature is to them a distant backdrop of their work, their home place, their familiar environment. Some enjoy parts of nature but are repelled by other parts (allergies, rodents, reptiles, insects). I realize that such a typology of relations to nature is an abstraction and cannot describe any actual human being's specific sensibility to nature. My own relation to the flora and fauna of nature is not simply romantic or aesthetic. I have never been entirely comfortable in settings of possible danger (sharks, bears), and enjoy these settings with eyes and ears alert for such predators. Reptiles and insects have never bothered me. Like the average person, my relation to nature is aesthetic, a fascination with its complexes of sounds and sights, even smells, its unfathomable, impenetrable variety of interdependent life-forms. This fascination is a frequent theme in my poems for children, *The Magic Window*. The poems depict ways of relating to nature that are not primarily, negative, anxious, or indifferent, but appreciative, aesthetic, fascinated.

This may be why I am drawn to the entangled world of swamps more than deserts and plains, more to the lush lagoons of Florida and Louisiana than the arid Western plateaus. I realize that the most arid desert has its own flora and fauna. Perhaps this preference has something to do with my relation to water. (At this point Sigmund Freud would interject his notion of memories of the womb.) My earliest memories have to do with water, sitting as a toddler in the shallows of a river, being bathed in a bathtub. I learned to swim at eight years old and the experience of floating free in water is still a vivid memory. Thus, my fantasized place for retirement is a place on inland water, and having little exposure to water is one of the impoverishments I experience in retirement. Throughout my life, I have enjoyed the feel, sights, sounds, and even smells of water. (The Kentucky River at dawn had a certain delightful smell.) As a city person, I did not grow up sailing, and never developed a real sailor's spontaneous reactions to wind shifts and the like. Canoeing is a great pleasure not only because it is close to water, but because it calls for constant bodily responses to the behavior and qualities of water. Less enjoyable is motoring, which I have done mostly in order to fish.

My fascination with the (eco)systems of nature is at the base of a certain sadness as I watch the inexorable displacement of the wilderness by a growing human populace: forests, ocean reefs, tropical isles endangered by invasive animals and plants, desertification of North Africa, the melting of the polar ice packs. Countering this trend are several things: a drop in population growth in a few places (Japan), the creation of National Parks and National Forests, the global projects of the Nature Conservancy. My fascination with the various systems of nature could have pushed me toward a career in the biological sciences, but I think, unlike my brother who was an enthusiastic and groundbreaking researcher, I would not have been very good at it. This fascination is not simply evoked by the complexes and systems of nature but is attuned to the way specific entities look, sound, and behave. In the biosphere, these entities like human beings have their own self-active, creative, and self-enjoying integrity. Nor is it possible to experience the actual experiencing (responses) of any perceived entity in nature. We do not directly or immediately experience the *experiencing* of another human being, nor that of a bird, insect, or amoeba. The best we can do is observe, perceive, calculate, interpret; we cannot *be* the other life-form. This is not to say I see no "causes" at work as entities act, react, and behave in various ways. I tend to be alert to causes as I move about the out of doors, and look for anything out of the ordinary: a scarred tree (by deer, beaver), a dying part of a marsh, a slight movement on the surface of creek. Such is my fascination with what individuals are doing when they behave or react. Is the singing bird trying to get a date, chasing a competitor off its territory, or just plain singing (cf. Hartshorne, *Born to Sing*)? I must confess that my fascination increases in intensity with the so called higher forms of evolution: thus, with the macro life-forms of animal life. It may have been different if I were more scientifically astute, and familiar with the world of the electron microscope.

Religion

"When the Lamb opened the seventh seal,
there was silence in heaven for about half an hour."

REVELATION 8:1

*"Christians have burnt each other, quite persuaded.
That all the Apostles would have done as they did."*

—LORD BYRON, *DON JUAN*

To leave religion out of this memoir is tempting. Like so many old terms (this one goes back to ancient Rome), the word is at best simply ambiguous and at worst a ruined term. But there it is, endlessly disputed by those who study it, linked to proud and powerful institutions, displaying a bloody history of persecution perpetrated both by religion itself and its oppressors. I would just as soon not deal with the subject. But in some of its meanings, religion was, and in a way is, an important part of my life and to ignore it would be a prevarication. Because religion is what it is, a vast, historical and cultural phenomenon that displays the whole range of human cruelty, profound insights, and just plain silliness, my relation to religion is many sided. It includes anger and disgust, indifference, fascination, and awe. From childhood on, religion has played a role in the person I was becoming. So I will try in a few pages to first tell the story of how religion is part of me and then say something about my ambivalence about it. I may repeat some of the things I covered in Chapter 2 and in the essay, "Vocation."

Religion became part of me (or I a part of it) first of all by way of my mother. She grew up a "country Methodist," and although she became a Presbyterian shortly after my birth, her personal religion was always Methodist. She had lost a baby, a daughter, due to a fall while pregnant. Apparently, conception was not easy for her, and when she found herself pregnant again after a number of years, she experienced her baby's birth and childhood in a religious, prayerful, even visionary way, "giving the child to God." She was, in other words, deeply pious, intuitive, and whatever she experienced, felt, believed was by way of strong emotions. Religion, then, was a deep strand of the maternal side of my family, and my relations with my mother. In this sense, I grew up in a "religious family" and in a small Presbyterian congregation in the West End of Louisville. This congregation was a kind of second home. From infancy through adolescence, I was active there in many ways: learning the hymns and Bible stories, memorizing the very Calvinistic Child's Catechism, acting in pageants, singing in the choir.

Woodland was a congregation of the 1930s and 1940s southern Presbyterian Church. Compared to Southern Baptists, Pentecostals and the like, the congregation was a moderate form of Protestantism. I do not recall hearing any modernist-fundamentalist debates discussed in the congregation, such as evolution or biblical inerrancy, or the virgin birth. For the most part, those issues, debated in the 1920s in the northeast, had not crossed the Mason-Dixon Line into the South. The minister of my childhood was probably a fundamentalist (but he may have been simply a traditional Scottish Calvinist). The aura of this congregation then was a kind of mild Calvinism, conservative in the sense of being untouched by the winds blowing through American Protestantism from German scholarship. I was never a fundamentalist. That term is, of course, a taboo term in most circles now, and even extremely conservative Christians (megachurches, independent community churches, southern conservative denominations) refuse the term. For them the term means "narrow-minded," "fanatical." For me the term works best to describe views or attitudes or ways of being religious that, for religious, doctrinal, or "biblical" reasons reject what has become a consensus among natural scientists or historians. To insist that the earth is flat, is 6000 years old, that species never evolved into other species, that legendary stories are literally true is to be religious in the sense of fundamentalism. I don't remember any time in my life when such a thing was a temptation for me. When I encountered Darwin and evolution in college biology, it was simply an intriguing issue of scientific evidence.

Adolescence was probably the most intense period of my religious life. In those years religion, along with Doris, music, books, and the out of doors, was a primary focus, even passion. Several things contributed to this. First of all, there was my religious childhood, family, and congregation. Second, in my high school years, my best friend was Dan Hunt, a superb athlete and a fervent, self-conscious Christian who recently had experienced a conversion in his Southern Baptist church. He was not as I remember it a fundamentalist, but very much an Evangelical, a "Jesus person." He and I were very close friends and a shared piety was part of that relation. Third, these adolescent years were emotionally volatile and painful. Religion, thus, was a powerful resource as I struggled with the exaggerated emotions of adolescence. Finally, being a typical Presbyterian, I never experienced a revivalism type of conversion, but there were some life-changing events. The first took place at a YMCA camp (Piomingo) when at fifteen I served as a junior counselor there. The leader of our small group was a Methodist minister. As I observed his behavior, listened to an occasional sermon, and conversed with him, I became conscious for the first time that the needs of others, not just my own, deserve sympathy and attention. This was not entirely a new idea or behavior, but somehow I became aware of it as a whole life-orientation. The second event took place sometime in my early teens. I was alone at night, walking in downtown Louisville, probably returning home from playing trumpet for a dance. I passed a large, stone Methodist church that had placed the following words on its sign: "Is it nothing to you, all you who pass by? Look and see if there be any sorrow like unto my sorrow which was brought upon me." I heard these words of Jeremiah as the words of Jesus, and for some reason, his suffering and my own merged. For some reason, that event was life-shaping.

In high school and college, I continued to be religiously active, hanging out with Southern Baptist students when I went to Centre. I was aware of my differences from them but participated in their Evangelicalism and pietism. Thus, over my three years at Centre, I dutifully read through the entire Bible, a venture that was part piety and part curiosity about what was in those texts. I had some background doing this. When I was a child, I spent most of a winter and part of many summers on a farm in Henry County. One of the two books in the house—there probably was a Bible somewhere—was Hurlbutt's *Stories of the Bible,* which I read through more than once. Actually, there wasn't much else to do. In my third and last year at Centre, I had the chance to serve a small Presbyterian church in Carrollton, Kentucky on the Ohio River. It was about eighty miles away and required hitchhiking or bus treks on several roads. Looking back on this, I regret that I took it on. I was too busy with all sorts of things already, and it meant leaving Doris, in her first year as a student at Centre, every weekend, and missing out on all sorts of campus activities. I think I did it not from piety but ego, attracted to the idea of occupying a pulpit. I will not repeat my account of how I decided on ministry as a life work, attended seminary, and gradually moved toward teaching in the area of religion and theology.

As one would expect, the religious part of my life, my way of being religious, changed as I moved from adolescence to adulthood. In addition to maturation and life experience, my everyday activity of study, teaching, and writing on religious issues prompted me to constantly reassess and alter my previously held views and opened up new ways of interpretation and even new sets of values. I will not pursue this in detail. Much of that story, at least pertaining to intellectual change, is in my books. But a few general comments about belief, worship, and church are in order.

Experience and study did not turn me into an "unbeliever," disillusioned with religion as mythical, irrelevant, or wrong. They did change my way of being a believer. This means in part an ever growing sense of the limits, even failure of language as an expression of the contents of religion: thus, the negative (mystical, mysterious) and metaphorical character of anything believed, proclaimed, even disbelieved. It also meant that I became distanced from the importance and centrality of a specific list of beliefs. ("Belief" does seem to have a centrality in the history of Christianity that it does not have in other world faiths.) I still "believe" but always with tongue-in-cheek, humor, and qualification. I believe but leave the (cognitive) door ajar. A variety of personal and social convictions and attitudes were operative in the displacement of beliefs at the center of religious life. (See "The Poetic," "The Ethical," and "The Tragic" in chapter 4.) These attitudes no doubt reflect some of the earth-shaking changes in Christian theology in recent generations having to do with race, gender, textual and institutional authorities, and other faiths.

Among the changes I have experienced in religious orientation is worship, the corporate event whose center and theme is the presence of the Mystery. For me this event is both central and peripheral. It is central because the presence of the Mystery of things is the one and only thing which can break the lure and hold of absolutes. One could argue, of course, that skepticism can de-absolutize one's convictions and loyalties. I agree that it can, but I also think skepticism can itself become a self-absolutizing ideology. Human history is an endless tale of a pitiful and anxious clinging to things (anything) that can bestow meaning, power, security on an individual or group. What makes the Mystery available to break the power of the lures and liberate the self is "worship," a personal or community activity of prayer, song, contemplation. Yet, in my own life, worship as a cultic ritual is peripheral. I have not abandoned that activity and never will. But I experience it (in church) as too bright, too casual, too intellectual to be a medium of the Mystery. Perhaps I am simply a Christianized Druid. For me the ideal venue of worship is a cave. A few candles flicker in the dim light. A faint smell of incense drifts about. A chant resounds in the background. In all these things, shimmering through them, is the Mystery. (I can do without the human sacrifice.)

Church or at least a specific congregation is still a part of my life. Even as I am ambivalent toward belief and worship, so I am ambivalent toward religion as it organizes itself into congregations, denominations, sects with innumerable laws, broad mythical-cosmological narratives, and aggressive self-promotions. On one side of this ambivalence is a negative reaction to certain features of religion itself. In saying this, I try to avoid the moralizing clichés about churches as havens of hypocrisy. Of course such criticisms are not simply pointless. They remind us of the tragic character of religion. When human beings associate with each other, nothing they create to help that association can exist over time without institutionalization. To be a tribe, committee, school, musical group, company, government body, or anything else requires social structures that enable the entity to exist over time and pursue its aims. And no human institution is an ideal entity. Made up of human beings, institutions develop conflicts within themselves and with other institutions, exaggerate their own importance, and react violently when threatened. The same holds for religion. Religious institutions have always suffered and perpetrated the human problems of frailty, self-exaggeration, conflict, and even corruption. The reason religion must be institutionalized is because, like everything else, it cannot survive over a period of time without some organization. Like clans, families, governments, corporations, and even committees, religions cannot survive as social entities without enduring traditions, rules of behavior, cultic practices, leaders (shamans, priests, ministers, gurus), stories, and in some cases texts. But something about religion itself, namely the Mystery at its heart, lays on it a unique problem. Deliverance and the easing of suffering and human wrong doing are what orient a religious community to the Mystery. On its ideal side, this is what at least some religions are all about.

But to have to do with the Mystery is to name it, render it into language, apply human adjectives and verbs to its being and activity, and claim that the naming group (race, gender, sect, nation) is the embodiment of the Mystery's activity. Religion, therefore, must mundanize, humanize, finitize, and even institutionalize the Mystery in order to worship it and enjoy its liberation. It not only needs the paraphernalia of an institution but the grammar of language so it can speak of it, worship it, and, empowered by its metaphors, practice its transforming freedom. It is just this tragic necessity that makes religious people "hypocritical." The inadequacy of human language, traditions, institutions, and even personal experience before the Mystery is religion's fate and tragic character. This observation is general and abstract. When we consider the actual history, institutions, and practices of religious groups and individuals, we find they are self-promoting, sometimes dangerous, often just loony. But the more one is a part of a specific congregation and interacts with its individuals, the more one senses the pitiful, tragic plight of trying to be religious. The distinction reminds me of Reinhold Niebuhr's book title, *Moral Man* (individuals) *and Immoral Society* (the ugliness of power-oriented institutionalized groups). So I, like so many others, find it easy to scorn, ignore, criticize religion as an organized phenomenon.

As I review my dark portrait of religion, I realize that it is a reduction, an abstract narrowing that is a kind of falsification. One can portray any human phenomenon this way (sports, universities, corporations, entertainments). But I must pose the question to religion that I could pose to any of these institutions. Does anything survive the idolatry, the silliness, the conflicts that makes being part of a congregation tolerable and even joyous? Of course, there is no universal answer to such a question, an answer that would appeal to all human beings, or apply to all religious groups, institutions, traditions. (Some I see as more or less demonic and to be part of them would compromise my feeble sense of what is good, fair, important, beautiful.) As it pertains to me, the question is this. How important is it to be part of a face-to-face community (not just an institution) whose distinctive aim and reason for its existence is to remember the stories, conduct rituals, and interpret texts which have to do with the Mystery? This question prompts me to ask myself whether I really would prefer the tradition-less "Brave New World" of Aldous Huxley (the postmodern), a world where every trace, story, and metaphor of transcendence has been forgotten or suppressed, where all issues posed by such things as karma, Enlightenment, idolatry, and forgiveness have disappeared and in their place is simply entertainment, buying and selling, and war making? When I pose that question, I realize that a community (of course, of a certain type) that thematizes the Mystery is important to me. My life (and death) would become shallower, lonelier, more turned in on itself, if I utterly abandoned all relations to such a community. Thus, even though my piety, beliefs, and practices have changed much since my adolescent days, I remain active in a community that is conscious of and embodies the tragic phenomenon, religion.

Politics

"I know not who may conquer: if I could
Have such a prescience, it should be no bar
To this my plain, sworn, downright detestation
Of every despotism in every nation."

—LORD BYRON, *DON JUAN*

"And yet nearly all men, deceived by a false good and a false glory, allow themselves voluntarily or ignorantly to be drawn towards those who deserve more blame than praise."

—NICCOLÓ MACHIAVELLI, *THE DISCOURSES*

In a politically fractured society, words that have long functioned to interpret human experience and to express deep values often lose their original meanings or become ambiguous: *morality, reality, community, nature, love.* This is not to say that at one time the people who used them had arrived at a consensus about what they meant. The more a word survives the ages and accumulates layers of connotations, the more it becomes a candidate for disputes over its meanings. Everyday life conversations are rife with misunderstandings and disagreements over definitions, and these are eventually recorded in dictionaries: e.g., Denis Diderot's *Encyclopèdie*, Grimm's *Deutsches Wörterbuch*, Samuel Johnson's *Dictionary*, and the *Oxford English Dictionary*. It may be that in our postmodern society words have become ambiguous in another sense. Formerly, in good Socratic fashion, people might argue about the "meaning" of love, evil, or knowing, an activity that presupposes some sort of manifested actuality that might determine meaning. The postmodern is not at all sure about the "manifested actuality" and is suspicious about the possibility of such disputes. Dictionaries then have tended to abandon their function (if they ever had one) as arbiters of meaning. The fate of words in the era of the postmodern is the fate of Humpty Dumpty. Once the meanings topple off of the wall of modernity, they cannot be reassembled. They remain fragments even when we use them as if they had a stable meaning. Not only are the meanings and usages of words dispersed by the cultural sea change; the very status of meaning and usage is altered by political, ethnic, and subcultural differences. Words take on specific meanings (functions) in their locations in subcultures, age-groups, communities, even political groups, and in some cases they are deliberately deployed by seekers of power and influence. For all of these reasons, quotation marks are placed around words to indicate that the "real" meaning of the word is disputed or there is no "real" meaning at all. The quotation marks tell the reader that the writer is aware of this but will use the word anyway. Thus we speak and write of "reality," "morality," "values," "justice," "virtues," "evil," even "meanings."

The following two words have long histories and have now become propaganda terms for political movements: "liberal" and "conservative." These words are "good" or "bad" words depending on which group, pundit, newspaper, religious community, or political movement uses them. Politically, the deployed term offers a negative stereotype which evokes fear or antipathy. Given such a development, it is easy to forget that both words were once positive terms, denoting something which societies or their individuals need for their well-being. As to the term, conservative, no society exists *de novo*, inventing itself anew in each moment. Societies like biological entities consist of enduring structures pertinent to their survival and endurance. These structures (organizations, deep values, institutions) embody the long history of the society's responses to crises, responses that in the past have contributed to the society's survival. It goes without saying that the *conserving* of these responses is a condition of the society's health and even existence. In its traditional meaning, a "conservative" is one whose primary orientation is to the elements (traditions, values, institutions, symbols) that protect, stabilize, and conserve. On the other hand, no modern society can simply repeat its past and survive. To exist at all is to be in process, and process (historical, biological, cosmological, personal) involves adapting to situations and events that never before existed. Life itself is a flow of novel situations, and all life-forms from fruit flies to koala bears must constantly adapt to them. Accordingly, to survive and to enjoy stability, societies must not simply conserve but adapt, solve the problems of new situations, and even bring about new patterns of organization. To be "liberal" is to be committed to the adaptive, creative activities appropriate to changing situations. Such is the traditional positive core of meaning in these two terms. Curiously, both conservatives and liberals think of their foci, their agendas, as necessary for the society's stability and health. And both seem to be right.

It does seem to be the case that these positive or ideal meanings of the two words have more or less disappeared from current usage. The reason is that acts of conserving or adapting are never merely general; they are embodied in particular institutions, alignments, movements of social power. As such they serve the self-interests of these movements and thus compete with other self-interests and evoke conflict. Being embedded in actual movements of power, the terms become instruments of propaganda, labels for caricatured positions. The "conservative" becomes someone who is closed, narrow-minded, obscurantist, sexist: the "liberal" someone who would sacrifice the general health of the society on the altar of bleeding heart obsession with an endangered species or an ethnic group.

The above analysis is simply a wordy preface to voicing my relation to "politics," another more or less ruined word with a traditional, positive core. For reasons I am not proud of, I may be the least political member of my family. Thus my attention to politics and politicians tends to be more dutiful than enthusiastic. I am not sure why this is, but I shall explore it in a brief and shallow way. My parents were for the most part not highly active or involved in the political elections of their day. The word "independent" floated about our family. The word would not describe the political orientation of my father, formed as he was in the urban conflicts between the new Catholic immigrants and their leaders (Tammany Hall) and urban Protestants. For him "Democrat" meant first of all local and corrupt Catholic politicians in Louisville. This early orientation was solidified when he became a white collar (accountant) rather than plant and labor union employee of the Ford Motor Company. My mother was apolitical, voting on the basis of her very personal take on the candidate. My parental orientations caught my attention early but were not very important to me, and throughout my early years as an adult I was more or less innocent about the power struggles and issues of both local and national elections.

I was not awakened to political issues until graduate school at Union Seminary. There, for the first time, I met and conversed with people (students and faculty) who were politically impassioned and very well informed. The civil rights movement was just beginning at this time, and the subsequent years of the 1960s and 1970s were the years of the Cold War with Russia, the Vietnam war, the radical student movements, and the witch hunts of the McCarthy era. Ours was a nation very much divided, and I was very much on the side of the anti-war activists and civil rights protesters. These divisions were not synonymous with the two political parties. (I have always regretted that our country has only two major parties.) Lyndon Johnson, a Democrat, was the war's most powerful defender. Most Southern anti-civil rights Dixiecrats were Democrats. Many moderate Republicans defended civil rights, and were appalled at McCarthy's tactics.

If I have a political philosophy at all, it is centered in three notions of the way social and institutional power works. In my judgment (no doubt aping Reinhold Niebuhr), the best kind of modern society is one in which various competing powers are limited by a structure of checks and balances. Checked or limited in power would be the government, the military, the wealthy, corporations, the unions, education and anything else that has power. Any government, be it a dictatorship, a republic, or a military junta, quickly becomes corrupt, that is, has little orientation to the common good, without being checked by a constitution, a legal system, a voting populace. When corporations are unchecked, the society drifts toward an oligarchy and plutocracy and an enormous gap develops between the top stratum of power and wealth and the middle and lower classes. In the early years of the American Republic, a system of checks and balances was more or less in place, but it seems now to be seriously weakened.

The second notion of my no doubt overly simple political philosophy has a moral root, based on what looks to me like a primary structure at work in the ways human beings relate to each other. At the level of individual persons, this structure, the very basis of morality itself, is a kind of natural empathy, a mutual concern for the rights and welfare of others. Human individuals also have other primary structures: for instance, a natural self-interest and competitiveness. The empathy structure is what engenders a sense of personhood applied to any and all human beings and is the root of the notion that human beings have certain rights that should be acknowledged by their families, communities, governments, and also the notion that human beings can be violated by rape, torture, incest, insult, not just by other individual human beings but by governments, laws, units of enforcement and institutions. It is because of this principle, which is also a kind of moral sensibility, that political pragmatism, inevitable as it is, has limits. It is the morally based sensibility of the possibility of human violation that prompts governments and other institutions of power to draw a line that they refuse to cross, a line that their own policies and laws must recognize. With such a line, a government will take on a certain ethos that says, "These are things we will never do," and "These are the policies and limitations to power we will try to implement." Such a principle, sensibility, or ethos is ever compromised in the actual practice of governing, making war, maintaining national security. But a commonwealth that retains even a vestige of this moral core will pursue its pragmatic ends by way of a constant self-monitoring and self-restraint.

A third notion could be called the principle of democracy. It is a broader principle than the notion of government by the people, and points to the rationale of that principle. It is the notion that a legitimate and well-functioning government is oriented to the common good, to the well-being of its citizenry, to the protection of the rights, freedoms, and opportunities of all classes, ethnic groups, genders, and ages. One might argue that government by the people is a correlate of that. Negatively expressed, the "moral" element—quotation marks again—of this principle is that each and every individual human being needs protection from certain kinds of violation. Positively expressed, it is a republic's commitment to procuring the best living conditions possible for its citizenry. An extreme version of this principle could mean the welfare society. I do see welfare programs as inevitable to a society committed to the common good because of unpredictable cycles of a free market economy, weather disasters, international conflicts, and other contingencies of modern life. If the common good of the total citizenry is what provides the general aim of governance, then governments must constantly limit both their own power and the power of the society's institutions. It seems evident that if a society is large, complex, and is constituted by very powerful institutions, the only thing that could limit them would be a very powerful legal system and government. I do see a difference between a governing body's commitment to create the conditions of the common good and that of other societal institutions. All the institutions I know of (universities, businesses, media) are structured to pursue their own good and have their own distinctive aims and projects. An institution may see itself as contributing to the common good of its society but that is not what brought it into existence or defines its everyday aims and behaviors. These institutions thus have such aims as the education of professionals, manufacturing and selling a product, publishing the news, providing an age group with musical entertainment. A government, ideally, has no such aim. Its general and basic function is to procure the common good of its citizenry. These three notions are only general principles. (I have given a more detailed version of them in chapter 7.) They do not amount to a refined, savvy political philosophy or economic expertise. They do indicate why many people would label me a "liberal" rather than a "conservative."

To return to a former theme, I continue to be only marginally political in know-how, study, and activity. (Doris is much more "political" than I am.) The reason has to do with one of my idiosyncrasies. (Some would call it an idolatry.) I am ever puzzled by, frustrated by, what might be called "political knowledge": that is, the grounds and evidence for political preferences and policies, and the arguments candidates and partisans use to support their views. My reaction to most such debates is usually one of skepticism or agnosticism. Whatever political disputes are, they clearly are not explained by the presence or absence of intelligence. People of intellectual brilliance, possessing the highest IQs, marked by long-term technical training and political experience, take opposite positions in political debates even on very detailed issues. I am not talking here about the kind of political arguments that are mere harangues, exercises in bigotry, or contests of stupidity. But high level political differences are distributed over a whole range of intelligence. A political issue has almost endless dimensions and elements. It is shaped by very general values, ethics, and class, ethnic, and personal orientations. Thus, it is always a mixture of "facts," worldviews, values, and power. Its proponents may marshal what appear to be "facts," but all the different positions on the issue claim the same thing. Its arguments are conducted in words loaded with ambiguity. A political argument often makes predictive claims, but predictions in the complex world of economic or societal outcomes often tend to serve ideological agendas. This conceptual and even emotional morass, I fear, produces in me a certain disinterest. I realize that a certain elitism may be at work here. Hence, I am not enthusiastic about talking "'politics" even with true believers on the liberal side. To repeat, I am not proud of this. High level, serious political debate and discourse is crucially important for a democracy and for "the common good" and should not be despised or ignored.

SEVEN

"From Sea to Shining Sea"

Thoughts on the State of the Union

"Every old man complains of the growing depravity of the world, of the petulance and insolence of the rising generation. He recounts the decency and regularity of former times, and celebrates the discipline and sobriety of the age in which his youth was passed."

—SAMUEL JOHNSON, *RAMBLER*, 1750

"'At least for a while,' said Elrond. 'The road must be trod, but it will be every hard. And neither strength nor wisdom will carry us far upon it. This quest may be attempted by the weak with as much hope as the strong. Yet such is oft the course of deeds that move the wheels of the world: small hands do them because they must, while the eyes of the great are elsewhere.'"

—J. R. R. TOLKEIN, *THE FELLOWSHIP OF THE RING*, 1954

To think about, much less to write about, the drift of a whole nation-state toward the future seems abstract to the point of absurdity. I do it not with great confidence that I (or anyone else) have gotten it right. I do it partly because my attempt to communicate something about myself in this memoir would be incomplete if it didn't include my general take on the state of things. The reader will quickly discover that while I do have reasons for my slant or interpretations, I do not argue for their facticity or accuracy. They is not comparable to the research-based analyses of historians, economists, or cultural anthropologists, and in many cases, my opinings are little more than vague intuitions, suspicions, and generalizations. But they do disclose something about me as I read the newspapers and think about what I read. I begin with a few general comments.

First, I am aware of the well-known phenomenon or tendency among those fortunate enough to live into their elderly years to be pessimistic, even apocalyptic, about what is going on in the present. We expect a good-old-days way of talking from those of us in their retirement years. I have not avoided this tendency. What follows here is a dark reading of things, so I struggle against being too certain, too closed, too hopeless, and try to keep alive my sense of serendipity and pleasant surprises. Nevertheless, at times, these comments may seem to be those of an elderly apocalypse-monger. The Greek word, *apocalypse*, simply means "unveiling," but because it was the title of the final book of the New Testament, a fantasy-like vision of the passing of "Babylon" or the Roman Empire, the word now connotes end time scenarios. "Apocalyptic" does describe the mood of many in our society who sense the decline and ending of the "West," (cf. Otto Spengler's work) or Europe, or America, even the prospects of all peoples on the planet. Apocalypses are scattered through the poems and novels of the last one hundred years. Now Hollywood delivers apocalypses to the movie theaters on a monthly basis. In some cases the world end is triggered by a natural catastrophe, but in most instances human folly (overpopulation, nuclear war, economic-governmental systems) bring on the end of things. Even in the nineteenth century, there were writers who yearned for an earlier, simpler, more agrarian time (e.g., William Morris). In this sense, apocalyptic is a kind of nostalgia for an older and better time. I do not find such a view attractive and suspect that it is always more a literary device than a serious conviction. Would these writers really prefer living in the colonial era of Europe that absorbed or exploited weaker peoples? Do they prefer the old bigotries, classist, gender, and ethnic hierarchies, absolutistic and authoritarian religions? Would they willingly embrace eighteenth-century dentistry, surgery without anesthetics, disease without immunization and antibiotics, a lifespan averaging three or four decades? Most of us would refuse a time machine transportation back to the villages of medieval Europe, the London of Dickens, the cannibalistic isles of Oceania.

Second, not being a historical determinist, I cannot take seriously religious, philosophical, or "scientific" future scenarios in any other sense than statistical probabilities. Of course things happen that appear to be the inexorable outcomes (effects) of preceding events, trends, causes. The application of a certain force (a moving car) to a human leg will break the bone, and the movement of huge tectonic plates will separate Pangaea (the older single continent on the globe) into what are now continents, and will eliminate vast numbers of species that occupy continental shelves. I am very much a Darwinian both in the sense of thinking that the history of life on our planet is an evolution of species and that all species of living things come about by way of mutation, competition, and changing environments. With some qualifications, I also see human history this way, proceeding by way of spontaneous events and responses (cf. mutations), conflict, competition, and the preservation of past traditions. While the general direction of things in a specific locale or epoch may be toward complexity (e.g., towns develop into cities), such a notion is not synonymous with progress. Evolution offers no guarantees that a species will develop features that assure its survival or even its improvement, and historical process offers no guarantees that civilizations, nations, or ethnic groups will improve or even survive. Given certain values and criteria, we can speak of progress if our reference is specific enough: a developing stability in a society in a particular era, a trend of discovery in a science or technology. Most of us enjoy and take for granted at least some features of modern life that have replaced (to a certain degree) brutality, shortness of lifespan, slave-based economies, sadistic tyrannies. But all such societies eventually end. Furthermore, measured by the quality of life of their members, human societies at their best generate new forms of peril and brutality. Perennial and ever recurring are various forms of slavery, ethnic suppression, warfare, poverty. Modern and postmodern societies have not ended these things but have fostered unbelievably powerful versions of them. In other words, the drift of human history as a whole is neither toward utopia nor apocalypse. We are aware that apocalypse, a worldwide period of social chaos, can occur, brought about by an event of nature (a very large meteor) or techno-political fanaticism (nuclear war). But what we expect in history is more of the same: ever new economic, medical, energy-related technologies, experiments of governing, new lifestyles, new forms of artistry or scientific expertise. And each of these things carries with it risks and corruptions that in turn call forth corrective responses and new, powerful institutions.

Third, I do not have a cyclical view (e.g., Toynbee) of history. I don't see the present state of things as part of some long-term cycle, or as some inevitable return to something worse or something better. While there are some parallels in past history to what may be happening to us (e.g., the decline and end of the Roman Empire), I see the present state of things as unique in world history: that is, a global situation in which the lives of people in most of the nation-states are altered by new institutions, political alignments, economics. These alterations include the decline of European colonial domination, the merger of digital and other technologies with war-making, the new cultural and economic influence of the East, new international systems of economics, super-powers, corporations, gradual changes of millennial-long sexism of both East and West, and the possibility of a history-ending nuclear war.

A single theme unites these reflections. I do not assume that the theme is so obvious or well argued that it will be persuasive. It is a theme of transition, and I do see this transition as a decline. A political-cultural shift or dominating influence has come about in recent decades and is an element in the current (early twenty-first-century) situation in the USA. This shift is reshaping every aspect of American culture as the nation moves from its ideal of being a democracy to a plutocracy. The setting of this shift is the broader scene of world events, trends, cultures, and even events having to do with the planet itself as a stable environment of human life. The planet's biosphere is a story in itself, a tale of growth and demise of its flora and fauna. Over the eons, multiple species arise, flourish, decline, and disappear. The slow movement of continent-size plates so changed the continental shelves that many species were erased. A massive meteorite falling into the Western Atlantic appears to have ended the age of dinosaurs. As far as I know, these biosphere changing events were never the effects of one of the planet's species. It may be the case that we are living in the first era in which that is the case. One species, the human race, has so overpopulated the planet and so rapidly used up its resources that its forests are disappearing (desertification), its coral reefs are under stress, its fresh waters drying up, many of its species of both flora and fauna have disappeared and many others are endangered. Ours is a species capable of being its own massive meteorite, bringing to an end its own existence as a species and possibly most other life-forms as well by nuclear war.

As to human societies over the world, the direst development (in my opinion of course) in recent centuries has to do with over population. *Population* density is surely a factor in the inability of many nation-states and ethnic and language groups to create or maintain the conditions of stable and healthy life, find sufficient resources, avoid internal conflicts and external wars, and avoid polluting their own spaces. The human part of the planet clearly needs to be put on a diet, but no Weight Watchers is available to the world's nation-states, tribes, or ethnic groups.

The solution to many of the problems of securing and maintaining viable standards of human well-being rests with finding and using non-destructive and relatively inexpensive sources of *energy*. At the present time, fossil fuels continue as the primary suppliers of energy, a source that will apparently disappear after a few decades. The race is on to find alternative sources of energy, at least in a minimum way. Overall, the problem has not received much attention from governments, corporations, and peoples throughout the world.

In the twenty-first century, an event is underway that will change the global political *structure* that was formed by the hegemonies of the industrialized nation-states of Europe, and that in various degrees established colonializing relations with Middle Eastern and Asian populations. I have only the vaguest grasp of what it means to say this, but a major shift of world powers seems to be taking place, and when we look into the future, a huge question mark lingers over the developments of Asia, the Caucasus, the so-called Middle East, Africa, and India. Is one of our future possibilities a new "hundred years" war, this time between European peoples and Islamist states? Will giant world powers other than the USA compete for economic and military hegemony? Will European peoples become marginalized by the ever growing populations of China, India, South America, Africa? Will technological and military success turn the "Third World" peoples into postmodern technocracies like Europe and the USA, and Japan? In that scenario, the USA may lose its economic and military position and the new kids on the block will lose their cultures. A major factor in the way this future will unroll is the *cultural* (not just military) strength of the USA, to which I now turn.

The USA: What We Were and What We Became

The very phenomenon of the New World, the successful break with a colonial power and the creation of a new society along an expanding frontier, has long fascinated historians. The European political and literary (Wilde, Dickens) intelligentsia saw the USA as rootless, violent, unpredictable, dangerous, and anti-intellectual. Yet in a very brief historical period, what was a small population of pioneers, hunters, farmers and clever merchants had created a major power on the world scene. Its very contradictions (as a culture) were intriguing. As the USA moved out of the eighteenth century, populated the West, and gradually became a cultural multiplicity, it took on the following features.

The USA first of all was a *Republic* committed to a single government strong enough to establish order and security with states independent enough to pursue their own aims. Thus, the new Republic existed from the beginning in a mode of tension, even conflict between individual and corporate entities (states, government, regions, business) and whatever ideals and principles the nation embraced as the foundation of its health and the welfare of all citizens. The USA was also a constitutional democracy that created ways of limiting the power of both individuals and institutions by the Enlightenment principle of human rights set in writing in the form of a constitution. Thus, a strong commitment to the Constitution and to law and the judiciary was part of what brought about the new nation. From the beginning, the new nation found a way to mix its stratum of powerful merchant families with its populism and commitment to the citizenry. Thus, it labored to make land available to citizens, and while a few urban areas could claim a cultural elite, the lines created by wealth and power could be crossed. The new nation was without a true peerage. Until well into the nineteenth century, the USA was primarily rural, with farms surrounding its hamlets and small towns, and large cities as the exception. Although both the Spanish and the French made a serious run at creating a new Spain or new France in North America, most of the population south of Canada and north of Florida was made up of English-speaking peoples from the British isles. The initial organization of states, central government, Constitution, judiciary, was the creation of English-speaking Anglo-Saxons, and from the beginning, a central linguistic-cultural establishment (Anglo-Saxon) dominated other populations on the scene: Native Americans, African slaves, newly arriving European and Asian immigrants. The population of the new nation was divided between a landed and more or less ruling Anglo-Saxon community and marginalized immigrants, defeated natives, and slaves. Native Americans were enemies to be defeated and isolated; Africans were slaves to be owned and managed. Italians, Chinese, Jews, and other immigrants were second-class citizens whose growing political participation was resented. In spite of this Anglo-Saxon hegemony, the direction of growth was toward a melting pot of peoples.

Education in some sense was one of the deep values brought to this country by the first settlers. From the days of Plymouth Rock and Jamestown, this Anglo-Saxon population tended to be literate, educated, quasi-seventeenth century, and Protestant, and its leaders were intellectually the children of the European Enlightenment. In the early generations, future clergy and children of the elite were either sent back to England for their education or educated in schools (e.g., Harvard) that were imitations of English institutions. The classical languages and authors of ancient Greece and Rome were the defining core of education. Part of the framework of education was the new "rationalism" of the seventeenth-century Enlightenment. Both of those traditions were very much at work when the new nation adopted its basic legal principles and shaped new institutions.

Much has been made by religious conservatives of the *religious* roots of the Republic, the Puritan story. It does seem to be the case that religion was from the beginning a major strand of the villages spread over New England. Although the "deist" framers of the Constitution use the occasional religious term, there was never an official act that established one religion as something to be sponsored by the government or even by the states. In the first century or so after the creation of the Republic, the religious hegemony of the new nation was a Protestant establishment (Anglican, Congregational, and Calvinist) to which was eventually added Methodist, Baptist, Lutheran churches and the churches of the left wing of the Reformation. In most of these churches, there was tension and conflict from the beginning: thus between the settled congregations of the cities and frontier religion, educated clergy and charismatic movements (e.g., Old School and New School Presbyterians). Possibly because of roots in the Enlightenment, the religious element, and even the old traditions of Europe, the new nation and its populace took for granted a strong moral tradition: thus, ideals of generosity, compassion for the needy, fairness, and justice. We sense this when we read the Federalist

Papers, the correspondence of early leaders, the Constitution, the literature and poetry of the period.

Like almost all newly founded commonwealths, *violence* was a feature of its founding, survival, and growth. A strong regional dependence on slavery and the laws and customs of American apartheid began long before the American Revolution and planted the seeds for later conflicts and cultural instabilities: civil conflict (war), the virulent racism of the Reconstruction era and after, racial uprisings (riots). The nation committed itself to slavery and racial oppression in spite of their contradiction to its Enlightenment principles of equality and the nation's deep moral strain. Different elements were at work in the new nation's relation to the tribes of Native Americans: Western expansion, colonizing ambitions, warfare. The new nation had been born in a military conflict with England, and had fought relatively brief wars with both the French and the Spanish. Further, it subjected itself to a long, devastating civil war both to end slavery and preserve the union. Thus, the violence of both external and internal warfare plus racial suppression was very much a part of the nation's beginning, heritage, and mindset.

To the above themes of religion, education, and violence, we must add a very important but elusive trait of the new nation. Viewed from abroad, this trait, almost synonymous with the adjective *American*, had negative connotations. A number of American poets have voiced this trait (Whitman, Sandburg, S. V. Benet). All three poets celebrate but also describe the dark side of this *élan:* thus, for instance, Benet's "Ode to Walt Whitman." It is a certain *energy*, a restless, never satisfied drive toward confronting crises, solving problems, tackling new frontiers. One could say it is a kind of hastiness, a readiness to jump into things and make them work. Thus, Americans have a tendency to exaggerate (cf. American humor), to overreact. We sense this energy in Whitman's *Leaves of Grass* and Carl Sandburg's poetry, the danger and hardships of the Westward movement, the unbelievable carnage of the Civil War, in the music of George Gershwin, the instantaneous amassing of military power after Pearl Harbor, the mushroom-like growth of cities, small businesses, corporations, and schools. We even sense it in our way of being religious from the Great Awakening to the revivalism of Billy Sunday and Billy Graham, and the merger of conservative religion and entertainment in present-day megachurches.

Perhaps it is the American *élan* or energy that is responsible for another trait of the American experience and character, an ethos and even a
world-view of *manifest destiny*. I have no idea how this originated or how
widespread it was. The framers of the documents of the American Revolution seem to be aware of it. We find the point expressed in certain poets,
in war-time orators, in most politicians running for office. H. R. Niebuhr
offers a brilliant historical account of the theme in *The Kingdom of God in
America*. To be American is to be part not only of a new land and nation
but an experiment destined for growth and success: something muscular,
manly, and backed by divine power. We find it in Lincoln's phrase, "This
nation, under God, shall have a new birth of freedom," and in Theodore
Roosevelt's oratory. We do not find it in Emily Dickinson, Conrad Aiken,
or Masters's *The Spoon River Anthology*.

To summarize, the constitutional Republic that arose in the late
eighteenth century was that of a primarily Anglo-Saxon and rural (farming) people gradually exploring and occupying lands to the southwest,
north, and east, committed to human rights, religion, moral values, a
government of freely elected representatives, but subject to the principles
of a Constitution and to local laws. This new land, this experiment in
democracy, was torn by disputes with other nations, between its own
states, and prepared to violently defend itself, occupy a vast territory, and
control its slave population.

The rural and Anglo-Saxon America of great energy, manifest
destiny, slavery, and piety is not the America of the twenty-first century.
These character traits have not disappeared, but they have undergone
a cultural sea change. The story of the change is neither a story of decline nor progress but both together. The USA now is largely a nation of
medium to large-sized cities, although small towns do continue. From
northern Virginia to Boston and beyond stretches an unbroken urban
area. In some regions, a city has filled out the county and is partitioned
into an inner space of minority, poor, and lower-middle class families
and an outer space of relatively affluent whites. The old Anglo-Saxon political and merchant hegemony is still more or less in place but gradually
changing. With the assimilation of immigrant peoples (Jewish, Asian,
European) into the society and feminist and other liberation movements,
the USA now has women, blacks, and non-Anglo Saxon minorities in its
governing bodies, the military, the universities, and businesses. Blocks
of Spanish, Asian, Muslim and African-Americans are large enough to

shape elections, the work force, and religious constituencies. Before the twenty-first century is over, the Anglo-Saxon contingency of the society will be a minority. For some Americans, this means decline and even apocalypse, for others cultural enrichment.

We continue to be a *religious* nation measured by churches built, regular church attendance, money donated, and even religio-political clout. We may in fact be the most "religious" people on the globe, although in their own ways both South Korea and India could vie for that dubious title. And some of the fiery emotions of the Great Awakening, (fanaticism, extremism, and fundamentalism) are very much part of the culture. But the changes of American religion are deep, massive, and public. The churches of the old Protestant Establishment have not completely disappeared but they are no longer the religious majority nor the most public and popular religious group of the USA. Having embraced the civil rights movement, feminism, and moderate to liberal biblical scholarship, all of the traditional mainline denominations are either in decline or seriously divided, or both. Denominational divisions had been taking place since the Great Awakening, and they continued on north and south lines during and after the Civil War, and conservative-liberal lines due to the fundamentalist-modernist controversy, and the civil rights and feminist movements. Division and decline continues as the mainline churches affirm and embody the rights of gays and lesbians. In place of the old Protestant establishment is a new politically and culturally influential religious center, a mix of the traditionally conservative denominations (Southern Baptists, Churches of Christ, Nazarenes) and their neo-Evangelical, non-denominational competitors. The energy and popularity of the new forms of Protestant conservatism may be misleading as a picture of religious America. The USA is more religiously pluralistic than any time in its history. There are more Muslims than Presbyterians, a growing population of Hindus and Buddhists in the cities, and in spite of declining priesthood and religious orders, a growing Roman Catholic population. Added to these traditional groups is a large segment of New Agers and boomers committed to quasi-religious movements. But the American way of being religious has paradoxically been shaped by the wider cultural movements of the postmodern and secularization. Committed to an entertainment-oriented Sunday morning, the conservative churches adopt elements from the secularized subcultures of the young. The mainline denominations welcome (in various degrees) ordained gays and lesbians, worry over the gradual loss of their small congregations, construct new complexities of bureaucratization, and canon law, and experiment with the pop-rock and advertising styles of the successful Evangelical churches.

The Enlightenment principles of *equality*, civil rights, non-state-established religions, have not faded over time. On the contrary, the logic of these principles has been applied to women, African-Americans, immigrants, gender relations. One result of these applications has been the current class wars between the newly energized Evangelicalism and secular (trans-religious) or religiously liberal followers of these principles. The general direction of American history, like all European countries and possibly most nation-states throughout the world, has been toward secularization. As the USA grew in population, became urbanized, and culturally pluralistic, its institutions of education, entertainment, law courts, and corporations became secular in a thoroughgoing way.

Classes, that is, strata of culture, education, literacy, and wealth were present from the beginning by way of differences between rural hamlets and cities, frontier traders and the settled East, farmers and merchants, professionals and artisans (e.g., clergy), owners or citizens and slaves, Anglo-Saxons and the new immigrants. But with the disappearance of the frontier and also slavery, and with the displacement of the farm and hamlet with the city as the locale of most citizens, and the new pluralism of minorities, language groups, and cultures, "class" has not only undergone a sea change but has taken on new virulent forms. The former slave population has changed into a city-dwelling and largely poor community of unstable neighborhoods, single parent families, and minimal economic opportunities, with a significant percentage of its males in prison or on the streets as homeless. This grim situation is offset in part both by a small percentage of gifted, highly educated and affluent individuals and by the distinctive religious and ethnic characteristics and contributions (humor, athleticism, artistry, traditions) of the black communities. In the new situation, "class" is exacerbated by the growing disparity between rich or affluent, educated groups and a large poor and welfare-dependent population, part of which are the recently arrived Spanish-speaking immigrants. The boundaries of these classes are somewhat blurred, and occasionally individuals can move across them from poverty to wealth. Yet the population does seem to be constituted by classes in the sense of groups that resist cultural assimilation and have little interest in integrating with each other: Asians, Kurds, various Middle Eastern peoples, African-Americans, Spanish-speaking peoples, and Caucasians. In addition to strong ethnic self-identities is another factor that sets classes in cement, namely national and local policies that promote the isolation of the nation's assets into an ever smaller percentage of the population, thus resulting in impoverished cities with their marginal school systems, gangs, ex-cons, and welfare-dependent single parents.

Is the American *élan* or energy still with us? We no longer have a geographical frontier (the West). After the Western expansion, the colonializing impulses of the USA have been minimal compared to nineteenth-century Europe. We do have our colony-like territories: Puerto Rico, American Samoa, Hawaii. At the peak of our military power and global influence, we have pondered a project of "Americanizing" (reproducing the American experiment) the so-called Third World, but for primarily economic reasons, we seem to be cooling toward such a project. We do face certain domestic challenges: diseases to be conquered, the social instabilities of a nation divided between affluent and poor. Perhaps a certain *élan* shows signs of life when we overreact to crises, make too much of novelties and fads. But for the most part, the old *élan* seems displaced by the perpetual sorting out of the complexities of modern institutions, financial worries, our new toys. Perhaps we sense that our manifest destiny has been fulfilled. I venture another explanation. We sense that our old narrative (Christian, religious, exploratory, expansive) has been eroded by many things: a new apocalypticism of what is in store for the world, the West, the USA, the decline if not the replacement of the Anglo-Saxon hegemony with a plurality of cultures, a mode of life that is not driven by a sense of challenge or opportunity but by fending off boredom by various amusements. The new gratifications and amusements may be the replacement for the old American energy and *élan*. Whatever the explanation, our poets, novelists, pundits, scientists, and even politicians do not speak from the old narrative or use the discourse of energy and destiny. When they do, the words have a hollow ring.

Constitutional law interpreted by those appointed by whatever party is in power is still in place, but its very meaning and function are matters of dispute between legal fundamentalists (literalism) who would stick to the intended letter and those like myself who see the Constitution's authority as residing in certain basic principles and thus open to interpretation and application. Because they are human, fallible, historical,

graduates, lowered homicide rates in cities. At the same time, statistics show darker sides of modern societies, things that are in decline, going awry, not working. Paradoxically, these numbers can put a human face on movements, trends, groups. The statistics of incarceration in the USA are shocking: the sheer numbers of people in prison, on death row, the numbers of teenagers with life sentences (in some states), the enormous percentage of young black males who were, are, or will be in the prison system, the costs of the system as a whole. Crime statistics are shocking: the billions of dollars lost to fraud, the cost of law enforcement, the overburdened judiciary. Statistics having to do with the economy are scary, expressing as they do the degree to which the USA is in debt to or is owned by foreign countries, the imbalance of imports and exports, the loss of manufacturing to foreign competitors, the average debt of the citizens, the percentage of the nation's assets held by a small group of the population, the average cost of a funeral or a hospital stay. All in all, and as a country, we now seem unable to pay for our military security, the education of our people, the maintenance of our infrastructure, our health care, even our toys and lifestyles. Statistics that describe how much college students learn in their years of study are discouraging as are those that poll the general population's knowledge of geography, science, history, arts and culture, the ability to speak grammatical English, the popularity of cult-like, anti-scientific movements. Such statistics may not mean that the apocalypse has already taken place (except for the urban poor), but they do paint a picture of something seriously wrong, a society headed in the wrong direction. We live in a society in which the basic conditions of health, well-being, and stability are not available for a huge portion of the population, a society unable to deal with what imperils it, unable to pay its bills. The "state of the union" is not simply a matter of corrupt or inept governing bodies but something deeper having to do with intrinsic weaknesses, tensions, clueless policies and behavior in the culture and its institutions. In more "rationalistic" mood, I sometimes think that collective or individual human intelligence is simply not able to handle the problems that arise with a modern bureaucratized, technologically dependent society. A similar gap between human capability and its life-situations probably structures every epoch and people of human history. I do not think, however, that the limitation of human intelligence is the primary cause of society's ills. Such a view assumes that, given intelligent foresight, analysis, and know-how, a society would evolve into or create its own utopia. On the contrary, the dynamics of societies, their institutions, and their leaders are the dynamics of the exercise of power. In other words, the realities behind the statistics are pre-rational needs and hungers for power and gratification. Such a notion is background to what follows, my account of the "idea of democracy" and what has happened to that idea in recent history.

Democracy in Peril

Traditional terms like *republic* and *democracy* are not exactly suitable for what I am about to describe. Both terms mean governance or rule by the people. "Republic" connotes rule through elected representatives. "Democracy" is an umbrella term for a broad variety of ways in which people participate in their own rule. In what follows, "democracy" is an idea or even ideal that occurs in history in varying degrees. Thus, nation-states are democracies or republics to the degree that they embody that idea. As a concept, democracy describes not simply a system of government under officials elected by the populace but a broader set of features of the society's deep values and institutions. I do think that "rule by the people" implies several features that fill out what the rule requires. The most general aim of a democracy is to procure and maintain the health and well-being (the common good) of the total community of human beings, including their environmental setting. This would be the "socialist" element in the democracy. This aim implies a second general aim, namely the maintenance of a balance between competing societal powers, each one of which is less attuned to the common good than its own power, values, or existence. Insofar as a society does embody this aim, it sets limits on the autonomy of its institutions, classes, or organized movements that vie for power, including governing bodies. Embodying or serving these aims are the following seven features of the idea of democracy, at least in a modern nation-state.

First, the *economy* of a democracy needs to be a relatively free and open system of competitive business and merchant enterprises. Thus, producing, trading, and selling constitute the "capitalist" element in a democracy and is neither simply government sponsored nor utterly controlled by the industries themselves.

Second, the *governing bodies* of democracy are relatively independent entities charged to pursue the common good of their constituencies, and thus to constantly monitor institutions including themselves (military, corporate, educational, entertainment) whose power would otherwise be excessive.

Third, in a democracy, the *electoral process* is relatively independent from control by governing bodies, economic institutions, media, and propaganda.

Fourth, the activities of the electoral, governing, and industrial activities of a democracy are subject to national and regional *laws* enforced by judicatories and embodied in traditions and customs. The general character of such laws is their embodiment of principles and taboos important for the common good of the nation or a particular community. The very idea of law becomes corrupted when its statutes serve the self-interest and aims of a single group such that harm is done to the commonwealth itself and to other groups. Thus, the responsibility of a judicatory (Supreme Court, federal courts) is to protect the law from that corruption by means of interpretation and application.

Fifth, all of the institutions of a democracy including the electorate, the judiciary, and the government, require *education* in order to properly function. In a minimal sense, to be educated means literacy both in the narrow sense of reading and writing and in a broader sense of a knowledge of the nation's historical past and how political, economics and other institutions work. In order to properly function, a modern democracy requires its citizens not simply to be minimally literate but acquainted with the society's history, culture, sciences, legal traditions, and economic conditions. Thus, a democracy declines or becomes compromised to the degree that its populace lacks the cognitive, informational, technological expertise necessary for choosing its leaders and engaging in governance, trade, production.

Sixth, the electoral process of a democracy can function independently only if there is access to up-to-date information on local, national, and global situations and a constant reportage of trends, events, threats, movements, opportunities, and issues: that is, information distributed by a *free press*. If some special institution or group (judiciary, government (as in Fascism) or industrial complex controls information distribution, it can also control the electoral process, and through that the application of law itself. In such a situation the democracy begins to decline as its relatively independent media is lost.

Seventh, it seems clear that all of these features of democracy are closely linked so that their positive functions depend on each other. But something else, something difficult to articulate, constitutes their linkage. This something else is a kind of *élan*, a moral energy at work in the deep values of the nation as a set of communities. I shall elaborate this notion in the last section of this piece. In my view, this *élan* or moral energy is the very condition of a true democracy. Without it the populace, the institutions, and governing leadership have only a minimum commitment too or even awareness of the aims of democracy, the procuring and maintaining the common good and the balancing of specific self-interests that would compromise that good. Apart from some vision or sense of the welfare of the whole, the very notion of "common good" is empty, and the democracy is turned over simply to competing institutions.

A mere glance at early stages of American history (e.g., pre-Civil War) reveals that American life and institutions have undergone a sea change. One could say the same thing about many present-day nation-states. This change has to do with population, emigration, cultures and subcultures, foreign relations, the global economy, and dozens of other things. My comments will be limited to what appears to be a transition toward a weakening of the seven features of democracy. This transition or sea-change is especially visible in two matters: *complexity* and *power*.

In the decades since the Civil War, the USA has grown in population, world influence, military capacity, technological wherewithal, and institutional complexity (bureaucracy and organization). Businesses, governments, universities, hospitals, sports, and entertainment have developed into Kafkaesque bureaucracies and are all entangled with other bureaucracies to which they must relate to survive. Many things have brought about the new institutional complexity: sheer population growth and density, the multiplication of laws, statutes, and policies plus the armies of people needed to formulate, monitor, and enforce them, the new technologies and what it takes to use, update, protect, and repair them. The new complexity has positive and negative aspects. On the surface, it seems as if the new technology simplifies production. The older populations of farmers, small merchants, and individual laborers constitute a small percentage of the employed population, most of whom function to keep the institution going by way of record-keeping, litigation, monitoring of other institutions, marketing. In medicine, a simple ten-minute surgical procedure will involve dozens, possibly hundreds, of people spread across the country in HMOs, pharmacies, insurance companies, office managers, accountants, sales specialists in medical equipment, medical personnel, nurses, and physical therapists. (In my naive opinion, such complexity is one of the reasons why there is little possibility of reforming health care. The system of health delivery is now unable to de-complicate itself.) Complex systems of governance, entertainment, taxation, litigation, and multi-layered systems of marketing and public relations structure and constitute all the major services-delivering systems of society.

The second alteration or sea change of our democratic legacy has to do with *power*, and that will be the focus of this analysis. The exercise of power is an intrinsic feature of any and all human groups: tribal communities, families, classes, governments. As our institutions (bureaucracies) of law, education, media, and government mushroomed in size, numbers, and complexity, they became centers of great power and influence. With the growth of power have come laws and enforcers of laws that limit power, and this in turn has evoked fear of and opposition to the limiters and enforcers. The paradox is that while our institutions may be more subject to external monitoring and control than any previous time, they have at the same time awesome power to influence, lobby, shape elections, and control media. Power like virtually everything else in the world exists in degrees. Therefore, it is not simply a word for absolute control or direct causation but for degrees of influence: that is, the capacity to attract, shape, alter, limit. Power then is not something only highly placed individuals (senators, generals, CEOs) possess. It resides in the whole cluster of postmodern institutions as they compete for attention, loyalty, positions of influence, money: thus, religions, businesses, political parties, schools, social movements, charity organizations, entertainments. The targets of these influence mongers is almost everything: other institutions, individuals, ethnic and age groups, government agencies, anyone and anything able to respond with money, votes, or public action. Thus, the everyday life of Americans has the character of a constant visual, verbal, and auditory bombardment by institutions in need of monetary and other sources of growth or maintenance. The cultural world of everyday life is a world of marketing events, a twenty-four-hour day of sounds, pictures, mailings, blogs, tweets, TV ads, speeches, coupons, conferences. Altogether, the influencers do not simply study, poll, and respond to the interests and "needs" of the populace but also create them. Even with a minimum of technological know-how, an institution or social entity especially when allied with other institutions can "have power," shape local and even national trends, and affect the social and natural environment for good or ill. The network of public and not so public exercise of influence via marketing is the second feature of the sea change taking place in postmodern America, and other nation-states.

These comments are about a certain trend or transition that is a weakening of the American commitment to democracy. I would flesh out an account of that transition by looking at how the new societal complexity (bureaucracy) and power has had an effect on the seven features of the American democratic experiment. I repeat once again that I offer such comments not as an authority, or expert, or researcher but as one trying to understand what has happened.

The operations of what constitutes the American *economy* mostly elude me. I have some concerns or worries that I realize are vague, difficult to express. My initial and rather vague suspicion is that the new bureaucratic complex of money, jobs, and banks resembles the fairytale about the king who is naked but self-deluded into thinking he is clad in beautiful clothes. The economic complex seems to be something feeding on itself, an internal system of what appear to be profits but minus many natural resources and without much production. There seems to be little true value or worth at the root of the whole system. There was a "true value" at the base of late Medieval and Renaissance England, namely wool. There is true value at the root of a Middle Eastern rich nation-state (oil), but its days are apparently numbered. At one time, we thought of true value as the possession of gold. Lacking such a "true value," our economy becomes more and more dependent on imports and on foreign owned corporations. The shift here appears to be from an industrial-manufacturing nation where natural resources and actual products ground the value of the operation to a system of primarily internal services funded ultimately by the printing of money. Further, the primary things that generate money appear to be the activities of record-keeping, selling, managing, litigating, organizing, and reorganizing. As a whole, the American economy resembles a small group of men and women who create a "business" whose primary operation is to market itself and keep its records, but without a product, service, or source of income, thus it prints counterfeit money to pay its salaries. American businesses do of course offer services (financial, legal, educational, health-related technological) and thus receive money for such, but the whole thing seems to be an internal system. Exacerbating the situation is the very high standard of living of most Americans. Compared to Third World countries, anything Americans do by way of products or services carries a very high price. The result is the inability to compete with such countries in the open market of goods and services, and with that the loss or diminution of whole industries (ship building, clothing). In this case, it looks as if the very success of the American economy up until now is one of its biggest problems. Middle class Americans are accustomed to a "high" level of comfort, security, and services: but our resourceless, manufacture-less economy cannot pay for it. Furthermore, we pay a price for our middle class standard of living beyond simply a lowered capacity to compete with other economies. There is a perpetual and gloomy gap between the massive costs of government, entertainment, medicine, education and military preparedness and what the economy generates. It appears that our labor, corporations, manufacturing, and exports cannot generate the profits needed for a stable, healthy, educated, secure, and entertained populace. This is not a phenomenon of an impending future but is the present financial state of the national government, state governments, and various institutions (medicine, public schools, and the like) where people work. I realize that people in the know, who grasp how economies work, may have rather easy and obvious answers to these queries. But for me, they are cause for, if not apocalyptic predictions, serious concern.

My second worry is also prompted by something I know little about, and perhaps I am foolish to voice it. My take on this is obviously that of a spectator, not a player. A set of circumstances seems to have come about which amounts to a certain fragility or instability of even the largest of American corporations. Gone are the days of large numbers of family-owned corporations. The typical CEO and Board of Directors of a corporation routinely juggle a variety of scary challenges having to do with the contingencies of the era, global trends (e.g., the effects of the creation of the Euro, the rise of China), taxation policies, the mood of investors, corporate raiders at the door. Many corporations meet these challenges by way of mergers and takeovers, thus becoming foreign-owned, international entities with multi-products. One of the results of this shaky situation is a new kind of corporate leadership whose expertise has less to do with the product than the guidance of the corporate ship through the seas of mergers, foreign ownership, and the economies of other nations. A second result is a shift from a focus on the long-term health of the company toward near-term survival (the new complexity), which includes year by year bottom-line performance, image-making, and political activities, and away from the long-term health of the company. The concern I have is that the near-term styles of leadership, the worry about investors and bottom line, the new challenges for the corporations, the dark clouds looming over the world economy, the American economy of internal systems of self-maintenance, all weaken the competitive capacities of our corporations and create a leadership whose priority is to display a strong near-term annual report. How might these developments have a weakening effect on the features of democracy? Corporations like all institutions create structures to survive, maintain themselves, pursue their self-interests. In an era of enormous competition, enormous threat, but great power, their leaders will concentrate their efforts on reducing, eliminating, or weakening what would limit them, namely other corporations, ideological movements, governments, even the judiciary.

How does the era of the postmodern affect the democratic institution of *government* and governing bodies whose relative independence enables them to work for the common good of the commonwealth? While such independence has always been relative, varying in degree from age to age, there seems to be a drift away from such independence as the governing process becomes ever more subject to the influence of very powerful groups. I hope this generalization is simply wrong. I offer it because government at all levels appears to be conducted as a negotiation between legislators and professional (salaried) lobbyists. Lobbyists are employed by groups large enough and wealthy enough to pay them, and this means that the primary face-to-face influences on legislators are the representatives of powerful institutions, not their needy but silent constituencies. Thus lobbyists press legislation, offer research, and even write versions of bills, are closely connected with the machinery of partisan politics, and even participate in party threats for non-support if the legislator votes the wrong way. And it is a political axiom that once elected, senators and representatives go about their business always looking over their shoulder at whatever will threaten their reelection. Such a system may not be outright corruption, that is, accepting money for voting the right way, but it is not very far away from corruption when party leadership, lobbyists, and Super-Pacs can determine (or threaten to determine) who stays and who goes. In such a system, money (for re-election), status, the power of office is exchanged for voting the right way. Thus, to be elected at all and to function in this system is to be virtually an employee of groups whose self-interests and agendas are not the good of the commonwealth as such. Accordingly, the relative independence needed by legislative bodies to pursue the common good (their primary task) is seriously threatened by such a system. There are some lobbyists on the scene who represent the rights and well-being of those who are marginal in the society (minorities, prisoners, death-row inmates, immigrants), but they seem to have little influence on the larger systems of party politics, little access to election-determining wealth. It shouldn't be necessary to say that the character, quality, and level of legislative activity is closely linked to the health and function of the various features of democracy, thus to education, the electoral process, the *élan* or moral energy. If these things are marginal, if they have been seriously compromised, the system of governance as oriented to the common good will surely be affected.

How has the *electoral process* fared in recent decades? Throughout much of American history, this process has been volatile, sometimes violent, marked by duels, libel, and corruption. The degree to which the electorate or the process of electing representatives to legislative bodies has some independence from manipulation, propaganda, and fear-mongering is difficult to determine. Every politician is aware of a certain basic feature of voting constituencies, namely that we human beings vote our self-interests. And these self-interests have to do with our basic fears (of foreign or domestic threats) and our anxieties about whatever threatens our mode of life. Thus, our voting reflects our race, locale, age, religion, financial situation. This feature presents every would-be politician with an initial decision: whether to defeat the opponent and get elected by becoming a rabble-rouser, a propagandizer, a manipulator of fears and prejudices, or work for the common good of the populace. This more or less inevitable orientation to self-interest becomes ever more intense in periods of conflict in which a dangerous enemy can be identified: the Suffragette, the "communist," the Negro, the illegal immigrant, the Islamist, the non-heterosexual. Such "threats" are gifts to politicians willing to appeal to fear.

As I look over American history, there seem to be cycles of fear-politics, so we are not witnessing anything new in the elections of the early twenty-first century. Yet, there seem to be new elements in election-time attempts to manipulate the voter. While at the very heart of elections are "the bad things that may happen," the insecurities of the day, there also are what we may call issues. Issues can be important but almost invisible, having to do with long-term trends and outcomes: the crisis of available water, the vast reduction of available fossil fuel, the radical reduction of the value of the dollar or the Euro. Issues can be important but broad and general, without apparent connection to the immediate needs of a family or individual; the effect of state gambling (lotteries) on the poor, the economic effects of crime and the prison system, the possible effects of certain policies toward the Middle East conflicts. Issues can be important but abstract, having to do with fairness, justice, mistreatment. Such were the issues of women's suffrage, of civil rights for African-Americans, of gay and lesbian rights, of policies of government torture, a city's response to homelessness, of taxation. "Issues" tend to be about complex situations. A taxation issue (even in a small rural county) has to do with what is necessary for the security, protection, education, and welfare of that area. Such an issue is about priorities, values, and needs, and calls for both solid information and debate. In my opinion, the electoral process of a democracy should be a mix of voting one's self-interest and assessing issues. When American voters simply vote on the basis of their immediate needs and self-interests, they invite into their bed propagandizing politicians whose pitch has the character of seduction and whose aim is power. But only a brief look at the electoral process reveals that fear and self-interest more and more trumps issues. And if issues are absent from the rhetoric of those running for office, the electorate (and the candidates) have little prospect of being oriented to the broader issues of the common good, the good of the commonwealth. "The common good" is of course present rhetorically in every election as appeals to patriotism, "our great nation," and as appeals that arouse fear of our enemies. But as an issue, the common good is always a complex cluster of considerations pertaining to fairness, outcome, and a balance of power.

Are the disputes between politicians, the primary concerns of the electorate, the rhetorical themes of political parties "issues"? For the most part, they do not seem to be. There are a few sound-bite issues which to mention is to settle something one way or another; abortion, praying in public schools, taxation of the rich, any and all taxes, the Equal Rights Amendment. And it seems apparent that issues can be addressed in an election only if there is an informed electorate and the media functions in a certain way. At this point, we are told that only a small percentage of Americans (voters) subscribe to newspapers and other sources of local, world, and national information or attend to news programs on television. The American voter seems to have little sense of world geography, global trends, the recent history of events, the natural sciences, various religions such as Islam, even the governing process and structure, or the character of medical, educational, political or corporate institutions. This combination of minimal education and minimal awareness of what is going on in the country and across the globe produces elections that proceed by constant polling, inane debates, image-making, and the rhetoric of fear. "Issues" then seem to be at best a marginal part of the electoral process. In this situation, voters rarely hear (and maybe do not want to hear or read about) actual, argued, articulated issues. Insofar as this is the case, the democratic ideal of electing legislators by informed, debated, response to issues that pertain to the common good is seriously compromised. Our elections are "free." We (at least some of us) go to the polls without fear or coercion. At the same time, the process itself is primarily a war between political parties (and the economic and social groups behind them) that spend uncountable millions on political marketing. If our leaders are elected in this way, one has to wonder in what sense or to what extent our system is a "democracy."

We would all agree that a *free press* still exists in the USA. But I must ask, free from what? A narrow definition might describe a free press as an institution whose publishing, reporting, and broadcasting is not subject to governmental or judiciary censure, monitoring, or punishment. A broader view might see a free press as a feature of democracy, an investigative and reporting institution relatively independent from the other major powers of the society. Publishers at least in the traditional sense serve special interests: general readers, hobbyists, professional specialists, political parties, urban constituents. More general than these specialized publishing markets is the news-oriented free press which monitors the state of the union, the goings on of the world scene, the local events and personages. In the democratic ideal, this general publishing venture will distance itself as far as possible from the special interests and agendas of movements, institutions, groups. To say such a thing is of course naive since publishing ventures will typically have politically oriented owners. Even if that is the case, such owners have some responsibility in a democratic society to transcend their political or ideological commitments. Even if their news is slanted, they should make some attempt to be fair and objective. Insofar as the media simply carries out an ideological function, it has become a mere instrument of propaganda and is cynical about the idea of a democracy. Even if it is the case that much of the media has little interest in this idea, we can say that at present most Americans have access to a variety of fairly accurate and non-ideological sources of news. A free press in a society means both the availability of needed information and public critical analysis of what is happening. But the mere existence of these things does not guarantee a widespread, motivated, and discerning use of them by the populace. A free press does not guarantee an informed public. A free press can contribute to the common good, the general health of the society, only if it provides a fairly accurate account of what is going on and frames issues to be debated, and is utilized by a discerning populace, able in some degree to transcend ideology. But it appears that on both counts, there are signs that the free press of our society has only a minimum function. Apparently, only a small percentage of the populace attends closely to published or even broadcasted accounts (beyond the police blotter evening news of every American city) of domestic and international events. The typical local newspaper covers global and national events and frames issues minimally, poorly, and sometimes ideologically. What a free press should be free *from* is not only governmental pressure but the ideological agendas of other major social institutions. And it is apparent that a portion of the media is not "free" in the sense of transcending ideology but has a self-conscious, propagandistic character. To summarize, our "free press" is not very good at news dissemination and analysis of matters other than tabloid, local, or sensational events, and is not widely utilized by the populace. The explanation of such things seems to have something to do with what it takes to compete and survive as a newspaper, TV station, magazine, namely sufficient popular appeal to attract its advertising. Thus, the weakening or minimal function of the free press is part of larger economic, educational, and cultural trends.

A relatively independent *judiciary* (legal system of law schools, courts, judges, prosecutors, prison system) is surely a *sine qua non* of a democracy. Lacking such a system, whatever law that exists is simply directly applied by those in power. Law itself becomes synonymous with power and enforcement. A judiciary more or less independent of ideology and other societal powers is a strong tradition of American society. I do worry about the future of an independent judiciary when I read of states pressing for elected judges, a trend which gradually turns the judiciary into a redundant entity, an extension of whatever political party is in power. This is now the case at the federal level where the party in power appoints judges from the Supreme Court down. I realize there may be no sane alternative to this. In the actual world, how laws are interpreted and applied has an enormous effect on every institution of great power and virtually all lawyers and judges will have political leanings. Hence, no way can be devised that can create a politically neutral judiciary. The only hope I have is in the "idea of the law" itself, the origin and function of law in pre-law, moral sensibilities of fairness, justice, and the like. If the institutions of law (including the law schools) abandon "the idea of the law," the courts become servile to prevailing societal powers, and the legal process is reduced to skills of formal debate. Perhaps it is because I am poorly informed about what is going on in federal, state, county, and urban courtrooms that I am prompted to think that the judiciary is more or less functioning like it should in a democracy. I realize there are corrupt, ideological, and incompetent judges. In the worst cases, the system finds ways to discipline or oust them. My primary measure of a judiciary which contributes to the health of the commonwealth has to do with issues of jurisprudence and the status of what we call laws. Here the dispute is between legal fundamentalists who reduce law (and thus language, words) to a single, literal function, and non-fundamentalists who remain open to the intent and ambiguity of law, to spaces (in the ex- pressions) of application and interpretation, and to the larger good they serve. If law and the judiciary degenerate to legal fundamentalism, the primary function of law in the democratic experiment will be severely weakened. Law's origin in and relation to the moral *élan* of the country, the vision of the common good, would disappear, and what would sur- vive would be conformity to statutes, codes written by lobbyists and other representatives of power.

I argued (opined?) that a democratic populace is in some sense an *educated* populace. This is because the populace cannot be self-determin- ing, cannot function as a true electorate, if it cannot grasp its own societal problems, the issues posed by societal crises and conflicts. The electoral process requires a populace with antennae alert to ideology, propaganda, demagoguery, quackery, and equipped to discern issues crucial for the common good. A non-educated populace is a gift to demagogues and institutions who dream of power and control. I do not want to make this point in an exaggerated way, idealistically assuming that "education," knowledge, and cultural sophistication somehow create an immunity to propaganda. In the 1930s the most culturally sophisticated people of Europe (including the universities) caved into the Nazi propaganda machine. There is no guarantee, then, that the educated will have no fears, no bigotry, no self-absolutizing patriotism. Education is not itself a moral *élan* or energy, although such a moral energy may be at work in societies which value it. But I am naive enough to think education can do something, and I worry when there are signs in the society that it is weakening or not working. To repeat a point, literacy in its narrow sense means the ability to read and write in a primary language. I use it here in a broader sense. To be literate is to have some appreciation of the history, experience, and accomplishments of one's social environment and the capacity to interpret and assess the various events and trends of one's own era and situation. In an even broader sense, literacy is a certain sensibility to cultures (religion, politics, histories) other than one's own. I am assuming these broader meanings when I speak of education and an educated populace as a feature of democracy.

Given this broader definition of literacy, it does seem to be the case that the American populace as a whole is only marginally literate (educated), especially with respect to what the electoral process calls for. Of those eligible to vote, the percentage of those who do vote is small. Smaller yet is the percentage of actual voters who, oriented to the common good, struggle with issues on the basis of historical, situational, or cultural perceptiveness. While it is possible to interpret such things darkly and pessimistically, it is also possible to think that the average voter sufficiently intuits what is at stake in a specific election and does not simply echo the marketing machines of the parties.

At the same time, I cannot avoid the suspicion that our democratic heritage is at risk to the degree that the populace is only marginally literate. It may sound strange to say this. In our era our young people spend an enormous amount of time in schooling. More people attend and graduate from college than ever before. These statistical generalizations prompt me to say a few words about schooling (education) in America. I do so not as a close student of current trends but from my own limited experience and current observations. In general, I think we can say that at the highest, most technical levels (natural sciences, technology, engineering, medicine, law), American education is competitive with and possibly superior to that of any other nation. At the level of basic college education, the situation is so varied and hard to assess, I have little to say about it. Elementary through high school, the first twelve years of schooling, has received the most attention in recent years. What seems to be happening is the creation of several types or ways of schooling. Even as in urban areas, there are two cities, the inner city of the poor, the immigrants, the minorities, and low income families and the outer city of the white middle class, so there are now many types of pre-college schools: the inner city schools, the outer city schools, private schools, charter schools, and home schooling.

The gulf between urban and exurban schools originated in the 1960s when schools were forced by law to racially integrate and inner and outer cities came into being. Private or non-public schools have existed in small numbers for decades, but in the 1960s they mushroomed when "Christian" and other schools were created to avoid busing. Home-schooling is a fifth type and a newcomer on the scene. Accordingly, it is very difficult to generalize about the state of schools and schooling in our country, since each type of school has its own distinctive advantages and disadvantages. Where there are populations of minorities and immigrants more or less isolated in the inner city, the general problems of those populations (low income, financial difficulties, problematic buildings and equipment, a large percentage of single parent families, low literacy) will show up in their schools. The prevailing ethos for the students is one of social survival rather than high career expectation, thus one of the basic motivations for learning is absent or very diminished. The recent spasm of government-sponsored elementary through high school reforms has, through threatened punishments, stimulated principals and teachers to "teach for testing." The program has had occasional dramatic results: the "genius" principal who rescues a school, the "genius" teacher who turns around an out-of-control classroom. But the program is unpopular with teachers whose aim is to teach literacy in its broader sense. A doubt is planted about the overall quality of American education when we read the statistics that describe the percentage of high school graduates who need remunerative work in reading, writing, essays, problem-solving, math, and critical thinking when they enter college. I have no idea what is going on in the charter schools, but there does seem to be a significant difference in quality between the very best and the very worst. Nor do I know what kind of teaching and learning goes on in home schooling. My impression is that, measured by traditional standards, the prestigious private schools maintain rigorous standards. But I do wonder just how good education is in the "religious" private schools, county and rural schools, and in the high-ranked schools of the inner city. Education for testing may have made a difference in literacy (in the narrow sense) and rudimentary math. But this sort of reform has little to do with the learning of life-skills, specific career-oriented programs or tracks, and literacy in the broad sense of historical, cultural, aesthetic, and scientific understanding. Measured by such criteria, the elementary through high schools (also colleges and universities) do not do very well. The problem begins in the ethos and basic values of the broader culture. Compared to Japan, Germany, England, and some other countries, the USA does not seem very committed to learning (literacy in the broad sense) as an important component in the lives of individuals or the institutions of society. Teaching is at the bottom of salaried professions and one result of that is that the brightest career-oriented students are attracted to all the other career option: business, law, medicine, engineering. I see no signs that this hierarchy of value, with the various schemes to reward or punish poorly performing teachers, principals, and schools, will have a significant overall effect on the quality of education, unless they are supplemented by something we have never done before: introduce a new level of remuneration that would attract the best and the brightest, and reform the curricula of schools of education so as to abolish that appalling feature of teacher-education that interprets preparation for teaching a subject as a class in pedagogy rather than in the field of that subject. High school teachers of math, history, literature need masters degrees in those subjects, not in the pedagogy of those subjects. Here we have yet another feature of a genuine democracy under stress and possibly in decline; historical, linguistic, and cultural literacy. An illiterate (in the broad sense) populace is part of the larger mix of non-competitive industries, farcical election campaigns, a marginally competent media, a judiciary insensible to broader issues of the law, and lobbyist-dominated politicians.

As I have used the term, democracy is an idea (or ideal) we cite to explore the degree to which an actual society embodies certain features. Thus, a society becomes less of a democracy when its educational, judicial, electoral, governmental, and financial institutions weaken. At the heart of that idea is a certain degree of independence these institutions have from each other, the degree of their commitment to the commonwealth and its common good, and the degree to which their autonomy is limited by the nation's moral *élan* or energy, by laws, and by each other. Measured by these features, the USA has been throughout its history a genuine democracy, even if it has embodied or realized the features only to as degree. There has always been tension between the ideal of a common good and the striving for autonomy in various segments of the society. There has always been conflict and competition between powers, constituencies, and institutions. Having said this, I do see the recent decades of our history as a drift away from, not toward, this ideal in all of its major institutions. To speak generally, the drift is a relaxation or weakening of the tension between the common good element and institutions that regard the nation's health and their own ambitions and agendas as synonymous. To put the point differently, it is a drift from democracy (rule by the people under the ideal of the common good) toward a plutocracy/oligarchy (rule by and on behalf of a wealthy minority). This drift is evident insofar as all seven of the features of the idea of democracy (free press, literacy, the electorate, the judiciary and the like) serve the interests and welfare of the few and the affluent. The opposing or alternative drift is not to the welfare state. I do see a "welfare state" as an inevitable feature of all democratic societies. Welfare, the general community's support of needy, weakened, vulnerable elements in the society, is a perennial feature of democracy for two reasons. First, the contingencies of nature, global events, and economic systems produce, more or less unpredictably, events and periods of catastrophe (devastating floods, winters, wars, recessions) that affect industry, employment, and the financial survival of a portion of the populace. Second, the common good of the citizenry is what sets the primary aim of a democratic nation-state. In other words, committed to the idea of democracy, the nation-state will constantly monitor and react to events and eras which adversely affect its populace. It seems evident then that this commitment is undermined when the society separates into two "nations," the economically affluent and the economically marginal. In our case, this division means that a very large percentage of the society's basic wealth and assets are owned by a very small percentage of the population. Given the fact that both wealth and privilege reward expertise and high levels of responsibility, we should not be surprised that wealth becomes concentrated in a minority of the populace. Our present problem is not an inevitable or universal feature of all human societies but the fairly recent and stunning gap between a relatively small group of wealthy and dramatically growing group who live in or at the edge of poverty. This is what can and does happen when the laws, press, schools, and businesses relax their commitment to the common good and weaken their role in limiting the power of one group.

I can imaginatively construct an argument for plutocracy as a superior way to organize and govern a modern society. It would not be, at least on American soil, the old rationale for a peerage of inherited rank and wealth. Any society is best ruled by a natural hierarchy of the gifted, the intelligent, the equipped. In a sense, such a thing is inevitable. All societies (tribes, clans, ethnic groups) will usually be governed by a hierarchy of natural leadership that organizes and manages what the society needs, thus traders, shamans, generals, lawyers, scientists. The ungifted will not invent microchips, write novels, perform arias, run for touchdowns, and pursue quantum physics. And since the society depends on them for its security, its stability, and its amusements, it is natural that the gifted will have the lion's share of wealth and the power. This rationale more or less identifies intelligence and talent (giftedness) with wealth and power. This identification is the center of the oligarchy-plutocracy theory of societal rule. At the root of the theory is the old axiom: "might is right." Such a theory is devoid of any notion of a common good, and that is what differentiates the theory's idea of society (plutocracy) from the idea of democracy. It is thinkable that the common good might be incorporated into the idea of plutocratic rule, but only in the sense that a statistical majority is served. Rule *by* the wealthy minus the features of democracy turns out to be also *for* the wealthy, a rule whose primary concern is the preserving of institutions that are the conditions of the welfare of the few. But the problem is deeper than what a utilitarian theory would articulate. What grounds and energizes the very idea of the common good, the general welfare and rights of all, is a moral energy and vision. Thus, I conclude this reflection on the state of the union with this issue, the presence or absence of whatever would orient human beings to each other and their world other than self-interest and the exercise of power. The absence of moral energy and vision turned out to be one of the problems of the Marxist-Communist experiment, a rule which ironically turned to be a mix of tyranny (e.g., Stalin, Mao) and oligarchy (the party).

The Cultureless Society

The previous sections attempted an account of how the American democratic experiment has shifted toward oligarchy and plutocracy. I realize this account will evoke agreement by some readers and disagreement in others. I also realize that to argue it, to establish it in a more cogent way would involve study, expertise, and a mustering of uncountable details. Although I do not attempt such a thing, I do think the account has to do with observable events, information, historical trends, which when considered together add up to something going on deep in our culture itself: namely a change of ethos. I hesitate to explore this theme, partly because of its vagueness and partly because it signals one more example of an old person's tendency to idealize the past. I do think that in former eras of our history, our country had something of an overall ethos, an awareness of building something new, a commitment to certain values. Even if there were such a thing, I will try to avoid idealizing it. Whatever it was, our ethos was structured by various kinds of racism, an old and powerful male chauvinism, a religious triumphalism. It does seem that technology, global corporations, the new bureaucratic complexities, and many other things have given birth to a new ethos. I celebrate certain things in this ethos: the emerging religious pluralism, the more determined refusal to confer on any one religion a preferred legal status over the others, the logic of equality and rights applied universally, the new environmentalism. But I also note that several generations of historians, poets, novelists, and students of culture have a certain sadness, even apocalypticism, when they observe what happened in the shift from the modern to the postmodern. This tracking began early. Published in 1917, Edwin Arlington Robinson's poem, "Merlin," depicts the sad passing of an era, and ends with the words, "And there was darkness over Camelot." In 1935 Steven Vincent Benet imagined a visit from Walt Whitman to survey what has happened since his time, asking, "Is it well with the States?" The answer, "We have made many fine, new toys. . . . [T]here is a rust on the land, a rust and a creeping blight. There is a shadow on the streets. We walk naked in our plenty." Thus began a sad literature of passing, and the fear of a bleak future. H. G. Wells (*The Time Machine*) projects a time when techno-medical marvels have so reduced the challenges, frustrations, and strivings of human beings that imagination, creativity, and toughness decline, producing a passive, bovine-like race of beings preyed upon by other species (cf. *The Planet of the Apes*). In Aldous Huxley's *Brave New*

World, the new human beings are culture-less, shallow, technologically addicted, adult children. The occupants and setting of the Brave New World remind us of present-day sit-coms. To these early pieces we can add more recent authors: Wendell Berry's "The Mad Farmer's Manifesto," George Orwell's novels, Christopher Lasch's *The Culture of Narcissism,* Lyotard's *The Postmodern Condition,* the grim and scary novel *The Road,* by Cormac McCarthy. When we assemble this century-long genre of literature into a single phenomenon, we become intensely aware that the high tech countries of the world, Europe, the USA, and Japan, share a new ethos. For the most part, this literature is apocalyptic, a set of jeremiads about the Passing as decline, loss, ending.

What is lost and what is new in this cultural sea change? Whatever it is, it seems to elude fact-oriented research, polls, statistical studies, even psychological accounts of individual depressions and pathologies. It is doubtful that any actual human individual is reducible to the new ethos. Christopher Lasch's *The Culture of Narcissism* may be the most serious attempt to describe the new kind of person produced by this ethos. What prompts one's suspicion that we now live in a new "cultural" ethos is not so much our interactions with individuals as what we experience in the new complexity: the omnipresent sights and sounds of marketing, the dismal collection of TV offerings (surely these are the dregs, not the typicalities of our culture), what counts for entertainment and amusement, what politicians must say and do to get elected, the new adolescent subcultures of nihilism, the allure of self-help religion. Things of this sort signal what is important in the culture: what sells, what excites us, what evokes our efforts, what occupies our time, what amuses, what captures our loyalty and our votes. When I try to imagine just what the new ethos is, I find myself in a world of fleeting impressions, guesswork, suspicions. But I offer the following.

Perhaps Lyotard is right. The "cultures" of postmodern Western societies appear to have lost whatever master narrative they had which unified them as a community and bestowed on their people a shared history, set of values, literatures of remembrance. I have no special nostalgia for the narrative in place in former eras of our society, but it does seem proper to say that we are narrative-less. We are also, in some sense of the word, "culture-less." I assume that a society is culture-less insofar as it is wrenched loose from its traditioned past, and thus lacks whatever legacy, values, and corporate memories ground the values of its institutions of education, law, politics and the like. Of course it is not literally true to say that the past has no function in our present society. Obviously, the chauvinistic, patriotic, religious, racist, sexual, and even violent and bigoted past is still with us even if many of the old social structures have changed. And obviously, something of our musical, literary, and educational past is still part of our institutions. Being culture-less is a matter of degree, a phenomenon of drift in a certain direction. It may mean being "tradition-less." Particular groups of our society are certainly not tradition-less: Native Americans (although they struggle hard against assimilation), Jews, Muslims, Christians, Mormons, the black churches, the educational, political, and judicial institutions. But we seem traditionless when we inspect the "brave new world" of popular culture: the lyrics of popular music, the wasteland of TV offerings, advertising, and even certain kinds of poetry, music, and art.

The phrase "culture of narcissism" may mean roughly the same thing. In a narcissistic culture, the natural egocentrism that structures the everyday lives of human beings, thus the need for gratification, comfort, amusement, self-esteem, and freedom from anxiety, has become so paramount that it overwhelms and suppresses the empathetic ways human beings are oriented to each other. In a culture of narcissism, the way we humans are together in relation is in groups, institutions, organizations, not communities. Narcissism, both as a phenomenon of culture and as a personality syndrome, is a suppression of the moral dimension of empathy, mutuality, compassion, and the aesthetic dimension of being taken out of oneself by beauty and by the lure and experience of knowing and understanding. Difficult for the narcissist is the postponement of gratification demanded by rigorous sciences and even crafts. In its extreme manifestation, narcissism is a kind of distraction and drift, a moving from one gratification to another. The narcissistic person thus enjoys religion, family, work, sex as gratification, minus empathy, mutuality and obligation to the other. "No rules" (the repeated promise of a restaurant chain's marketing) appeals to the narcissistic temperament. "Rules" are associated with authoritarian teachers, parents, institutions (government) as well as difficult undertakings. To the narcissist, rules interfere with gratification.

In an earlier comment, I voiced the worry that our society was dividing into two quite distinct parts, each with its "culture": those who were financially stable, career-oriented, educated, and, those ever on the brink of poverty. (A recent book, *Coming Apart*, argues this thesis.) Both sides of the gap appear to be culture-less. On the one side are culture-less anti-intellectual and anti-aesthetic styles of life of the affluent; on the non-affluent side are the culture-less lives of gang members, lottery purchasers, drug subcultures, of the economically marginal. I repeat again that to say these things is to deal in generalizations and not concreteness. There are exceptions to these generalizations at every level; nor do the generalizations describe the life experience of any actual family or human being. If we as a people were exhaustively and without qualification narcissist, there would be no sciences, universities, corporations, armies, professions, even governments, all of which require preparation, focus, smarts, and rigor. But a drift toward a culture-less, tradition-less society seems to be taking place in the deep recesses of our institutions, manifest in the way we go about our everyday lives. If this is the case, we have before us what is at work behind the shift from democracy to oligarchy/plutocracy, namely the new ethos of narcissism, a weakening of the *élan* and energy which might be concerned about the common good. What has brought about the new ethos? Is it the culture-erasing power of technology, bureaucratic complexity, the replacement of an American *élan* with toys, fads, and the like? Is it the sheer success of affluence and the cultural deprivations of poverty, in other words, the two-tiered society? I do not know. The new culture-less ethos does call to mind Steven Vincent Benet's phrase. "There is a rust on the land, a creeping blight." It is no surprise that the citizenry of a narcissistic society would be less concerned with the common good, the overall conditions of the society's health and well-being than with the particular "goods" of gratification and immediate distraction. Such a citizenry is fair game for the demagogue, the propagandist, the power monger, the political marketer.

The metaphors used in these comments are those of drift, weakening, not apocalypse. To be sure, a national or worldwide collapse of the conditions of stable societies is thinkable. I can imagine future scenarios of national or global disaster: the disappearance of fossil fuel, fresh water, the corruption of the global gene pool, the tripling of the global population, the use of a nuclear weapon by some rogue nation-state, the collapse of debt-ridden economies brought to that point by endless military ventures, or an unbridgeable gap between the costs of maintaining a stable society and actual resources. These things are thinkable, but I am content not to dwell on them. What is worth thinking about is what might reverse the transition from democracy to oligarchy-plutocracy, or how to respond to the postmodern drift toward a culture-less society. The factors of reversal are easy to name: replacement of fossil fuel dependence by solar and other energy sources, the reversal of population growth; a renewed commitment to the democratic experiment and ideal, a balance of power between the government, corporations, electorate, judiciary, and electorate, a never-seen-before commitment to and reinvention of education. When I look into the future (the realm of possibility), I do not see such reversals taking place. Their occurrence seems undermined in advance by the culture-less populace playing with its toys and the new, bureaucratically complex structures of power.

I have little doubt that most people desire the reversals that would avoid apocalypse, and, possibly, even return us to the idea of democracy. But I do not see these reversals taking place by way of the electorate, the media, the body politic, the lobbyists, the policies of this or that party or political leader. The problem is deeper than legal enactments and policy changes. It is relatively easy to envision such policies: a massive program that lures both science and industry to address the thorny problems of cheap energy, a workable health care system. The problem is that at the present time, the groups that would be negatively affected by such are so powerful, they can undermine any political effort at the early stages of planning. This is why in times of party change or state and national elections, none of the items of the reversal of the shift toward oligarchy-plutocracy are on the agenda or even part of the debate. Not debated is cheap energy, environmental health, the absence of industrial production, population growth. And certainly something as vague as the drift toward a culture-less society and the culture of narcissism can never be a political issue. I do find it a little odd that what looks like a massive historical institutional change pertaining to the democratic idea is more or less overlooked. But then I shouldn't be too surprised, since it is one more sign of the shift itself, and its correlate, a narcissistic society unable to think in terms of the historical past, traditions, the common good. The issue is tacit, silent, and this silence is a silence of the electorate, the politicos, the educational institutions, the religions, the media, the tycoons of industry.

These are dark comments. I don't have much hope that the postmodern will go away soon or that the drift to plutocracy will be reversed. But human history has seen dark times before. Great civilizations arise, last many hundreds of years, spawn unbelievably beautiful things, and pass on. When I think of my family and others like them as individual persons and remember the good things that an open market economy, a free press, active electorate, and schools can do, my pessimism begins to wane. I don't see a light at the end of the tunnel, but I do see a lot of flickering lamps as individuals and even institutions help each other out, as people enjoy the treasures of past and present, and muddle through in tempers of hope and courage.

Family

"How many are you, then," said I,
"If they two are in heaven?"
Quick was the little maid's reply,
"Oh, Master! We are seven."
"But they are dead; those two are dead!

Their spirits are in heaven!"
T'was throwing words away; for still
The little Maid would have her will,
And said, "Nay, we are seven!"

—WILLIAM WORDSWORTH, "WE ARE SEVEN"

Genealogies

Given sufficient research, the genealogies of a family can easily grow into a book-length treatise. Needless to say, I have not done such research, and what I offer here is only selection of what is available. For most of this, I have drawn on the genealogical inquiries of Doris's mother, Theodora Kimbel, Wally Murray, the son of my mother's sister, and my brother's son, Charles (Chuck) Farley and his family. As is often the case, most of the ancestral data is lost, possibly unrecoverable. At this time, I have very little information about five of the family lines: the O'Daniels of the Lebanon-Loretto area of Kentucky, the Farley family prior to my grandfather, William E. Farley, Doris's paternal family, the Kimbel's and her paternal grandmother, a Holzheimer, and the Walker family prior to my grandfather. I am told that the census containing information about the Farley family was lost. Accordingly, the family lines I know a little about are Murray, Walker, O'Nan, Reager, and Roe.

As to how far back these lines go, the records I have access to provide almost no information about the lives or residences of these five families in the Old Country, that is, in England, Ireland, or Germany, their move across the Atlantic to this country, or their journey westward to Kentucky. Both the Farleys and O'Nans (Aunant?) can be placed in France, but I have no information about this. The Reagers (Riegers), Kimbels, and Holzheimers are from Switzerland and Germany. A Clemson who married an O'Nan is from Birmingham, England, and the Carroll (O'Carroll) family is Irish. The period of the Carrolls' arrival in America is the late sixteenth century. Both the Reagers and the O'Nans appear to have left Europe in the eighteenth century. When we think of the historical era in which these families immigrated to this country, we realize that the setting of our ancestors was the ceaseless flow of immigrants from Europe to the new nation-state created toward the end of the eigteenth century, and the Westward movements from the east coast during the eighteenth and nineteenth centuries.

I shall organize these genealogies as follows. The primary division is between the Edward Farley families and Doris Kimbel families. The ancestral lines of my family are Farley, Murray, Walker, O'Nan, and O'Daniel. The ancestral lines of Doris's family are Reager, Roe, Kimbel, Holzheimer.

The Edward Farley Families

THE FARLEY AND MURRAY FAMILIES

The four ancestral lines of my four grandparents are Farley, Murray (paternal), and Walker and O'Nan (maternal). I know little about the ancestry of my two grandfathers, William Edward Farley and Charles Walker. There are various speculations about Scottish, Irish, English, and French roots based on the names themselves. The two lines that have been tracked back to Colonial times are those of my two grandmothers, Elizabeth Murray (who married W. E. Farley) and Clementine (Tina) O'Nan (who married Charles Walker). My father's parents were William

E. Farley married to Elizabeth Murray. I have no information on the ancestry of William E. Farley, only the Louisville setting. My grandmother's ancestry (as I have it) begins with Samuel S. Murray (b. 1800) who married Elizabeth (b. 1800) of Maryland. A child of this marriage, John S. Murray (b.1842) married Sallie W. (b. 1842) of Lebanon, Kentucky. These were the parents of Elizabeth Murray, my grandmother. William E. Farley (b.1865) and Elizabeth (b.1865) married in Louisville and my father was one of the five children, all males, of this family: thus, Henry, William E., Patrick, Ernest, and Raymond Lee.

The Murray family of my grandmother became connected to the Walker-O'Nan family of my mother in the following way. Anderson C. Murray (b.1876) was one of the children of John S. and Sallie Murray. He married Margaret Enge (b.1882) of Germany, and one of their children was Wallace Murray (b. 1907) in New York City. On a visit to his aunt in Louisville, Elizabeth Farley, he met my mother's sister, Lillian Walker. Two children, my first cousins, Wallace (b. 1932) and Marilyn (b. 1933) were born of that marriage. Wallace married Phyllis Fisher, and their children are Alison, Karen, and James.

THE WALKER AND O'NAN FAMILIES

My mother's parents were Charles Walker (Madison, Indiana) and Clementine O'Nan (Lockport, Kentucky). As with my paternal grandfather's ancestry, I have very little information about the ancestry of Charles Walker. He was the son of Charles Lewis Walker who married Jeanette Wilhoite (Gest, Ky.), their four children being Oscar (a river boat captain), Robert, Ada, and my grandfather, Charles.

The O'Nan family hails from Pennsylvania and, prior to that, England. Dennis O'Nan (b.1705) married Rebecca Clemson (b.1707), whose parents were Alexander Clemson (Birmingham, England), and his son, James, and his wife, Sarah, of Philadelphia. A child of Dennis and Rebecca was William O'Nan (b.1753) of Virginia, who migrated to Henry County, Kentucky and married Charity Brewer. Dennis O'Nan (b.1850), my grandfather, was one of their children. In or around the Kentucky River town of Lockport, he married my great gtrandmother, Cassie Angelina Hall (b. 1848). Nine children, my aunts and uncles, were the progeny of this marriage: Sarah (Sannie), Seldon (Sel), America (Mec), Verdie (Birdie), Rowden (Rowd), Willard, Lillian (Ninnie), Myra Mae,

Dora Mae (Dode), and Clementine (Tina), my grandmother. The Walker and O'Nan families came together with the marriage of Charles Walker and Tina O'Nan in or around Lockport, Kentucky. Their two children were Lillian and my mother, Dora Mae,

THE WALKER AND O'DANIEL FAMILIES

My grandfather, Charles Walker, lost his wife, Tina, to tuberculosis when she was around thirty-five years old. After a brief period of farming on Pea Ridge above Gratz, he married Sadie O'Daniel, who came to New Castle for the funeral of her brother who was the husband of one of the O'Nan sisters, Myra Mae O'Nan, had died in a drowning accident. After the marriage, Charles and his two daughters joined Sadie in Loretto, Kentucky, and a number of boys and girls, my new cousins, were added to the family. I never spent long periods of time in Loretto but did make many visits. Thus as a child, I knew Virgina, Susan, Nell, and Buddy. I treasure this family, and still enjoy visits with them in Bardstown and Loretto. Virginia became a Sister of Loretto (Sister Charles Maureen). Others in the family worked at jobs in Louisville and environs, and the marriages of the children of Charles and Sadie produced several generations of cousins.

The Families of Doris Kimbel

Doris's parents were G. Dewey Kimbel and Theodora Reager. I have no information about her paternal ancestry beyond the names of Dewey Kimbel's father, Edward Kimbel. The following genealogy thus traces the family lines of Doris's maternal grandparents, the Reagers and the Roes. This Swiss and German family, as far as I have information, begins with Anthony Rieger, a Swiss who immigrated to Philadelphia. His sons were Anthony, Burkhart, and Jacob. Jacob emigrated to the East Coast of this country and from there traveled to the Louisville area on an Ohio River flatboat just as Louisville was being founded. His son, Frank Rieger (at one time in Stuttgart, Germany) married Bena Riece. Their son was Doris's grandfather, Henry Reager (b.1861).

Doris's maternal grandmother was Rose Carroll Roe. Strong family traditions plus genealogical evidence connects this family to Charles Carroll of Carrollton (Ireland, Philadelphia), a wealthy participant in the American Revolution. Two generations of ancestors of Charles Carroll are known. Charles O'Carroll (b. 1660) was married to Mary Darnall. A son of theirs was another Charles Carroll (b. 1702), and in the next generation came Charles Carroll of Carrollton (1735–1822). At least one son from every generation afterwards was named Charles Carroll, one of which was a Charles Carroll (1775–1861). Apparently, a sister of this Carroll (Mary Carroll) married into the Roe family, and from that marriage came the generation of Doris's grandmother, and various aunts and uncles: Kate, Blanche, Lucie, Charles Carroll, and Rose Crawford Roe. (I note that one of the Roe family sons was a much published Victorian-era novelist.) Henry Reager and Rose married in 1884, their children being Allen, Harry, Madeline, Charles Carroll, and Theodora, Doris's mother. Theodora and Dewey Kimbel married, their children being Virginia Catherine and Doris.

A Family Narrative

Times and Places

I begin the narrative part of this family story with the settings, origins, and progeny of my father's family (Farleys, Murrays), my mother's family (Walkers, O'Nans), and Doris's family (Reagers and Roes, and Kimbels). The physical setting of our parents is Louisville, Kentucky and various central Kentucky towns: New Castle, Gratz, Bardstown, Loretto. As the child of a minister, Doris lived in small towns in southern Indiana (Speed), Kentucky (Springfield and Bowling Green), and finally, Louisville. For the most part, her paternal aunts and uncles lived in other states, so the intimate family of her childhood and adolescence was fairly small. The Walkers, the large Catholic family of my grandparents, Charles and Sadie, resided in and around Bardstown and Loretto, Kentucky, My mother's sister married and moved to Long Island (New York) thus I kept up with both the Loretto and Long Island families by travel and visitations. Most of my relatives lived either in Louisville or in Henry and Owen Counties. The Louisville of my childhood (1930s) was experiencing transitions made possible by electricity and gasoline-driven vehicles. The occasional horse-drawn delivery vehicle plodded the streets, thus iron water containers for horses could still be seen on street corners. My childhood and adolescent years were spent in the West End of Louisville (Parkland), and my family resided in at least six different rental houses before they purchased the house next door to the manse of our church. Newcastle (the farm) and Gratz (a Kentucky River town) in Henry and Owen counties were about fifty miles southeast of Louisville. These sites were a second home to me, not simply places of occasional visits. My mother, my brother, and I, and on his vacations, my father, spent long summertime stretches in these places.

Both Doris's and my families were, in the Depression years of our youth and young adulthood, traditional in the sense that the men earned wages from an out-of-the-home occupation and the women were at-home caretakers. The two exceptions I can recall were my Aunt (Myra Mae), who was New Castle's telephone operator, and another aunt (Dode), who worked as an independent seamstress. Thus, there were no women factory workers, ministers, physicians. The occupations of Doris's family (Kimbels, Reagers, and Roes) and my family (Farleys, Walkers, O'Nans) were vastly different. According to Doris's mother, the Reager family was an educated, cultured group of teachers, ministers, company owners, and high-level craft workers. Doris's maternal grandfather, Henry Reager, owned an insurance company, sat on hospital and other Boards of Directors, and was honored as a philanthropist. The Roe family sported a well-known novelist, and Doris's paternal grandfather was a Louisville builder/contractor who oversaw the building of major bridges and civic structures. As to the Farley and Walker families, education beyond high school was not pursued until my own generation. Two women (O'Nans) married college educated men, one a physician (Rawlins), the other, a lawyer (Harrod). My cousins and I were the first college graduates of the Farley, Walker, and O'Nan families. My paternal grandfather was a postman. The Farley males (uncles) were firemen, printers, office workers. As to the Walkers and O'Nans, their occupations did not issue in either wealth or prestige, but did have a romantic air about them. The Walker and O'Nan males included a river boat gambler, saloon keeper, prison guard, small coal company owner, barber-musician, various farmers, and even a Roman Catholic nun (Sister Charles Maureen). In my generation the first college educated family members became ministers, teachers, scientists, lawyers, professors.

In Switzerland the Reager (Rieger) family had been Jewish, but their Judaic heritage seems not to have survived the trip across the Atlantic. The O'Carroll family, the root of the Roes, were Irish and thus Roman Catholic. The O'Nans, also Irish, were probably Catholic in their

European period, but became Methodists in the course of their move west to Kentucky. When my grandfather, Charles Walker, married a Roman Catholic (Sadie O'Daniel), the children, and finally he himself, were Catholic, living in and around Loretto, Kentucky. The O'Daniels immigrated from Maryland to Lebanon and Bardstown near Louisville. The O'Nan sisters, my aunts and uncles, and my mother were all Methodists. This is why I was baptized as a baby in a Methodist church. But the Farley family in Parkland was Presbyterian, my grandfather being an elder in the church there. Thus, shortly after my baptism, my mother joined my father as a member of the Woodland Presbyterian Church located in Parkland.

Many of the quaint and beautiful names of these families reflect their ancestry in Germany, England, Ireland, and Colonial America: thus, Jeptha, Clementine (Tina), William Tell, Cassandra (Cassie), America (Meck), Sadie, Bena, Rose, Charity, Sanny, Birdie, Rowd, Ada, Kate, Sel.

Family Portraits

Family is the theme of this first appendix. But "family" means more than simply origins, roots, ancestry, and places. These things are the setting, the framework for what in fact are people of flesh and blood. To know my family, any family, is to experience each personality, including the their relations to each other in the family, their idiosyncrasies, ways of speaking, pathologies, skills, humor, and many other things. I cannot of course re-create this flesh and blood family. I would come closer if I had the skill and time to write a novel about each individual, but even a full-length novel by a gifted writer (which I am not) could not reincarnate what it would be like to actually experience them. The best I can do is a few short vignettes that I hope will communicate at least something of their personalities. With the exception of my brother, I have chosen not to include my closest family (Doris or my children and their families) in these vignettes. As a proud father and grandfather, I am tempted to fill many pages with accounts of my intimate family, but these are the ones for whom this memoir is written. I hope they will enjoy these brief portraits of people in the broader family, and the people of my childhood, adolescence, and young adulthood. I will begin with my own family and continue with Doris's family.

As to my own family, the grandparents I knew best were my father's parents, *William E. and Elizabeth Farley.* We lived with them on the second floor of their house in Parkland. When I was about four years old, my grandfather would take me to the Parkland fire station where he routinely defeated all comers in checkers. He was, so people said, very intelligent, a post office worker who with education or inclination could have been an engineer or builder. Like other Farley men, he was adept at home repairs and mechanical projects. He invented a device for the automatic delivery of towels for the drying of hands, which eventually was placed on trains and in public restrooms. Unfortunately, his business sense did not match his inventive abilities and he sold it for very little money. When he was about forty years old, he experienced a religious conversion of some sort, and became active as an elder and Sunday school teacher in the Presbyterian Church in Parkland. When I was twelve, I did my first work for money, helping my grandmother in her garden. She had a reputation for winning baking contests.

My father, *Raymond Lee Farley,* was one of the middle children of the five sons. The family was neither wealthy nor poor. However, the salary of the father, a postman, did not go far to support a household of seven people. Most of the sons did not, I think, finish high school. If they stayed at home after they took a job, they were expected to hand over their earnings to my grandmother. My father's childhood was apparently severe, even traumatic, due to his own abusive father and his mother, whose affection varied from child to child. He was severely scalded as a child, and his experience of rejection by his mother was another kind of scalding. His personality was convoluted, a study in contradictions. On one side, he was very intelligent, humorous (the wit of his social circle, in his old age), altruistic, thus always available to his friends, neighbors, family in all sorts of ways. My father inherited the Farley genes for repair, construction, and mechanics, and wherever we lived, he was the one in the neighborhood or among friends who could and would address the challenges of home repair. He built the garage for the first house he and my mother owned, and in his retirement years, he designed and built a large screened-in porch for a neighbor. He was very much a caregiver both for my mother in the last decade of her life and of his second wife, Helen, until she died. At the same time, he was deeply marked by low self esteem, quick to anger, and super sensitive to what he experienced as slights. The result was a number of life-long alienations from family members and others, and even from institutions such as stores and banks, which "mistreated" him. Thus, he would draw his money out of a bank when a new teller didn't recognize him and asked for identification. His parenting style was that of a failed authoritarian, a mixture of occasional brutality and excessive pride in his two sons. From early on, he was able to find office jobs in various plants, and spent most of his working life as an accountant for the Ford Motor Company. He did this job with ease, but lost out in competitions for promotion because of the educational gap between himself and the new generation of college-educated men. He never spoke grammatically correct English, and that would have weighed against him when promotions impended. He was probably more intelligent than anyone in that office. He loved the out of doors, and was a dedicated bass fisherman. Although there was always an underlying element of estrangement between my mother and father, he was clearly very much in love with her. He also had real affection for Doris. In my late childhood and early adolescence, I spent a lot of time with him fishing in Kentucky ponds and lakes. When Doris and I married and bought homes in Pittsburgh and Nashville, what he liked best to do on his visits to us was to work on our house, and I learned a great deal about "how things worked" from working with him. His retirement from Ford lasted about thirty years. When my mother died, he haunted her burial place, Cave Hill Cemetery, for many months. Eventually, he moved to a retirement home, met and married Helen, whom he loved very much. Because of his care for her, she avoided having to reside in a nursing home.

Family and friends called my mother "Dormay," an elision of her name, *Dora Mae*. Her parents were Charles and Tina Walker, and she was born in a farmhouse somewhere near the town of Lockport on the Kentucky River. Her childhood was spent in various towns on or near that river, and after her mother died and her father remarried, she and her sister, Lillian, lived in Loretto, Kentucky. Her first fifteen or so years had two distinct parts: the time before her mother died when she was about seven, and the time she lived in Loretto. In the first period, she and her sister lived with their parents on a farm on Pea Ridge above Gratz until Tina became tubercular. Apparently against the doctor's advice, they moved to Eminence, Kentucky, where the girls could have better schooling. My impression was that Charlie Walker was never a very enthusiastic farmer. When Tina died and their father remarried, the two sisters moved with him to the Roman Catholic town of Loretto. They attended the parochial school there, having nuns as their teachers, but they were not pressed by their family to abandon their Methodist heritage and become Roman Catholic. Apparently, this was an unhappy time for my mother, and when she was fifteen or sixteen years old, she moved to a "girl's home" in Louisville and worked in a department store. This too was an unhappy time, and her journal for the period paints a picture of a severely depressed and lonely teenager. In these years, she met my father, and when she was eighteen she contracted tuberculosis and went to live with her grandmother in New Castle to recover. My father continued to court her in this period, visiting her in New Castle, and when she recovered, they married and lived in the Parkland area of Louisville. In one house, they lived on the second floor, and, pregnant with her first child, my mother fell down a full flight of stairs, an accident that resulted in the death of her almost full-term daughter.

Two things stand out in my memory of my mother. First, her intense, emotional way of experiencing and expressing in words what life had to offer her: people, nature, music, events. Second, her constant awe of and interest in "high culture," the worlds of learning, aesthetics, education, literature, religion. There was nothing phony or pretentious or social-climbing about her awe of cultured things. To know her and hear her talk about things was to sense a kind of aesthetic-personal perceptiveness, almost always positive in its tone or quality. Thus, she was not simply "religious" but intensely religious, and this was evident in her public prayers, conversations, teaching. As to "high culture," she had little formal education, perhaps to the eighth grade, but she sensed that behind certain closed doors were fascinating worlds of authors, composers, religious truths. She was never a "social climber," but she did linger longingly before the doors of learning and the art that had mostly been closed to her. She was in awe of Shakespeare, certain poets, and classical music. She loved to sing the classical repertoire of the church choir, and began taking me to hear the Louisville Symphony Orchestra when I was a young teenager. Thus, my brother and I needed no verbal prodding about the importance of education and going to college. Her fascination with "culture" was a kind of air we breathed in our home, and we knew that attending college loomed in our future. The last ten years of my mother's life were made very difficult by recurring ischemic attacks that reduced her sensibilities and by a period of time in a nursing home, hip surgery, drop foot, and other ills of old age. She had good care from my father and died of a massive stroke when she was eighty-one.

My brother, Charles Austin Farley (Austin) and I were seven years apart, a distance that prevented us from doing things together. When he was a child, I was a pre-teen, and my primary relation to him was that of protector. For some reason, I had a narrowed version of how to be an older brother, namely to defend him against what threatened him. For reasons I am not clear about, he was throughout his childhood and adolescence a target of my father's physical and emotional abuse. In that situation, I could do no "protecting," only retreat into angry resentment. This family pattern was one (but not the only one) of the reasons for my early and intense alienation from the family. My way of responding to this pattern was to seek isolation, to distance myself from the family, and this meant that I was not much of a brother to Austin in my teenage years. Eventually, we shared certain interests: natural history, herpetology, music, the out of doors. The Farley genes of repair and construction were more prominent in him than in me, but his primary passions turned out to be the life sciences rather than engineering. When he finished college as a biology major, he took a job in a government laboratory in Maryland, where it was quickly apparent that he had a natural gift for rigorous and important microbiological research. The result was a stunning career specializing in the pathologies of shellfish. Aided by graduate work at Johns Hopkins, he published many hefty articles in refereed journals including an article in *Science*, and made trips to Japan and Scandinavia where he shared the results of his research. Near the end of his career, he was given an important government award as recognition of his accomplishments. His life had deep tragic elements marked by the death of his first daughter, Lisa, in a pony accident, persistent money problems, and the early loss of his wife to cancer. Distance has separated Doris and me from my brother and his family, and visits now are unfortunately rare. Austin's son (Chuck) and daughter (Laura) are married with growing families filled with delightful, interesting, ambitious, and very religious people. I am sorry I do not know these nephews and nieces better than I do.

I never knew my mother's mother (Tina O'Nan Walker), who died when she was in her mid-thirties, and I did not know my grandfather (Charles Walker) very well simply because he lived in Loretto and visits were rare. But our family did visit Loretto often enough for me to know Sadie, my grandfather's second wife, and the children more or less my age (Buddy, Nell, Susan). My grandfather ("Papa," his children called him) was much loved and respected in his family. He was quiet, soft-spoken, kind, and a performing musician (fiddle, guitar) most of his life.

Among all of my relatives, the people I was closest to were the O'Nan sisters, my mother's aunts. These families lived in Henry and Owen Counties (Kentucky) on farms, a county seat (New Castle), a river town (Gratz), and Eminence. They were a close-knit family, united by their love for their mother, Cassie, who died when I was five years old. These aunts were my mother's primary family. Throughout much of her childhood and adolescence, she lived with or under the care of her aunts.

Aunt Dode functioned as a surrogate mother for my mother when my mother left Loretto for Louisville. As a surrogate mother to my mother, Aunt Dode was a surrogate grandmother to me. She worked all her adult life as a seamstress, making clothes for well-to-do women in the East End of Louisville. There were rumors of an early disappointed love affair, and she never married. She had her own apartment, but traveled with us, lived with us when ill, and stayed with my brother and me when my parents vacationed. Aunt Dode was the one member of the O'Nan clan always available to abandon her own work, pack her bags, and visit the family member who needed her on occasion of death and mourning, sickness and recovery. She did this all of her life until her final years, when she lived in a nursing home in New Castle. She was a beloved fixture in the family, taken for granted as an ever-available source of help and comfort.

In addition to my mother's surrogate mother, Aunt Dode, the family member closest to us was my mother's sister, Lillian Murray, born a Walker but married to Wallace Murray. Thus, both sisters, my mother and Lillian, married into the Farley-Murray family. The two sisters had shared the childhood trauma of losing their mother when they were five and seven years old, living a hardscrabble life as their mourning father tried to farm with another O'Nan sister and husband, and making the transition to a different family, school, and region (Loretto). Lillian, unlike my mother, did finish high school, going to Eminence, Kentucky with Uncle Roud and Aunt Kate, and later took a course in stenography. She was living with my parents in the Parkland area of Louisville when I was born, and, according to her taught me to sing "Bye Bye Blackbird" when I was one year old. My Grandfather Walker was the family musician, but Lillian was the family beauty. According to one story, in the jazz age of the 1920s, she dated (in Louisville) a nationally famous trumpet player, Clyde McCoy. It was no great surprise when the New Yorker, Wallace Murray, visited his aunt in Louisville (my grandmother Farley) that he was mesmerized by this local beauty. And she would be attracted to a good looking easterner who worked in Manhattan, played golf, and wore chic clothes. Their marriage took her to Long Island, and we made several visits there when I was still a child. The two sisters were always very close, and departures after visits were always teary affairs. Lillian and Wally were "family," helping us out in all sorts of ways when Doris and I were living in New York City. Doris and our new baby Mark stayed with them at the beginning of our second year as we waited for our apartment at Union to be finished. Wallace Murray worked in a New York City bank, commuting from Long Island, and retired from this difficult way of life as early as he was able. At this time, they moved to Florida (Sarasota), and when their two children, Wally and Marilyn, retired, they and their spouses joined them.

The O'Nan family of uncles and aunts was large (nine children of Dennis and Cassie O'Nan), scattered over several towns in Henry and Owen Counties. Being part of this family was an important part of my childhood and early adolescence. In addition to Aunt Dode (see above), two of the aunts were special in our family: Myra Mae (Auntie), and Lillian (Aunt Ninny). These were the two families we visited every summer, and the aunts and uncles I knew best. These summertime visits were longer than the vacation allotted to my father by the Ford Motor Company. My mother, brother and I would stay with Auntie (the Dunaways) or Ninny (the Smoots) for lengthy periods. Three places stand out in my memory, and with them the relatives who lived there: my great grandmother's two story brick house near the courthouse in New Castle, the Dunaway farm a mile outside of New Castle, and the Smoot house in Gratz on the Kentucky river.

When I was five, Cassandra (Cassie) O'Nan died in her bed in her two-story brick house in New Castle. How was she able to purchase and maintain that large house? I suspect she had some money from her husband, Dennis, possibly from the sale of his Inn ("saloon?") near Carrollton. I am told two things about my early childhood visits to that house. One was becoming very ill from gorging myself on cherries from the cherry tree in the front yard, thus earning a reputation for stupidity in the family. The other was my total affection for the African-American woman who apparently loved me very much and took care of me. I have sometimes wondered whether that "bonding" had anything to do with the fact that gut-level racism never took with me: that is, negative, fearful, or hostile feelings or stereotyping language about African-Americans. I do remember the occasional visit to that house when I was four or five. I liked where the house was located, directly across from the school where a World War I Howitzer canon was on display. But I didn't like the house itself. It was too big, too old, and at night, a creature would appear the adults called a "thousand legger." These harmless centipedes were on ceilings and walls, and there was always a great ado at bedtime about killing them. I was never a "good eater" in those years, but still remember the delicious biscuits and jams served in that house. "Grandmother," as she was called, was universally loved by everyone who knew her. She was tiny, and utterly sweet and gentle. Her one pride (as with most of her daughters) was her cooking. Her death was a devastating event for the family, and as a five-year-old, I could sense the intense grief of my mother and the O'Nan family. I remember being in her bedroom when one of her nephews (Dennis), a grown man, entered the room and stood sobbing by her now empty bed. As a five-year-old, I thought he had just discovered she had died by finding the bed empty, but in fact he was simply grieving her death.

The second location of our summer time visits was the farm not far from New Castle. Myra Mae ("Auntie"), the youngest of the O'Nan aunts, had married Leonard Dunaway. Her first husband had drowned swimming in a local pond. For a time she worked as the telephone operator for New Castle, inserting and withdrawing the plugs that connected or disconnected callers. On the farm she wore a bonnet while doing outside chores such as wringing the necks of unlucky chickens, churning butter, and tending a large garden. In the wintertime, she cooked on a huge iron stove that heated the kitchen. She had one daughter (from the earlier marriage), Mary Elizabeth, whose life story was filled with tragic elements: a terrible auto accident, drug addiction, a failed marriage to a physician, a second problematic marriage. My aunt and uncle left the farm to live in New Castle when he was in his late sixties.

How romantic it would be if the New Castle farm had a name. Perhaps if I had been an Anne (of Green Gables), I would have given it a name. Like Green Gables, the farm was for me a place of utter enchantment. It had no "Great White Way" or "Lake of Shining Waters"; at least, it had no such names. But it was ever a place of mystery and beauty, something that never became utterly familiar. Perhaps this was because the farm offered relations to nature not possible in the city. My friends and I would roam the city looking for vacant lots, river banks, specks of wildness where we could pretend to play jungle games. Compared to genuine and even dangerous wildness, the farm of course was tame. But to my childhood eyes and ears it was always a little wild. There was a mystery about the animals: their look, what they might do, why they acted the way they did. The "miracle" of the urban grocery store, the providing of instant and already prepared food, was replaced by another miracle, the experience of food coming directly from the earth and from animals. In one way I was never really at ease on the farm, even as I was never at ease in my childhood among downtown city crowds. In both cases I was among unpredictabilities, something a little scary. From the way the adults acted, I sensed the potential dangers of a bucking horse, the possible aggressions of sows, bulls, and the like. I don't mean that I went about constantly frightened, but I did have a kind of respect and alertness toward everyday living things: spiders, wasps, bees, snakes. Empathy with such living things (which came later) was not my mood. But my sensibility to their unpredictable behavior, their element of threat, was a way of experiencing them as real, that is, as self-determining beings. Confronted by wasps, roosters, and rams, I was unable to reduce them to the abstract pictures of a book or items found in a grocery store or a kitchen. Because I had to grant them distance and acknowledge what they might do, they were real. I came to know their characteristic sounds, smells, and ways of behaving.

Much of what the farm meant to me was its spaces. The farmhouse itself was large, a two-story frame house set back from the public road (gravel) about thirty yards. Its front yard was shaded with large buckeye trees and was flat, permitting occasional croquet games. I remember the buckeye trees because I spent many hours playing with these dark brown nuts, hollowing them out or hitting them with a stick as if they were baseballs. Like most farmhouses, the house had a central room and a distant, unused room. The central room, at least in function, was the kitchen, located in the back of the house and opening onto the back yard, thus to the well, the outhouse, the garden, and the underground smokehouse. In this room, the "house people," namely my aunts, mother, and others, in contrast to the "fields and barn" people, spent most of their time in both summer and winter. The primary items in the kitchen were its two stoves. The large black, iron stove was heated by wood and used mostly in winter for cooking and for heating the kitchen. I remember seeing a stove like that in Marjorie Rawlings's kitchen at Cross Creek. The kerosene stove was the summer stove. The unused or distant room was the living room, with its furniture covered by white sheets. I don't remember anyone other than myself ever going into that room. I cannot imagine any entertainment so important or so formal that my aunt and uncle would use that room. Its purpose, I think, was to provide a place to lay out the body of someone in the family who died. I have little memory of the rest of the house. Outside the house, the center of activity was the back yard. In or surrounding the back yard was the well, the smokehouse (a small cave-like structure), the outhouse with its Sears and Roebuck catalogues for toilet paper, and the chicken yard. Leaving the yard by way of the gate, I found myself in a large space surrounded by various buildings. (Most of these are still there.) The nearest structure was the chicken coop. Its proximity makes sense, for one had to feed chickens and collect eggs daily. Surrounding the large space were two large barns and a tool shed. One of the barns was the tobacco barn, and I had little interest in it. It was simply a big open space, to be filled at the end of the summer with racks of drying tobacco. The other barn was my second home. Cows were milked there and horses kept in its stalls. All the hay for feeding was stored in its loft, a place where I spent much of my time.

A couple of hundred yards away from the house were two ponds. These were magic places to me since beneath the surfaces of their waters swam small sunfish and catfish. One summer night, a loud explosion awakened all of us. Some locals had set off a dynamite stick in one of the ponds to kill the fish and gather them up quickly as they floated to the surface. The farm was about eighty acres, which was to my childish reckoning practically a whole nation, a space so large I never did explore it. I saw some of it riding behind my uncle on the back of an old work horse. The horse's back was so wide, I almost did the splits to straddle it. These acres were given mostly to corn, hay, tobacco, maybe some sorghum. Near the house was a sizable garden that supplied food for the summer months and for canning for the the wintertime. The routine was like any farm: planting, weeding, gathering, milking, calving, making butter, canning vegetables and jams and jellies.

How exciting it was to revisit the farm a few years ago. Apparently the farm had degenerated through lack of care in the years after my uncle and aunt sold it, but then it was purchased by the daughter and son-in-law of the poet, Wendell Berry. They restored the farm, and in their first years did traditional farming until they turned to winemaking. Today it is the Smith-Berry winery. Their daughter, an Ursula College student at the time, graciously took Doris and me on a tour of the house, the Green Gables of my youth.

Lillian (O'Nan) Smoot ("Aunt Ninnie") was married to Austin Smoot, for whom my brother, Austin, was named. He was one of two relatives in the O'Nan family I did not like very much as a child. The Smoots lived in a nice house in the tiny river town, Gratz, where he owned a small coal delivery company with one, maybe two, trucks. Gratz made New Castle seem like a metropolis. Fewer than 200 people lived in this tiny town on the Kentucky River. There was no town square. Gratz consisted of one main road through town, and "downtown" meant the area around the bridge that spanned the Kentucky River. Besides the two small churches, Baptist and Methodist, there was only one other building, a tiny store with an old fashioned ice cream bar and stools and the best ice cream I ever tasted. In spite of the intense pleasure of eating the occasional ice cream cone, I was much less interested in the drugstore than the area under the bridge leading to the river's edge. The town was a fishing town. Forty foot long circular nets for catching rough fish such as carp hung from the undersides of the bridge. A few rowboats floated at the water's edge, available to anyone who wanted to use them. In a recent visit to Gratz, I was disappointed to see that the space under the bridge was covered in weeds and there was no access to the river. A creek entered the river nearby, and a sulfur spring flowed into the creek a few yards away. Water from those springs smelled to me of rotten eggs and sewage. My uncle (and no doubt others) drank this water for "regularity." The Smoot house had the feel of a small farm. In the back was a small barn that housed a horse. There were also chickens, a garden, and a creek that provided bait (crawdads) for trot-line fishing in the river. Next to Aunt Dode, Aunt Ninnie was my mother's closest relative among the aunts. She was small, very shy, a little fearful of things, and much given to laughing with my mother at various quirky things of everyday life. She ended her days in New Castle, prone to blindness, in a small house near the courthouse.

Since our vacations were either at the New Castle farm or in Gratz, I did not know the other uncles and aunts as well as I knew the Dunaways and Smoots. Eminence, where Uncle Roud and Aunt Cecilia lived, was another town we visited. Betty Joyce, their daughter, was an occasional playmate. Aunt Meck (America) and Uncle Fred lived a few feet off the square in New Castle. She was a character, and I always liked her. Uncle Fred spent his days whittling and talking with a few other retired men at the courthouse. I never knew him to do anything other than that. Uncle Sel and Sannie were very old people who lived on a small rise outside of Gratz. When Sannie died, her funeral was the first time I experienced how the loss of a lifelong mate could evoke intense mourning. Sel had lost the wife of many decades and was beside himself with grief.

The O'Nan sisters and uncles were a generation older than my mother, hence their children had children they would be my parents age. Fortunately, there were a few nephews and nieces who were more or less my age. The ones I knew best were the children of Evan and Katherine Harrod. Katherine was the daughter of one of the O'Nan sisters, married to Evan, a lawyer in New Castle. He and the husband of Myra Mae's daughter, a doctor, were the only college educated people in the family. He was a giant for those times, possibly six and a half feet, and when he prayed at dinner table, it was an event of great eloquence and sincere piety. Their children were Pete and Carolyn. Pete was a few years younger, so my playmate, even into adolescent years, was Carolyn. As a boy Pete's close buddy was Wendell Berry, a friendship that lasted until Pete died. Carolyn, a beautiful woman, married and divorced early in her adulthood and lived near the courthouse in New Castle throughout her life. A delightful surprise came when I accidently discovered that one of Pete's children, Ginny, had continued the family tradition of both her grandfather, Evan, and her father by practicing law in New Castle and serving as the Henry County prosecutor.

One of the many gifts I received when I married Doris was a kind of second father, Dewey Kimbel. The manse of our church was next door, and the Kimbel family moved there when Doris was about thirteen. Dewey and I enjoyed a close relation through my high school and college years. He had been a famous Louisville area and Centre College athlete (track and football). He was part of the American army in France in World War I, and when the war ended won gold medals competing in track meets in France for the army. He was a member of the Praying Colonels, Centre's famous football team that beat Harvard in 1921 and has been installed in Centre's Athletes Hall of Fame. He had grown up in Parkland as I did. His personality, athleticism, and vocation as a minister, made him a natural idol and mentor before he became my father-in-law.

Yet it was not his fame, history, or role as minister but simply his person that was his primary attraction to me. As a human being, he totally lacked any features of stereotypical ministerial pomposity, "airs," or self-exaggerations. He went about his ministerial tasks of preaching and responding to the needs of those around him without "big steeple" ambitions or self-image worries. He was intelligent, honest, modest, compassionate, earthy, athletically competitive, tolerant and ever amused by the constant flow of quips and nonsense that rolled out of my mouth. His death (1962) was my first experience of intense mourning.

It should come as no surprise that I related to Doris's mother Theodora Kimbel in a very different way. Male-bonding, mentoring, religion, athletics, and a common vocation drew me to Doris's father. For me, Theodora was always "Doris's mother" rather than a mentor or close companion. She was very smart, and throughout her life displayed two seemingly opposite tendencies. On the one hand, her way of talking was a recital of the traditional values, roles, and principles of the late Victorian Presbyterianism of her era and her parents'. On the other hand, her traditionalism was never extreme, aggressive, or dogmatic, thus she could perceive and accept, not simply condemn, those about her who were different, vulnerable, problematic. Her perception of the problematic character of my own family and my internalized personality made her reticent about me as a future mate for Doris, but she was wise enough not to actually oppose the relationship. She did urge Doris to at least date other men in her first college year, a "wise and rational" parental counsel that almost brought to a close our years of adolescent love. She lived many years after Dewey Kimbel died, and in these years enjoyed many visits with our family and close relations with our children, especially with Wendy, her first granddaughter.

Ginny was Doris's only sibling, her older sister. She was in her own unique way a "presence": smart, talented, perceptive, and haunted by what is now called bipolar disease. She could be delightfully manic, the life of the party, and dangerously depressed. In those years, the biochemists had yet to come up with the drugs needed to treat this disorder. I have always suspected, however, that what prompted her to take her own life by an overdose was not simply a depressive phase of her disease but a grim prognosis for an advanced case of melanoma. Ginny was married (to Bob) and the mother of two children (David and Jim). She had many gifts. Friendships abounded in her life. She was a good writer, and had ambitions in that direction. She played the piano and organ. In her last years, the impending threat of melanoma and her more or less untreated bipolar condition made her increasingly anxious, almost frenetic in behavior. She and I were close, and Doris and I never really recovered from her death.

Ginny and Bob Nichols married shortly after their graduation (in psychology) from the University of Louisville. In these years of graduate work and early careers, the sisterly relation of Doris and Ginny and the mutual respect between Bob and me made them our closest family. There were many visits between the families each year, thus our children grew up together. Bob and Ginny gave us the loan that helped us buy our first house. Bob, like Dave Howe, was a graduate of Mayfield High School (Kentucky) and like Dave a "natural" mathematician. In his college years, he was drawn in the direction of clinical psychology by a group of gifted teachers. His hope at the time was, like some social scientists of that era, to transform the muddle of psychology into a genuine (mathematically based, causal-explanatory) science. He made progress toward that end in twin studies, sophisticated statistical methods, and eventually in the area of higher education (the National Merritt Foundation). He never abandoned his program for psychology but was discouraged that the field itself never really emerged as a true science. Bob and I were close friends, and our relation was sparked by endless arguments having to do with the quantification of human behavior and the philosophy of knowledge. His mathematical propensity and high intelligence were the grounds for his career-long hobby of Equities investments. After Ginny's death, he has enjoyed a second period of life marked by a new marriage, a new family, retirement, world travels, and companionship in Southern California.

Appendix 2

Friendships

Come walk with me, come walk with me
We were not once so few
But Death has stolen our company
As sunshine steals the dew.

—Charlotte Bronte, *Song 108*

To many who read this, what follows will simply be a list of strangers. Yet, friendships constitute much of my life and to omit them would surely distort the portrait I am painting. Friendship is a common theme in the stories and literatures of the past. It is there in the *Enuma Elish* of ancient Babylonia, in the Hebrew Bible (Jonathan and David), the *Iliad* (Achilles and Patroclus), an essay of Cicero, and a recurring concept (*philia*) in the New Testament. The concept is also puzzling. What exactly is friendship? Tersely expressed, it is an enduring, personal relation of mutual affection that takes many forms: short-lived and superficial, life-long and profound. Typically, it is an affection between people of the same gender, but there are of course exceptions to this. Some argue that cross-gender friendship is not a real possibility because sexual attraction always lurks in the background and draws the relation toward something else. The Billy Crystal-Meg Ryan movie (*When Harry Met Sally*) on a "platonic" friendship ends with that "something else." That may be a general truth but not an inevitability. Although most of my friends have been males, I have enjoyed friendships with girls since early grade school and in some instances, friendships that began in adolescence and young adulthood have endured through the rest of my life. I do have some long-term, deep friendships with a few women, and I cannot imagine my life

233

without them. When I look back over the friendships of my life, I realize that very different things formed their basis and each relationship had its own special character.

In all of my friendships mutual attractions, mutual respect, and shared interests set the tone and quality of the relation. In most cases, the friendship developed because we were thrown together in some common circumstance: an institution such as a school, department, musical group, summer camp. It should come as no surprise that schools where I have studied or taught have been the typical setting of many of my friendships. Friendships formed as I got to know students, served on committees, worked with other faculty on the problems of the institution. Nor is it surprising to me that many of my friendships, while intense at the time, did not survive when the friend and I were no longer together in the original setting. Many of the friends I shall mention are of this sort, friends known in an adolescent age music group (a dance band), graduate school, or the faculty of a school. Fortunately, for me, there have also been a few friendships, around twenty-five or so, which endured from their beginning to the present, or to the death of the friend. At this time, I remain in touch with these (living) friends. In what follows, I discuss my friendships in two parts: the friendships of different periods and institutional settings, and, some lifelong, profound friendships. For the most part, I will not include relatives here, although my relations with them were typically marked by mutual respect and affection.

A Narrative of Friendships

When I look back on seven decades friendships, I am tempted to spend many pages trying to recapture what each one meant to me. That in itself would require a book. These friends were schoolmates, neighbors, mentors, and my relation to each one had a distinctive quality. Instead, I shall quickly list the friends of various periods of my life and the sites and situations where the friendships took place.

I do remember a few special friends as early as first grade, but only one continued as a friend through high school, a boy named Don Scott. I also remember a few friends from my neighborhood and schools in the West End of Louisville. In junior high school (middle school), one of these friends was extremely intelligent, seriously abused by his family, and from the very beginning (I think) gay. He ran my campaign for election for junior high school president, and although he was smarter than just about everybody, he dropped out of high school in the tenth grade, ending his education there. In the sixth grade, I met the person who would be by girlfriend throughout junior high school, a Jewish girl, Debra Hoffman. We were too young to "date," but one of her aunts taught us to dance, and we wrote letters to each other almost every day of the school year. The relation, frowned on by her parents, ended when we went to high school. Another close friend (not a "girlfriend") was a church member, a year older than I, a budding musician (pianist) and eventual music teacher whose name was Jane Trinkle. We were "summer friends," playing tennis and traveling by city bus to a Louisville lake to swim. In these years, most of my time was spent with neighborhood boys, especially two: Larry (Posey) Gaslin, who eventually became an engineer, and Bob Keown, a victim of polio in the Louisville epidemic, whose PhD was the basis for a career in chemistry. Posey and I were "bicycle friends," spending our summer days exploring Louisville on our bikes when we were not working on people's lawns. Two life-long friendships were formed in this period (Bill Hopper and Jim Brown), and I discuss them in the next section. In my high school years, new interests, places, and schools meant new friendships. A large group of friends gathered in a teen club every weekend. A small group of high school aged boys and girls in our church congregation hung out together every Sunday afternoon. One of the boys was Bill Collins, the eventual owner of several car dealerships in the Louisville area. Another was Jesse Tully, who later worked in the graduate school administration of the University of Kentucky. Friends also came with my musical activities: church choir, the Male High marching band, also chorus, the Kenny Hale dance band, and other bands. These included Herbie Hale, a talented trumpet player who later turned professional and eventually became president of the Musician's Union in Louisville, and Bob Conklin, with whom I attended rehearsals of the Louisville Symphony Orchestra. I spent my summers outside of Louisville as camp counselor, and several close friendships formed there

The story of my friendships that began after high school is primarily a story of schools that I either attended (Centre College, Louisville Presbyterian Seminary, Union/Columbia) or at which I taught (DePauw, Pittsburgh Presbyterian Seminary, Vanderbilt). My close friends in these years were almost all men, since women were not as yet attending or teaching at seminaries, and only rarely pursuing graduate studies in religion. At Centre friendships formed by way of my fraternity, the pre-ministry students, and campus groups such as the drama club or the debate team. Some of these students became lifelong friends who remained in touch with each other for decades: thus Jim Brown, Mayo Smith (a Presbyterian minister and editor) and his wife Joanne, and Bobby Jones, who died as a young adult in an auto crash. At Louisville Seminary, I was a commuter student, and knew most of the students only in a superficial way. The faculty members I was closest to were Harry Goodygoontz (education, pastoral care), A. B. Rhodes (Hebrew Bible), and J. P. Love (biblical theology). Graduate school at Union was the site of many new friends. Friends in my own graduate field included Joe Elmore (eventually dean at Earlham College), Larry DeBoer, Jack Forstman, and Bob Lynn. The faculty members I was closest to were Bob Brown and Jack Hutchison, both of whom I assisted as a tutor and grader. Bob shortly thereafter left Union for Stanford

The philosophy and religion department at DePauw was a growing department when I arrived, staffed with a number of men my own age. These young professors and their wives developed close relationships: thus Bob and Ann Newton, Leon and Janet Pacala, and John Eigenbrodt. A close friend was the department chair, Russell Compton, who patched together a Methodist piety with far-left politics. Outside the department, two people especially were close friends. One couple was Clem and Sarah Jane Williams. He taught Medieval literature, she was a polymath who could and did teach in a variety of fields. Closest of all was E. K. Williams, with whom I taught courses on selected themes in literature.

The best and most enduring thing about my five years at Pittsburgh Seminary were the close friendships formed there. The school, a recent merger of schools from different denominations, was conflicted along several lines, and one group, not unlike the ship's crew in the movie, *Mr. Roberts*, formed friendships as they worked together on school politics. In these years, there were no women faculty members, but the friendships were always between couples, not just individuals. These included, Gordon and Phylise Jackson, Doug and Ruth Hare, Walter and Betty Wiest, David and Betty Buttrick, and George and Mary Lou Kehm. These friends who struggled together in school politics, visited an occasional night club, attended sports events, protested the Vietnam war, enjoyed their own and student parties. Most of these faculty members remained in-touch friends long after I left Pittsburgh.

Most of my teaching career was spent at the Divinity School of Vanderbilt University, and this meant a new set of decades-long faculty and student friends. During most of that time, the faculty was collegial, not politicized (as it was in Pittsburgh), was gradually becoming racially and by gender diverse. It was a relatively young faculty, in age not too distant from the students, thus, faculty and students partied together, satirized each other in skits, worked on school projects. Now for the first time, women were present both in the professional and graduate programs and on the faculty. The first women on the faculty were Sally McFague (theology, Dean), Peggy Way (pastoral care), Mary Ann Tolbert (New Testament). I will not try to list the dozens of graduate student friends of these years, although I remain in touch with some of them. Within this very collegial faculty, several groups of friends formed across the partitions of disciplines. One group included the Harrelsons, Harrods, Forstmans, Knights, Ogletrees, Peter and Eva Hodgson. In later years, I especially enjoyed the friendship of Joe (dean) and Heidi Hough and Victor Anderson (ethics), and, after retirement, John Thatamanil, a gifted teacher and scholar who was refused tenure at VDS. In the university itself, I enjoyed friendships with a number of professors in the philosophy department, especially those in continental philosophy, John Compton and Charles Scott. Joining a Big Band, the Establishment, was the occasion for a new friend, Del Sawyer, who eventually became the founding dean of the Blair School of Music. Our relation continued after both he and I left the Big Band, and I joined him in his sailing trips off of the west coast of south Florida.

In the course of my teaching and writing career, many friendships developed outside of Nashville as I attended conferences, worked on projects, and went to Europe on sabbaticals. It has been difficult to keep up with friends made abroad, but I am especially cognizant of those relations: thus, to the Irish poet, Michael O'Siadhail, and David Ford, the Regius Professor of Theology at Cambridge, and David Pailin at the University of Manchester.

Lifelong Friendships

What follows are a few short vignettes of friendships that have either continued over many years or have had a certain intensity of affection or mutuality. When I consider this list of twenty-five or so people, I realize there is something silly about it. Many others in fact belong on the list. To select these friends is something I am uneasy about, but they are friends in some special way: mentors, influences, colleagues, or simply those who have evoked a deeply felt affection. I will take them up in a rough chronological order, beginning with my adolescence. Every one of these friends is different from me in personality, interests, talents, even values, and those differences were a strong feature of the friendship. Of the twenty-five or so people, about eight of them have died. To the rest of you, I address these words of gratitude and appreciation.

Bob Allen was perhaps more of a mentor than a friend in my adolescent years (high school). He was the organist and choir director of my church congregation, played cello in the Louisville Symphony, and served as a school principal and administrator in Louisville. I learned in later years that he was gay. I was not totally surprised by the fact, but was grieved by the way it came out (front page of the newspaper) and by the nature of his and his partner's activities. He had tutored me in music theory and for a few months given me piano lessons. He was in my memory the only true "liberal" and "intellectual" in the congregation, and in fact, in all of my pre-college years. He was the only person I knew who delighted in reading and conversing about Plato, Darwin, political science, anthropology, labor unions, and dozens of other things. He was awesomely informed and also reflective. We argued about many things, most of which I was clueless about, and since that time I have come over to his side of the arguments. He was an idealist who thought people should, if possible, commit themselves to staying in and contributing to their own cities of origin, but the public scandal forced him to leave Louisville for, I think, northern Indiana. I regret losing touch with him. He was the one deeply reflective and critical mind I encountered prior to my post-High School education.

Bill Hopper, some three years older than I, was a neighbor and the son of a Presbyterian minister. He was also an unusually gifted and denominationally active minister. During my adolescent years, I knew him primarily as someone who was part of an older group. My very first date with Doris was a double date in which Bill (Bill's date was Doris's sister) drove his car to a party. Bill grew up in a family that was strongly Presbyterian and far to the left on racial and other social issues of the 1940s. In college he toured Kentucky with two or three others, breaking Jim Crow laws. After college he spent a couple of years in the Shah's Iran, where he met and married his wife, Molly. When he returned to go to seminary, he and I were classmates, and our close friendship really began at that time. He was my closest friend and counselor in those three years. Throughout his subsequent career in the Presbyterian Church, he held many levels of pastoral responsibility: pastor, Presbytery executive, missionary, mission board director, and author. He suffered a severe decline of health in the final decades of his life. Along with Bob Allen, he was the most liberal person I knew on social issues in my early years.

Jim Brown, also a neighbor, was someone I knew off and on from elementary school on. He was a fine athlete (football, track) in the army, in high school, and at Centre. He and I were roommates for two years at Centre and were lifelong friends thereafter. At Centre he was busy with football and I was spending weekends at a distant church. After a brief post-college job, he enrolled at Louisville Presbyterian Seminary, arriving there just as I graduated. He served pastorates in Washington, DC and Jeffersontown, Indiana. For years he was the "liberal" voice on a televised panel (*The Moral Side of the News*). Due to athletic injuries and other things, he had many debilitating surgeries in his retirement years. He was a gifted pastor, self-deprecating and modest, with a strong element of humor in his interactions with others.

Dan Hunt was my best friend in my high school years. We both attended Male High School but were in different circles; he in track and football, I in music. What brought us together was the YMCA camp near Fort Knox, Kentucky, where we were counselors for three summers. We spent every evening in the lodge of our unit after the campers were put to bed, listening to music, writing letters, and talking. He was a recent and fervent convert (Southern Baptist), an evangelical in the best sense, and our respective religious commitments served as a deep bond between us. He was a very fine athlete: football and track at Male and track at the University of Louisville. He could have played varsity basketball at most colleges. He was probably more attuned than I was to his high school classes, fascinated by English, writing, and poetry. His life-plan was to be a (Baptist) preacher, but that came to an end early on, and he became an elementary school teacher with occasional interim-type pastorates, and teaching in a church-based program for the education of black ministers. As a person he was smart, kind, compassionate, ever involved with his family. He was one of the gifts to my very difficult adolescence.

The next three friendships began in my years of graduate study at Union Seminary in New York. In each case, the friendship began almost instantaneously with our initial meeting. I met Jack Forstman quite by accident (a break from study in the Union quad). Each of us was drawn to something about the other. I can't really say what that was. Jack was in a course of study which would turn into a ThD in historical theology and a career as a professor (Stanford, Vanderbilt) and dean (Vanderbilt). He was gifted in many ways: languages, meticulous historical-critical scholarship, institutionally-related smarts, ease with human beings. As I think of it, humor and laughter is a factor in most of my deep friendships, and that was also the case with Jack and me. We were close friends at Union, and became closer when we were colleagues at VDS. In our retirement, we enjoyed regular sessions analyzing and sometimes disputing about textual and historical puzzles. To know Jack is also to know Shirley, his wife, who has been a close friend of both Doris and me through many decades.

It was my good fortune to run across and become friends with Bob Lynn at Union. Our friendship surprises me as I think of it. Graduate students tend not to form close friendships with people in other specialties. Education was Bob's area of graduate study. He had been a Presbyterian pastor, and his former schooling and natural gifts made him savvy in many ways I was not. His story is that I was an influence on him at Union, which always puzzled me. (I arrived at Union knowing little, and in my rush to finish early left knowing little more.) Yet, a real friendship began in those years, one that brought us together regularly when he became an officer of the Lilly Endowment. History, culture, institutions formed his ways of thinking, thus he was flexible, open to all sorts of new possibilities, framing new projects, opening up new horizons in theological education. He was an amazingly informed, careful, and critical administrator who left behind multiple strategies and programs.

I met John Fry through Bob Lynn. Fry, an editor in Presbyterian adult education in Philadephia, was looking for someone to write a series of articles and Lynn suggested me. We met in a room at Union and spent little time on his project and most of the time laughing at one thing and another. The laughing continued from that time until his death decades later. A book-length piece on John would not be sufficient to cover his interests, gusto, outrageous personality, smarts. When I met him, he had been a marine in the Pacific theater of World War II, a Colgate graduate (philosophy), a prize-winning graduate of Union, an associate pastor in Cincinnati, and now he was one of the Witherspoon Building (Presbyterian Center, Philadelphia) crazies. I finished the articles he asked for, and that began a friendship lasting until his death in 2011. As a personality he was brilliant, a natural, fluid writer, a social-political radical, a constantly amused and also outraged observer of the human comedy. I will not try to tell his story except to say that it was only because of the love and smarts of his second wife, Carol Alice, that he survived his alcohol and tobacco addictions to enjoy a retirement into his eighties. John's original passion was academic and philosophical, and that side of him showed itself in his writing and talk. As with so many of these friends, I remain puzzled by what attracted him to me. Philosophy? Humor? My internalized, cool personality? We were as different as night and day, yet loved each other over many decades.

The next three friendships formed in my years at DePauw University in Greencastle, Indiana. Don Hartsock was my (Presbyterian) pastor there. Our friendship was instantaneous. He made sure I joined the Presbytery of Indianapolis, thus moving from the "Southern" to the "Northern" branch Presbyterianism. He had been a college fullback, was a World War II and Korean war veteran, and moved through life from day to day with a mixture of great passion and deep insights. It was not a surprise that in the turbulent 1960s he was appointed Ombudsman on the UCLA campus, and later became a Peace Corps director on Palau, Micronesia. He and I played handball regularly (I always lost). The injury that ended that sort of thing for me meant an eight-day hospitalization and visits from him every day. We still enjoy occasional phone conversations.

I mentioned in a former paragraph the many friendships of my years at DePauw University and the department of religion and philosophy there. The one person (with his wife, Janet) who remained an in-touch friend over the next four decades was Leon Pacala. (He too has written a memoir for his family.) Our mutual academic interests (philosophy, theology) were close enough for us to attempt a joint project, a collection of texts in historical theology. (We never finished it.) In this case as with most other friends, we were almost polar opposites in our ways of thinking. I thought "poetically," historically, contextually, with eyes and ears focused on change, relation, and depth. He thought inferentially, beginning with a first principle and tracking deductions. He was an Aristotelian-Thomist-Barthian. I was a Platonic-phenomenological-Tillichian. He was conservative on most issues except politics. I was gradually shedding most of the conservative elements of my religious past. Yet our friendship was deep and lasting, and was renewed after he became director of the Association of Theological Schools. From that time on, we enjoyed conferences, visits, arguments. His wife Janet died in this period of his life, and after years of intense mourning he married the lovely Virginia.

At DePauw I was still young enough (middle twenties) to be close in age to my students, the result being a number of friendships especially with the majors in the department. Among these students, one friendship continues to the present day. Bob Williams and I were close even in DePauw days as he struggled with vocational decisions and grieved over the death of his father. We stayed in touch, and the friendship deepened when (for rather odd reasons), I ended up supervising his PhD dissertation on Schleiermacher in his Union Seminary PhD program. Since that time he has taught in several small colleges and the University of Illinois in Chicago. Gradually, he expanded and deepened his dissertation area, Schleiermacher and nineteenth-century German idealism, to an amazing expertise as a Hegel scholar and translator. I remain in awe of my friends (Bob, Peter Hodgson) who deep dive in the ocean of Hegel. Diving into one sentence of Hegel intimidates me.

The next three friendships began in my five years at Pittsburgh Theological Seminary. Many other faculty members (and some students) were also friends, but due to proximity, visits, or communications, these three remained especially close in the subsequent years. A constant exchange of humor was probably the initial basis for my friendship with Lynn Hinds. In my years in Pittsburgh, Lynn tried (he failed) to turn me into a pool shark. Our families greatly enjoyed each other. We went to the occasional Pirates' or Steelers' game. We both enjoyed an acquaintance with the Damon Runyon type characters, the lowest echelon of the Pittsburgh Mafia, who worked as barbers, restaurant owners, numbers runners a few blocks from school. Lynn's graduate study and field was homiletics and communications. In these years he became a well-known local TV personality due to a popular talk show. Eventually, the homiletics dropped away, and he taught and headed departments (University of West Virginia, Drury) in journalism and communications. He was sharp, articulate, witty, informed, and at the top of his field as a teacher and writer.

David Buttrick arrived at Pittsburgh Seminary after serving as a pastor in upstate New York and a stop-over with the crazies in the Witherspoon Building. He taught homiletics and worship, and continued to serve as a writer and editor for Presbyterian liturgical matters. He was a proud ex-New Yorker (Manhattan) and Union graduate, and he and I became good friends in those years and really close friends when he joined the VDS faculty at Vanderbilt. In Pittsburgh he talked about various writing projects in homiletics including an ambitious field-changing work. At Vanderbilt the talk turned into texts and over the years he wrote over twenty works in homiletics, including the promised tome. He was a sought-after preacher and lecturer, an amazingly gifted teacher of preaching, a writer and poet. He and I also shared a kind of tongue in cheek, bemused (when we were not actually appalled and outraged) perspective on the general culture, the institutions in which we worked, and our own undertakings.

In most instances, the friends of these years were very different from me in personality, interests, and abilities. In the case of George Kehm, the difference was minimal. We are in many respects very much alike. We shared a kind of *eros* or passion for theology, and looked at its challenges and issues much the same way. He was a workaholic scholar, laboring into the wee hours of the night over the whole range of biblical and church historical texts and the issues posed by Reformed and contemporary theologies. He has an encyclopedic knowledge of Continental (German) theology and had a clear-minded grasp of the issues it posed. But another common interest sealed our relation, the out of doors. Beginning in Pittsburgh days and continuing for many decades were our western Pennsylvania fishing trips, and when I moved to Nashville, we enjoyed wilderness canoeing (and fishing) from the Everglades to the Adirondacks.

I moved to Nashville in 1969 and many new friendships were formed there over the next four decades: neighbors, colleagues, musicians, church people. I can mention only a few. Robert and Kim Maphis Early were students at VDS in the early years. Music and the human comedy brought Robert and me together, and over the years we played trumpet together, haunted various bars and concert venues listening to friends and various groups, including our friend, Beegie Adair. My relation with Robert has been a constant flow of mutual comic exchanges, sparked also by his shrewd insights into almost everything. My friendship was with both Robert and Kim as individuals and with them as a couple. My life (and Doris's) has been fuller, more enjoyable because of the trips, parties, sports attendance, with Robert and Kim. I have always been awed by how Kim's intelligence, beauty, and compassion came together in one person, and our mutual sharing of each other's concerns has made us something of soulmates.

My friendship with Howard and Annemarie Harrod was also with the two of them as a couple and with each one as an individual. In my initial years at VDS, Howard and a few others constituted a small circle of very close friends who partied, politicked (in school), and went on the occasional trip together. More than anyone else in the group, Howard was willing to share his convoluted emotional life with the rest of us. My friendship with Annemarie revolved around a mutual interest in nature, the setting, the flora and fauna, the ecology of the out of doors. My relation to such things was primarily aesthetic. Her relation to nature was broader and more complex, combining aesthetic, intellectual (research), and activist dimensions.

Another four-way friendship lasting over forty years is between Doris and me and Peter and Eva Hodgson. Peter was already teaching at VDS when I arrived. His theological and pedagogical interests were both specialized and comprehensive. They included historical theology (especially of the nineteenth and twentieth centuries), systematic theology, ethics, philosophy, and the feminist and African-American theological movements from the 1960s on. At the same time he was an author of works requiring the most meticulous and linguistic scholarship, especially the German texts of Hegel. As a person and teacher, he was flexible, fair, compassionate: the very opposite of the isolated pedant. Both his published works and the multiple dissertation projects he guided are indications of a rare, energetic, and creative intelligence.

In my teaching years at Vanderbilt, I always counted it as a gift when a pedagogical relation also became a friendship. I cannot name all of these friendships. My friendship with Betty DeBerg has continued to this day. She has enjoyed a highly successful career as a college teacher (American studies and religion), administrator, and researcher in higher education. In the early years she and I introduced the new MDiv classes to the subject of inclusive language. Over the years, we have fished together, partied, and enjoyed many conversations. Treasured are my memories of and continued relations to a number of graduate students (Linda Tober,

Sister Aquin O'Neal, Linda Holler, Steve Gordy, Debbie Dodson, Father Bill McConville, and many others.

The chief administrative officer of a Divinity School (or any school of a university) is the dean. The four deans of VDS in my years of teaching were superb leaders, each with a different set of gifts, and I count all four (Walter Harrelson, Jack Forstman, Sallie McFague, and Joe Hough) as good friends. Joe Hough is in his own way an amazingly creative administrator and leader as well as human being. My friendship with Joe was also a friendship with Heidi, his wife. A cluster of personal traits make Joe a gifted academic and creative administrator. He is smart, tough, speaks with utter candor (what you see and hear is what you get), is compassionate and caring, an omnivorous reader, an incisive and risk-taking decision maker. And he has a gift for friendship, for deep relations of real affection for many people.

Different academic settings and projects have provided occasions for a number of friendships over the years. I can mention only a few. I especially enjoyed a number of friendships with people in the Vanderbilt department of philosophy. My closest friend there was Charles Scott. The Scotts were one of the families with whom Doris and I owned some acreage in the wilds of Hickman County. The two couples spent much time together in the primitive conditions of that land, and Charles and I were closely associated in our studies and writings on Continental philosophy. A series of profound and beautifully written books show why Charles became one of the leading American philosophers working in that framework. I also enjoyed knowing and learning from John Compton, another cohort in Continental and phenomenological philosophy. The Blair School of Music at Vanderbilt was of course a natural attraction to me and through the years I made a number of friends there. Besides the dean, Del Sawyer, my best friend turned out to be a late arrival, the multi-talented Carl Smith. He taught music theory—auditing that course was how I met him—and other courses in the history of harpsichord music and various esoterica. An organist, former choir director, and harpsichordist, he composed choral music including a Masque on the life of Michelangelo. His intellectual passions were broad and included religion and the sciences, poetry, film, aesthetics, and of late, Michelangelo, on whom he has written a book. A mutual interest in that strange phenomenon, theological education, served as the occasion for a deep and affectionate friendship with Barbara Wheeler. It developed over time as we were together in multiple conferences. Eventually, we coedited two books on the subject, and visited each other in Florida and at the upstate New York retreat that she and Sam own. Barbara is another person whose story calls for a book-length effort. Her intelligence is awesome and rises to the challenge of whatever she is working on: an institution, a text to be interpreted, a social trend. I have no doubt that she knows more about the details and the situation of American theological education than anyone else in the country. Her expertise also includes the issues, institutions, and history of American Presbyterianism. She is a researcher, a social analyst, a resource, and many other things. Her interests are much broader than theological education and include Europe, art, gardening, literature, politics.

Two friendships began in my several stints at Clare Hall in Cambridge University. David Ford, the Regius professor of Divinity there, warmly welcomed me to Cambridge and gave me access to a number of "inside" events and circles I would not have known about. Unfortunately, I lost touch with him when I no longer pursued my writing ventures at Cambridge. It was David who introduced me to Michael O'Siadhail, a polymath who seems to know and speak almost all the languages of Europe but whose teaching area was Celtic (Irish) languages. At one time a professor at Trinity College, Dublin University, he decided to pursue a lifelong dream of becoming a poet. He has written the most commonly used grammar and introduction to the Irish language, a number of books of poetry, and because of those books has done several tours and residences in this country.

I met Harry Douma quite by accident. He and his English wife, Sue, resided next door to the Buttrick's vacation place in Michigan, and I met him when Doris and I vacationed there. Our friendship was almost instantaneous. Neither of us ever figured out why this was so. He was the chief engineer of Ford Tractor International, an executive at the highest echelon. His world was the world of business, numbers, mechanics, administration. He was highly intelligent, tough, skeptical (his most frequent phrase was, "I don't know"), a natural mechanic, a committed Republican. On the other hand, I was an academic, a wordsmith, a musician and aesthete, a liberal Democrat. Yet, we became friends in the full sense of mutual respect and affection. He finished an upstairs garage apartment so I could spend significant summer time in study and writing there. We spent a year in Florida living near Harry and Sue in the east coast town of Stewart. Harry and I worked together on various projects in Michigan and simply enjoyed being together. In his later years, and to my regret, we fell out of touch.

I met Grant Browning in my first year in Nashville. Someone said he would be a good person to talk with about investments. (The amount of money I had to invest was laughably small.) Grant was a successful real-estate entrepreneur who in his former life had been a PhD student (ethics) at VDS and had flirted with the idea of a ministry career. His circle of friends included Nashville's most famous lawyer, a former mayor, a nationally known editor. That we would become friends is a bit of a surprise to me, but we did have some things in common. Grant never abandoned the set of issues (only the beliefs) that had lured him to graduate school, issues of religion, ethics, philosophy, and worldview, and he enjoyed probing those issues in conversations with me. He was also available on several crucial occasions of my life for advice and assistance in business matters.

Another friendship outside of the Vanderbilt faculty was with a couple, Pat and Alice McGeachy. We were initially brought together by our daughters, who were middle school friends. Pat was a Presbyterian minister who applied his considerable gifts to the challenges of pastoral ministry and at the same time was burdened with what seemed to be a family-rooted fatedness toward a clergy career, working hard to evade and avoid clerical stereotypes. He was highly intelligent, a person of multiple intellectual interests, a persistent performer (music, speeches), a political and social liberal especially focused on prisoners and ex-prisoners. Alice, who died in 2012, was a close friend of Doris, and was an actress, musician, wit, and calmer of Pat's exuberances.

APPENDIX 3

Problematics

"'You may seek it with thimbles—and seek it with care,
You may hunt it with forks and hope;
You may threaten its life with a railway share;
You may charm it with smiles and soap—'"

("That's exactly the method,") the Bellman bold
In a hasty parenthesis cried,
That's exactly the way I have always been told
That the capture of Snarks should be tried."

—LEWIS CARROLL, "THE HUNTING OF THE SNARK"

Men [*sic*] are moved to act by the lure of what looks good to them.
They eat because they hunger for food, they run because they want to
catch the train, they think because they want a prospering business,
and they also think because they want to know the fun of knowing, and
the pleasure of solving a puzzle.

—W. M. SHELDON, *GOD AND POLARITY*

Teaching and writing (various research projects) were at the center
of my thirty or so years at Vanderbilt University. In most cases, the
projects originated as I confronted, usually in the setting of teaching,
some puzzle or enigma. Most of the puzzles began with almost child-like
questions. What does it mean to think theologically? Is theology teach-
able? Is a biblical passage the defining subject of a sermon, that which

ministers preach? Are faith, human freedom, justice, or creativity in any sense beautiful? Questions of this sort have been for me the primary units of my theological work. Except for the collections of essays, most of the books I wrote had at their center a single puzzle, a problematic which called for exploration. My account of my years at the Divinity School at Vanderbilt (chapter 3) highlighted events, students, leaders, and faculty but omitted the substance and content of my work. The omission was deliberate, an act of compassion for the reader who would not eagerly enter the dense thickets of a theo-philosophical synopsis. Yet some account of what I have been up to is called for in a work of this sort. This account is not simply a quick march through my published works, something I did in the essay, "Writing," but rather a brief review of the problematics, the main puzzles, at work in my teaching and writing. I begin with a preamble on two rather general subjects: "influences" and "public theology."

Influences

I have never given much thought to how these problematics were related to my studies of ancient and modern texts, contemporary theological movements, or my peers and colleagues. I am largely unaware of just how these resources shaped my reading of the situation. Furthermore, I realize that many influences and sources of these problematics were not "theological," academic, or even "religious." I also know that any effort to track down these influences would be highly selective and even misleading. A lifetime of reading literary (poetry, fiction), scientific, cultural, and historical works as well as non-textual influences from conversations, arguments, and the mentoring from others was a constant, often subliminal source of ideas, insights, even writing styles. I am especially aware of the influences behind five recurring themes of my work. These themes are not so much the puzzles themselves (although I did extensive work on them) as the tools, the key notions of the framework for the problematics. The five themes are: dialectical thinking, determinacy, the interhuman, the negative theology, and *eros*.

Dialectic

In recent years, I have become increasingly aware of the presence of Reinhold Niebuhr in my thinking/teaching and even my life. Insights abound in virtually every line of his writings. I did include a chapter on his work in my dissertation, but after that, I did not make extensive use of his works. (Reinhold Niebuhr, ever suspicious of academic discipleship, would have approved.) What I now realize is that Niebuhr's one point—his students used to say he had only one sermon—was something I took for granted, something that became a part of my basic attitude, my responses to things, even my way of talking. That one point was the powerful dialectic, the yes and the no, the affirmation and its qualifier, ever present in his thinking, talking, and even living. His alertness and even genius was directed to the perpetual and universal tendency of human beings to "absolutize" the things they valued, depended on, worshiped. The root of this Niebuhrian dialectic was not ancient Greece, and only at a distance Søren Kierkegaard. My best guess is that the prophets of the Hebrew Bible were the voices drumming in his ears. But I also think his yes and no came from Niebuhr himself, not from his autonomy or creativity, but his experience of fallibility and grace. Graced by Niebuhr's one point, I tried to apply his dialectic to everything: psychological impulses, personal attachments, political and religious loyalties.

Determinacy

A second influence was Friedrich Schleiermacher. In graduate school I was able to give only brief and superficial attention to Schleiermacher. When I did finally turn to those difficult texts, what grasped and held me was not the "traditional Schleiermacher" of most of his interpreters, the father of liberal theology's turn to the self, experience, feeling, and the like. It was his determined resistance to abstraction. Platonist (of a sort) though he was, he was ever alert to the seduction of the general, the principle, the essence. Thus, his explorations of things tracked the alteration of features (essences) by determinacy (*Bestimmtheit*), by the unique specificity of the particular. This is why he could not and would not reduce "Christianity," an abstraction, to individual feeling, the standard misreading of his work. For Schleiermacher, "Christianity" arose and persisted through time as a determinate historical community, something that is lost when the interpreter ignores its particularity. In this sense Karl Barth's theology is a Schleiermacherian theology.

Via Negativa

The 1,500-year-old tradition of "negative theology" (perhaps even a 2,500-year-old tradition found in the Hebrew prophets and Brahmanic Hinduism) generates another kind of dialectical thinking that the term, *mystical theology* tends to obscure. Pseudo-Dionysius, the anonymous source of some sixth-century works in the Platonic tradition, formulated the most radical version of "negative" or qualifying language in the history of Christianity. It was radical, not because it affirmed the metaphorical (*kataphatic*) character of liturgical and theological language but because it called for a negation of the negation itself. If one does not do that, then the negative statement takes on the character of a description, a positive claim. For instance, "God does not and cannot change" becomes a straightforward, literal or metaphysical claim. For Pseudo-Dionysius, God is beyond, not coincident with any affirmation and negation, and with that, we have a new theological ball game. Eventually, I realized that this radical undermining of direct language applies not only to God but to all language about anything actual.

The Interhuman

I have already given an account of the importance of Edmund Husserl and the phenomenological movement in the beginning phases of my projects. While never completely abandoned, Husserl's initial venture in "transcendental phenomenology" focused more and more on concreteness (e.g., life-world), uncovering the way the modes of experience (intentionality) and the contents or objects of experience were inseparably linked to each other. This general structure led Husserl to life-world, intersubjectivity, and "phenomenological psychology," elements or dimensions of the activity of knowing, meaning, experiencing. Fascinated with the theme of intersubjectivity, I broadened my textual inquiries to include a group of Jewish philosophers (Rosenzweig, Buber, Schutz, and Levinas), each of which offered new and profound analyses of human interrelation. Their works opened up the dense structure of human sociality, the phenomenon of meeting or encounter, the "face of the other," the mysteries of the ethical. Thus, the interhuman became for me a theological constant, present in some way in all of my subsequent analyses.

Eros

No single author is the source of this fifth influence. In mid-twentieth century, one would expect Sigmund Freud to be the primary source on those who stress the pre-rational needs, drives, passions, and subconscious inclinations at work in human beings. In my case, what got my attention to such things was the great "rationalist" of the ages, Plato, and his notion of *eros* as a way of understanding human beings. Later, I would broaden the notion with the help of Jonathan Edwards, Maurice Blondel (*Action,* 1893), and Henri Bergson (*Creative Evolution).* What these texts have in common is a philosophical anthropology of passion, striving, desire. In a sense, I find such an anthropology in Kant (the Third Critique) when he discusses *Lust,* and *Unlust,* forces more primordial than even human knowing. What such anthropologies do is to display the ways the intellect (knowing, experiencing, understanding) is engendered and shaped by the pre-cognitive strivings of the human being. Such a notion was, along with the intersubjective, at the center of my book *Good and Evil.*

Public Theology

The problematics, that is, the puzzles and issues of my published works, are continuous with those we find in centuries Western academic settings. When I reflect on that fact, I am torn between the need to issue an *apologia* (defense, justification) and a *mea culpa* (a confession of guilt and regret). These problematics arise in and express the "modern" era more than the pre-modern or postmodern. The religious and academic influences of my adolescence were pre-modern (conservative),and those my graduate education were modern. In the mid-twentieth century, civil rights and feminist issues were just beginning to impact the field of theology and its educational settings. In that era, only the occasional theologian allowed these issues to alter the very meaning of theology and change the traditional problematics: thus, Robert MacAfee Brown, Beverly Harrison, James Cone. A number of theologians of my generation began their work as modernists, addressing the traditional *loci* of theology and problems of method, but in later years turned their attention to nuclear, racial, and feminist and gender issues: thus, Gordon Kaufman, Langdon Gilkey, Sallie McFague, Peter Hodgson, John Cobb. It is clear to me that if my projects had had their beginning in the 1980s and 1990s, they would have struggled with a different set of problematics, and to my great pleasure, my students typically moved to the postmodern when they placed the burning moral issues of oppression and liberation at the center of their work. Such is my *mea cupla*, my regret for my preoccupation with a tangled, obstinate set of puzzles when everything is blowing apart and when new paradigms of theological thinking are being born.

In the past four decades, the frontier, or to change the metaphor, the center of theological work in many theological schools has been the struggles of oppressed or marginalized peoples: women, LGBTs, African Americans, the disenfranchised poor. That frontier or center appears now to be broadening. The present generation of theologians face a new problematic, the fate of "religion" itself, the very character of religion, the new and bitter conflicts between religions, the profound insights of ritual communities other than their own, all of which call for a new kind of theologian, a broadened agenda for theology, and a new kind of education. Most theologians, even recent graduates, are not prepared for life on this frontier, and the issues typically have not been part of their education and dissertation research. Here lies another set of problematics, calling for *mea culpas* to be voiced in the future.

Given my *mea culpa*, my *apologia* has failure built into it from the start. The *mea culpa* undermines any self-confident defense or justification I can marshal for my problematics. Thus, I can only say at this point that these problematics are perennial and deserve attention. I remember my initial reaction to the new liberation theologies, combining both deep sympathy (an "of course" response) and serious criticism. As to criticism, I was less than enthusiastic about the theological traditionalism, a kind of neo-orthodoxy, which seemed to characterize much of the literature. I did see these authors as opening a space for a new anti-authority theology, but the old authorities and the traditional way of using them were still in place. Further, I resisted what seemed to me to be a narrowing of the whole venture of theology to ethical issues, thus implying (or stating) a discrediting of centuries of theological movements and texts and most of what was happening in the present. This resistance may be simply an after-the-fact rationalization on my part, but I saw theology ever open to many frontiers: ethical and local, public, confessional, apologetic-philosophical, systematic, speculative. I still think this because all historical eras and cultural situations are multi-dimensional and stratified, and these situations call for a pluralism of callings, gifts, and agendas. All of these styles and agendas together, at least so I hope, can and do "change the world." The nit-picking linguistic and textual criticism of certain specialists in New Testament undermines fundamentalist paradigms and the authority theologies that serve as rationales for oppressive movements. Similarly, Medieval historians whose work expose the fallibilities, the cruelties of an era, a movement, a church leader, or whose work discovers a long ignored textuality (e.g., women contemplatives) make their contribution to world change. Accordingly, I resist the bicameral or dualistic separation of world-change theologies versus all other kinds. In past eras, there were controversies over "academic" issues, the outcome of which "changed the world" in important ways: for instance, the fundamentalist-modernist controversy of the first decades of the twentieth century. I remain convinced that wherever there is "religion," there are self-absolutizing, literal-mythological, and oppressively cruel tendencies toward conflict and violence, and the best and most vital religions (or periods of religion) are those in which various kinds of critical explorations confront these dark tendencies. These tendencies ever generate ideologies, paradigms, of interpretation and imageries, which call for exposure and analysis. This in fact is what deconstructive, post-modern movements are doing. My *apologia* is that my own problematics may do something of this sort, uncovering and criticizing centuries-old, deeply buried paradigms that provide the framework for institutional oppressive policies. In other words, I see these problematics of method, education, or human transformation as paradigm critique and the paradigms in question have been operative in slavery, sexism, homophobia, and ethnocentrism. Such an *apologia* does not, I realize, erase my *mea culpa*, my regret that I have not sufficiently and explicitly addressed the social issues of my era.

Four Problematics

"Problematics" as a term may mislead more than clarify the subjects of my writings. It does point to the *problem* as the unit and focus on my inquiries. But these problematics are not simply discrete puzzles but also "phenomena," dense clusters of things in process. Thus, for instance, a particular kind of community has arisen and endured over time that confronts the interpreter or inquirer with a "problematic," as does a set of behaviors whose matrix is some sort of vulnerability and anxiousness.

In the broad sense, each of my works is a journey into a problematic, a kind of unraveling or sorting out, but each work contains many problematics, each of which is a challenge to the inquirer: thus human beings as "self-presencing," "human evil as intersubjective," or language about God as a mixture of metaphors and qualifiers. In this brief account of my work over the years, I shall select four general areas of problematics: the problematics of method (knowing, procedure, assessment), the problematics of human beings, the problematics of the manifested and unknown God, and the problematics that arise with "practical theology," especially education.

The Problematics of Method

Prior to writing *Ecclesial Man* and *Ecclesial Reflection,* I had worked for a number of years assembling certain tools of reflective inquiry that might help uncover whether, how, in what sense religious communities (and their members), traditions, teachings, and religious convictions have to do with anything actual or "real." To put the question this way signals that the "authorities" (textual, synodical, papal, hierarchical) that preside over or embody such things have no immunity to error, nor are their contents in an *a priori* way identical with what is true, real, or factual. That the beliefs, teachings, doctrines, and narratives of those communities display genuine insights seems evident. One cannot read the Psalms, sing the hymns, pray the prayers, peruse the confessions, or review the controversies of these communities without sensing the presence of profound insights. The problem was how to get at that which generated these insights, made them possible. I have already described one of the results of my application of social phenomenology to the problem, the exploration of how a community's intersubjectivity (the structures of human co-intentions enduring through time) could deliver and even constitute certain facticities about the world, human beings, their fragility, corruption, and possible remaking. In other words, relations of mutuality and other liturgical and narrative expressions manifest things (mysteries) about certain human possibilities.

The general problem of faith's cognitive dimension included a second challenge, namely how one could use philosophical tools (social phenomenology) to study a community of faith without losing or violating its determinate character. I learned later that all inquiries, acts of knowing, research projects involving categorization, explanations, claims, faced this challenge. Even in the everyday world, we know what we know by way of types or categories, thus we identify our dwellings as "houses," our religious particularities as "religions," "denominations." But any actual thing is a uniquely specific flow of processes, never the same from second to second, comprised of uncountable events and contents, and occupying a distinctive place in space and time. Thus, its similarities to other things (generalizable features) such as bodily organs, scales, rationality, typical behaviors do not as such constitute its concreteness. A specific human person, constituted by uncountable organic events taking place in 75 trillion cells is never simply a type or category. And all the category terms ("humanity," "evil," and "freedom") are modified in actual processes of being or behavior. Accordingly, the inquirer's task is not only to discover the type, cause, structure, or behavioral pattern but how these things are modified by the particularity of individuals and communities. This was my challenge and task as I tried to understand faith, the ecclesial community, its narratives of redemption. I tried to be alert to the ways general categories could obscure and suppress the distinctiveness of any existing entity or group. I realize that the categories strewn throughout my writings are abstractions. There is nothing distinctive about that, since abstraction is inevitable to knowing itself, not only in its formal or "precise" mode (the sciences, the philosophers, humanistic scholarship) but in everyday cognitive acts. But I tried to voice the abstractions in a way that would disclose the way the particularity of a thing undermined or qualified the concepts used to communicate it. I tried to show how the features born in social science or phenomenology were altered when embedded in particularity. Thus, desire, intentionality, even evil and freedom, undergo alterations of meaning in their setting in ecclesial existence, and that existence itself undergoes alteration in every individual instantiation, every person. I called this modification of types and generalities, even the specific adjectives, names, verbs, by concreteness, "the principle of positivity," and in the course of many investigations over the years, I applied it to such things as beauty, preaching, education, symbols (deep social values), and even theology.

The principle of positivity found explicit expression in *Ecclesial Man*, and it became a bridge to my second work on method, *Ecclesial Reflection*. Here I faced a new problematics, not the question of the "realities" (mysteries) that haunt the world of faith but how one might assess and make judgments about the discourse of faith. If we are not simply citing textual and other authorities when we do this, what are we doing? The first step in this project was negative, a clearing of weeds, a historically oriented deconstruction of authority theology that identified it as a paradigm, uncovered the assumptions it was built on, and tried to expose why those assumptions are arbitrary, absolutistic, or even contradictory to faith itself. The result of this negative step was an abandonment of both the traditionally conservative and the liberal versions of how theological judgments could be made. The traditional version, citing "authoritative" texts, authors, confessions, had the character of a restatement, and called for a second interrogation that asked why or how the original text or synod was an unquestionable unit of truth. Placement in the flow of historical events, fallibility, moral ambiguity, and many other things made it clear that no authority had an unquestionable status. The liberal version, translating the accumulated doctrinal contents of tradition into general moral or philosophical maxims, was purchased at the cost of the particularity or concreteness of the faith community. In the land of the theological liberal, the moral generality reigned. I was satisfied that "something" was there, a mysterious facticity, in the ecclesial community. (I would say the same thing about other religious and non-religious communities that arose in history, left their mark, created texts, endured through time in distinctive kinds of mutuality.) That "something" was not the "house of authority," not the accumulated interpretations of councils, theologians, or prelates but the "thing itself," the set of freedom-bestowing, human transforming events manifested both in the community's narratives and its distinctive intersubjectivity. What else could theologians or believers be subject to but that which occurs when they believe, proclaim, teach, make judgments? This second problematic theme, then, set the task of discerning how the mysteries and insights displayed in the texts and narratives of the ecclesial community originated in transformative freedom. Is this Schleiermacher, Paul Tillich, Reinhold Niebuhr *redidivus*? Probably so. In saying this, I realize that I, like many of my peers, have not left the land of liberal theology.

The Problematics of Human Transformation

Methodological or foundational inquiries were my major projects in the 1980s. (Some colleagues thought I would never emerge from the cavern of foundationalism.) But a second trans-methodological problematic had been astir in my teaching and reflection all along. This had to do with the possibility that even in their corrupted historical setting, human beings could be transformed. "Something" seemed to be at work in the narratives, liturgies, history, and even structure of the ecclesial communities that was transformative, a "good news" or gospel of human empowerment and freedom. Apart from this Mystery behind the mysteries, none of the other themes of theology and liturgy (God, eschatology, church, Christology, even scripture) came to life or even made much sense. Presupposed by these thematics was something actual and available to human beings in their fragile lives, their pitiful struggle for meaning, their various enslavements and idolatries. Here then is a problematics, a task of inquiring into human salvific transformation not just of individuals but of human beings together in communities, societies, and institutions.

The structure of this problematic was not unlike the others. My aim was to understand the dynamics that bestowed on human beings a liberating freedom. The location of these dynamics (self-transcendence, anxiety, suffering, desire) was the human being in its concreteness. I couldn't grasp human frailty, evil, or freedom and ignore the particularity of human beings themselves, and that meant their biological constitution, strange temporality, intersubjectivity, meaning-orientations. It was just such things that were operative in but altered by the impact of suffering, the lure of idolatry, the loss of self-esteem. The problematic, thus, was not a single logical puzzle but a tangled concreteness. And although the things I list here are "general," all of them undergo modification in their actual presence in the human being's (including each human individual) situation. Thus human self-absolutizing presupposes and alters the *eros* structure of the self, and human transformation presupposes and transforms corrupted *eros*. Tracing these alterations was the project of the work *Good and Evil*.

The Problematics of Divine Concealment

A similar problematic arose when I took up the "theme of all themes" in theology, the creative power at work in human transformation. The situation and dynamics of human transformation was that which supplied the discourse about God with content (metaphors, anti-metaphors, narratives). Here too we have an ever-present undermining of the interpretive language at work, but in this case, what qualifies the language and renders its metaphors unstable is not a concreteness we experience but the ultimate mystery of God. No term stands still, not even the name, God, not the negations and qualifiers, not even formal terms like "exist" or numbers. This problematic then is unique. How can one understand the way in which this unthematizable (non)entity comes to discourse, belief, worship? (It never comes into view.) More specifically, how is it that the salvific transformation of human beings is unthinkable apart from "God" or "Gods"? As quantitative and mathematical terms, singularity and plurality are both metaphors, not direct descriptions of sacred power. The problematic then was to understand why an ultimate Mystery was connected to human transformation, and why that connection brought about a specific cluster of metaphors: power, love, creativity, justice.

Practice and Practices

The fourth problematics was a set of curiosities and puzzlements which arose in my graduate school years, and found expression in my earliest published essays. I was active in those years as an ordained minister in a variety of denominational and congregational settings, and therefore struggled with the challenges and issues presented by preaching, church education, pastoral care. I concluded early on that the primary meaning of "theology" was not a noun, a body of beliefs or doctrines, but a verb, an activity or process of reflection, interpretation, inquiry. If that is so, then it seemed utterly arbitrary to restrict that activity to ordained clergy, to teachers in degree-granting schools, to professionals of various sorts. Because of their setting and vocation, ministers and professors do have distinctive ways of pursuing theology, but why the restriction? My growing suspicion was that theology originated in the puzzles, curiosities and even spiritual needs of people whose lives are shaped in a religious community, thus the term is applicable to any and all who would draw on the community's narratives to interpret their own situation or the events of their world. In the broadest sense of the term *theology*, atheists and agnostics may be theologians even if they eschew the term. It is only a short step from thinking about theology in this way to the notion that both youth and adult education in congregations should have a theological character. This early broadening of the meaning of theology was the background for three closely related themes of activity and inquiry in later years: theology as irreducible to clerical or academic settings, the suppression of education in adult church education, and the reduction of theology to a single field or department in theological education.

As to the first theme, it seems evident that to restrict theology to church leaders or scholars is at the same time to withhold it from the laity. This withholding, this assumption that others (pastors, et al.) do theological thinking on behalf of or to instruct the laity, turns theology into a kind of priestly mediation of insight, truth, relevance. As to the second theme, the Protestant Reformation, eschewing as it did all things Catholic, made the act of preaching so liturgically central as the means of grace and the presence of a divine Word that the centuries-long tradition of contemplation was marginalized. With contemplation out of the picture, and preaching (and ministers of the Word) at the center, the education of the laity could not have and should not have a theological character. Furthermore, the various roots and contents, texts and issues of theology having to do with the New Testament, the history of Christianity, the confessions and controversies, all fell outside of lay education. The result was that "education" in the congregations could only mean nurture, spiritual formation, personal (psychological) issues minus study and minus theology. I have no quarrel with "spiritual formation" except to say that it is something that one would expect to occur in and through all the events of a congregation: its music, liturgy, pastoral care, outreach activities, and, of course education. As such, spiritual formation is too general a category to define or constitute the church's education.

Theological education, the third theme, was the institutional setting of my teaching and writing. In this setting, "theology" suffered a third narrowing, not just to clergy expertise or scholarly work, but to a specific department in a curriculum. This narrowing had the unfortunate consequence of separating other academic fields of the theological school from their matrix in the faith community and forcing each field to create its identity and sphere as a professional guild and (non-theological) academic specialty. This narrowing took place when specific schools or programs of pastoral education came into being, the result being a curricular structure (encyclopedia) of more or less separated academic fields. Thus arose the problematic that was the focus of a number of my practical theology writings from the 1980s on.

These three problematics, a broadened way of understanding theology, church education, and theological education, gave rise to a fourth, rather general, problematic and question. If theological thinking is something that can and should go on in the everyday lives of church people and across the fields of theological schools, what is the character of that theology? I had worked on the problematics of method using philosophical and other instruments and sources of reflection, a task quite appropriate to my "field," systematic theology. But what might theological thinking mean to a layperson, to a pastor preparing a sermon or doing counseling, or to teacher whose area is homiletics or church polity? There does appear to be something all of these have in common, a certain way of thinking, namely a reflection (contemplation?) whose occasion is the practices of everyday life, the life-situation at hand, life amidst the corruptions and possibilities of institutions. In the theological schools, there was a general term for this activity: "practical theology." The term, however, reflected the field-oriented, professionally narrowed meaning of theology, and therefore was a category used to organize a cluster of pastoral fields and give them a professional identity. As a field or cluster of fields term, it too excluded the reflective life of ministers themselves and of the laity, an exclusion that had at the same time the character of a suppression. In actuality, laypersons, pastors, church leaders were constantly struggling with, assessing, applying the narratives, texts, and symbols of faith in their life situations. Pastors did this in their preaching, counseling, and their decisions about liturgy. Church leaders (elders, denominational leaders) did this when they wrestled with matters of church growth, conflicts, polity. I concluded that there was at a general level a distinctive theological activity common to laity, church leaders, and teachers in seminaries, a thinking about and critical response to a variety of life situations in and through the resources and narratives of faith.

Curriculum Vita

Edward Farley

Personal

Birth, 1929, Louisville, Ky.
Parents, Raymond L. and Dora M. Farley.
Family: Brother, Charles Austin Farley. Spouse, Doris Kimbel Farley.
 Children, Mark Kimbel Farley, Wendy Farley, Amy Catherine
 Howe.

Education

Louisville Male High School in Louisville, Kentucky.
Centre College in Kentucky, BA, 1950.
Louisville Presbyterian Seminary, BD, 1953.
Graduate Study: Union Theological Seminary, New York and Colum-
 bia University, PhD in Philosophy of Religion and Ethics, 1957.

Post-Doctoral Studies

University of Basel, Switzerland.
University of Freiburg, summer 1970.
Clare Hall (Cambridge University), 1994, 1996.

Teaching

Summer programs of Centre College and the University of Louisville.

Graduate Assistant at Columbia University and Union Theological Seminary.

Instructor, Assistant Professor at DePauw University, Indiana, 1957–63 (philosophy and religion).

Pittsburgh Theological Seminary, Associate Professor, 1962–68, Professor, 1966–68.

Vanderbilt University, 1969–98, Professor of Theology.

Drucilla Moore Buffington Professor Emeritus, Divinity School, Vanderbilt University, 1997.

Awards and Fellowships

Fielding Lewis Walker Scholarship in Systematic Theology, Louisville Presbyterian Seminary.

Kent Fellowship.

Lilly Fellow in Religion, 1962–63; Lilly grant, 1982–83, and 1986–89 (theological education), and 1994.

ATS Fellowship, 1969–70; 1975–76; 1988–89.

University and summer Fellowships (Vanderbilt): 1975–76; 1988–89, 1993.

Who's Who in the Southeast; Who's Who in Religion; Outstanding Educators of America; Dictionary of International Biography.

Outstanding Alumnus, Centre College, 1985.

LLD, DePauw University, 1985; Phi Beta Kappa, Beta Chapter of Kentucky, 1991.

Earl Sutherland Award for Excellence in Research, Vanderbilt University, 1991.

Lifetime Fellow, Clare College, Cambridge University, 1994.

Festschrift, *Theology and the Interhuman: Essays in Honor of Edward Farley*, ed. Robert Williams, 1995.

American Academy of Religion, Award for Excellence, theology area, for *Divine Empathy*, November, 1996.

Hall of Fame, Louisville Male High School, 1998.

Outstanding Alumnus Award of 2004, Louisville Presbyterian Theological Seminary.

Doctor of Divinity, Centre College, May 23, 2004.

Unitas alumnus, alumna award, Union Theological Seminary, NY,
October, 2004.

Professional Societies

The New Haven Theological Discussion Group.
American Philosophical Association; American Academy of Religion.
The Society of Religion in Higher Education.
The Society for the Study of Process Philosophies.
Society for Phenomenology and Existentialist Philosophy.
American Theological Society; Workgroup in Theology.
"Theology and the Phenomenological Movement," a Seminar of the
American Academy of Religion (1985–91).
Phi Beta Kappa.

Miscellaneous

Member of editorial board, Vanderbilt University Press, 1993–96.
Member of Board of Advisors, "Theology through the Arts," Cam-
bridge, England (1997–2000).
Member of American Federation of Musicians, Local 257.
Retired from Nashville Presbytery.
Member, International Advisory Board, "New Critical Thinking in
Theology and Biblical Studies," Ashgate Publishing Ltd., 1999.
Member, Committee of Visitors, *Harvard Divinity School,* 2004–2008.

Music

[trumpet, flugelhorn] 1940s dance bands, Louisville, Ky.; 1960s, jazz
combo, Pittsburgh; Member, The Establishment 1975–95; John
Bell band (occasional); Falcon Flight, jazz combo; Vanderbilt
Symphony Orchestra, late 1980s.
[voice] Amati, Amahl and the Night Visitors (1960), Bach Choir and
Pittsburgh Opera; Theatre Nashville 1970s.
[piano] Member, Monday Night Jazz Band, 1999–2010; Duo, Patsy
Kirby, Ed Farley, 2011–present.

Lectureships

The Schaff Lectures, Pittsburgh Theological Seminary, 1975.

The Mendenhall Lectures, DePauw University, 1985.

The Rauschenbusch Lectures, Northern Baptist Seminary.

The Larkin-Stuart Lectures, Trinity College of the University of Toronto, 1992.

Caldwell Lectures, Louisville Presbyterian Theological Seminary, 1994.

Fall lectures (with Wendy Farley), Memphis Theological Seminary, 1999.

Ferguson Lectures, University of Manchester, 1998.

Cole Lecture, Vanderbilt Divinity School, 1997.

Killeen Chair Lecture Series, St. Norbert's. Fall, 2001

Hastings College Pastor Series.

Publications

BOOKS

The Transcendence of God: A Study in Contemporary Philosophical Theology. Philadelphia: Westminster Press, 1960.

Requiem for a Lost Piety: The Contemporary Search for the Christian Life. Philadelphia: Westminster Press, 1966.

Ecclesial Man: A Social Phenomenology of Faith and Reality. Philadelphia: Fortress Press, 1975.

Ecclesial Reflection: An Anatomy of Theological Method. Philadelphia: Fortress Press, 1982.

Theologia: The Fragmentation and Unity of Theological Education. Philadelphia: Fortress Press, 1983.

The Fragility of Knowledge: Theological Education in the Church and the University. Philadelphia: Fortress Press, 1988.

Good and Evil: Interpreting a Human Condition. Minneapolis: Augsburg/Fortress, 1990.

Divine Empathy: A Theology of God. Minneapolis: Augsburg/Fortress, 1996.

Deep Symbols: Their Postmodern Effacement and Reclamation. Edinburgh: T&T Clark, 1997.

Faith and Beauty: A Theological Aesthetic. Hampshire, England: Ashgate, 2001.

Practicing Gospel: Unconventional Thoughts on the Church's Ministry. Louisville: Westminster John Knox, 2003.

Wheeler, Barbara and Edward Farley, eds. *Shifting Boundaries: Contextual Approaches to the Structure of Theological Education.* Louisville: Westminster John Knox, 1991.

Long, Thomas G. and Edward Farley, eds. *Preaching as a Theological Task: World, Gospel, Structure.* Louisville: Westminster John Knox, 1996.

Chapters In Books

"Psychopathology and Human Evil: Toward a Theory of Differentiation," in eds. R. Bruzina and Martinus Nijhaff Wilshire, *Cross Currents in Phenomenology.* The Hague. Vol. 7 of Selected Studies in Phenomenology and Existential Philosophy, 1978.

"Toward a Contemporary Theology of Human Being," in eds. J. William Angell and E. Pendleton Banks, *Images of Man; Studies in Religion and Anthropology.* Macon, GA: Mercer University Press, 1984.

"Theocentric Ethics as A Generic Argument," in eds. Harlan R. Beckley and Charles M. Swezey, *James M. Gustrafson's Theocentric Ethics: Interpretations and Assessments.* Macon, GA: Mercer University Press, 1988.

"Praxis and Piety: Hermeneutics beyond the New Dualism," in eds. Douglas A. Knight and Peter Paris, *Justice and the Holy: Essays in Honor of Walter Harrelson.* Atlanta: Scholars Press, 1989.

"Truth and the Wisdom of Enduring," in ed. Daniel Guerrière, *Phenomenology of the Truth Proper to Religion.* Albany: State University of New York Press, 1990.

"Phenomenology," in eds. D. Musser and Joseph L. Price, *New Handbook of Christian Theology.* Nashville: Abingdon Press, 1992.

"The Tragic Dilemma of Church Education," in eds. P. Palmer, B. G. Wheeler, and J. W. Fowler, *Caring for the Commonweal: Education for Religious and Public Life.* Macon, GA: Mercer University Press, 1990.

"Ecclesial Contextual Thinking," in ed. Darren C. Marks, *Shaping a Theological Mind: Theological context and Methodology.* Aldershot, England: Ashgate, 2002.

Selected Articles

"Can Revelation be Formally Described?," *Journal of the American Academy of Religion*, Vol. XXXVII, No. 3, September, 1969.

"Phenomenology and the Problem of Metaphysics," *Man and World*, Vol. 12, No. 4, 1979.

"The Place of Theology in the Study of Religion," *Religious Studies and Theology*, Vol. 5, No. 3, September, 1985.

"Thinking Toward the World: A Case for Philosophical Pluralism in Theology," *American Journal of Theology and Philosophy*, January, 1993.

"Theological Education and the Arts: Four Comments," *Theological Education: Sacred Imagination, the Arts and Theological Education*, Vol. XXXI, Number 1, Autumn, 1994.

"Four Pedagogical Mistakes: A Mea Culpa," *Teaching Theology and Religion*, Vol. 8, no. 4, 2005

"Fundamentalism: A Theory," *Cross Currents*, 2005

Unpublished Books

The Magic Window: Poems for Children Young and Old

Teaching What is Unteachable: The Abstract and the Concrete in Religious and Theological Studies

Bibliography

Ager, Ben. *The Decline of Discourse: Reading, Writing, and Resistance in Postmodern Capitalism*. New York: Falmor, 1990.

Arum, Richard, and Joseph Roksa. *Academically Adrift: Limited Learning on College Campuses*. Chicago: University of Chicago Press, 2010.

Bloom, Harold. *How to Read and Why*. New York: Scribners, 2001.

————. *A Western Canon: The Books and School of the Ages*. New York: Riverhead, 1995.

Butler Books (with the Louisville Chamber of Commerce and the University of Louisville). *Louisville Then and Now*. Louisville: 2006.

Caplan, Brian D. *The Myth of the Rational Voter: Why Democracies Choose Bad Policies*. Princeton: Princeton University Press, 2007.

Cardozo, Benjamin N. *The Nature of the Judicial Process*. New Orleans: Quid Pro Law Books, 2010.

Cicero, Marcus Tullius. *Old Age; On Friendship; On Divination*. Translated by W. A. Falconer. Loeb Classical Library, No. 154. Cambridge, MA: Harvard University Press, 1923.

Delbanco, Andrew. *College: What It Was and What It Should Be*. Princeton, NJ: Princeton University Press, 2012.

Ferguson, Niall. *Civilization: The West and the Rest*. New York: Penguin, 2011.

Gergen, Kenneth. *The Saturated Self: Dilemmas of Identity in Contemporary Life*. New York: Basic, 1991.

Graetz, Michael J. *The End of Energy: The Unmaking of America's Environment, Security, and Independence*. Cambridge, MA: MIT Press, 2011.

Handy, Robert T. *A History of Union Theological Seminary in New York*. Grand Rapids: Eerdmans, 2002.

Johnson, Dale A., ed. *Vanderbilt Divinity School: Education, Context, and Change*. Nashville: Vanderbilt University Press, 2001.

Kohan, Erazim. *The Embers and the Stars: A Philosophical Inquiry into the Moral Sense of Nature*. Chicago: University of Chicago Press, 1987.

Lasch, Christopher. *The Culture of Narcissism: American Life in an Age of Diminishing Expectations*. New York: Norton, 1978.

Lessing, Lawrence. *Republic Lost: How Money Corrupts Congress and a Plan to Stop It*. New York: Twelve Books, 2011.

Levinas, Emmanuel. *Humanism and the Other*. Translated by Nidra Poller and Richard A. Cohen. Champaign: University of Illinois Press, 2005.

Lyotard, Jean-Francois. *The Postmodern Condition: A Report on Knowledge.* Theory and History of Literature, vol. 10. Translated by Geoff Pennington and Brian Massumi. Minneapolis: University of Minnesota Press, 1984.

McKim, Donald, and William J. Carl. *Ever a Vision: A Brief History of Pittsburgh Theological Seminary 1959–2009.* Grand Rapids: Eerdmans, 2009.

Murray, Charles. *Coming Apart: The State of White America 1960–2010.* New York: Random House (Crown Forum), 2012.

Niebuhr, Reinhold. *The Self and the Dramas of History.* New York: Scribners, 1955.

Noah, Timothy. *The Great Divergence: America's Growing Inequality Crisis and What We Can Do About It.* New York: Bloomsbury, 2012.

Nussbaum, Martha. *Not for Profit: Why Democracy Needs Humanities.* Princeton, NJ: Princeton University Press, 2010.

Nutt, Rick L. *Many Lamps, One Light: Louisville Presbyterian Theological Seminary, a 150th Anniversary History.* Grand Rapids: Eerdmans, 2002.

Rieff, Philip. *Fellow Teachers.* Chicago: University of Chicago Press, 1972.

Schuler, Gunther. *The Swing Era: The Development of Jazz 1930–1945.* New York: Oxford University Press, 1991.

Scott, Charles. *The Lives of Things.* Bloomington: Indiana University Press, 2002.

Simon, George T. *The Big Bands.* New York: Macmillan, 1967.

Stiglitz, Joseph F. *The Price of Inequality: How Today's Divided Society Endangers the Future.* New York: Norton, 2012.

Strode, William. *Centre College.* Louisville: Harmony House Publishers, 1980.

Szwed, John Francis. *Jazz 101: A Complete Guide to Learning and Loving Jazz.* New York: Hyperion, 2000.

Taylor, Charles. *Sources of the Self: The Making of Modern Identity.* Cambridge, MA: Harvard University Press, 1992.

Taylor, Mark C. *Crisis on Campus: A Bold Plan for Reforming Our Colleges and Universities.* New York: Knopf, 2010.

Whitehead, Alfred North. *Modes of Thought.* New York: Free Press, 1968.

Wood, Nicki Pendleton. *Nashville: Yesterday and Today.* Nashville: Westside, 2010.